Deliver
Our Children
from the Evil One

Noel and Phyl Gibson

Sovereign World

Sovereign World Ltd
PO Box 777
Tonbridge
Kent TN11 9XT
England

ISBN 1 85240 108 7

Other available publications by Noel G. Gibson

'The Fisherman's Basket'
A text-book of evangelism both outdoors and indoors.

'Konfused'
A teenage tract published by the American Tract Company.

'20 Minutes to Decide'
An evangelistic tract.

By Noel and Phyl Gibson

'Evicting Demonic Intruders and Breaking Bondages'
A deliverance manual for adults.

'Excuse Me, but Your Rejection is Showing'
How Christians who feel walled in by rejection may receive freedom.

Typeset by CRB (Drayton) Typesetting Services, Drayton, Norwich.
Printed by Richard Clay Ltd, Bungay, Suffolk, England.

Acknowledgements

It is with grateful thanks that the following acknowledgments are made:

... the use of the New International Version in Biblical references
Unless otherwise stated, all Scripture quotations in this publication are from the Holy Bible, New International Version. Copyright © 1973, 1978, 1984, International Bible Society.

... the manuscript review by three highly respected members of the medical profession
We especially thank three dear friends who have blessed us greatly by devoting time they really could not afford to reviewing the manuscript medically, and ethically.

Dr Wade Brett from Auckland, New Zealand, is a specialist physician, and Director of the Health Care Foundation. Wade is also actively involved in the Mercy Ministries division of Youth with a Mission.

Dr Ernest Crocker, a specialist in nuclear medicine and ultrasound, is in private practice in Sydney, Australia. An Anglican layman, Ernest is actively involved in spiritual ministry within his own church, and to members of his own profession.

Dr Martin Panter is a specialist physician from England who has served the Lord and his profession in many countries, including regular visits to Thailand to assist in medical missionary work. At present Martin and his family are based in Norfolk Island.

The authors

Contents

Preface

You, the potential parent – present parent – or post-graduate parent, are probably confused by the profusion of advice being offered on the prevention and cure of common problems experienced by children and teenagers.

With so much expertly researched material available from the medical profession, psychologists, educationalists, and child welfare specialists, some eyebrows are bound to be raised when two grandparents toss another book onto the already large pile.

Frankly, we have not written from choice, but from pressure. For many years, grateful parents have been asking for written materials after seeing their children being freed from the influences of the evil one, through prayer. The audio tapes of some of Phyl's lectures have circulated far and wide, causing more and more parents to seek freedom for their children; they have provided them with clues to the childhood origins of the problems they encounter in adulthood.

Phyl and I make no claim to be experts on children's problems. We are merely parents and grandparents with practical experience; we believe that God has given some spiritual insights into the causes of, and solutions to, many vexing problems amongst the young. Revealed truth is like seed – it must be scattered before it can propagate. We pray that the Holy Spirit will quicken the seed in these following pages as you read.

How this book began is an interesting story. Being under pressure to write is one thing; how to commence, and what to say are entirely different matters. I had the urge to write, but nothing more until Phyl and I were conducting a one-day seminar on deliverance at a Uniting Church in the Sydney suburb of Liverpool. During the afternoon, when Phyl spoke on the subject of children's problems, she obviously was doing so under the anointing of the Holy Spirit. As I listened, I also became aware of a similar quickening. I reached into my Bible case and took out a sheet of note paper, and with only a fine point Indian ink pen available, wrote an outline of the first chapter. Phyl noticed me writing, and was somewhat puzzled as she knew I was conversant with her lecture material! She did not realize that this was the birth of chapter one.

Since that day, the Holy Spirit has added a little at a time. So in the context of God's word and His revealed wisdom, chapters have been added, and clearly defined sections have become visible. Written as the Holy Spirit has directed, and constantly in fellowship with Phyl, my most supportive and kindest critic of all, the book has reached its present shape. God has given it, and to Him alone belongs any credit which may be given.

Together, we dedicate this book to our three daughters whose love, tolerance, co-operation and forgiveness have made such a contribution to what we have been able to achieve in God; and through them, to our nine grandchildren who are such a blessing to us.

Noel and Phyl Gibson

Foreword

The breakdown of families is one of the symptoms of almost catastrophic societal upheaval in our days. Social, political, educational, legal, and psychological remedies have been vigorously applied, but to little avail. Many are wondering now if spiritual approaches may not bear more fruit.

As we see history unfolding, it seems clear to us that a strong word which the Spirit is speaking to the churches in the 1990s has to do with spiritual warfare in all its dimensions. Some leaders are specializing in exposing demonic powers working through the occult. Some are dealing with principalities, powers, and territorial spirits. Some are dealing with personal deliverance from demonic forces.

For almost a decade, Noel and Phyl Gibson have been widely used of God in ministering personal deliverance. Much of this ministry has brought them face-to-face with the heart-wrenching problems of family breakdown. Many of these, they soon found, can be traced to demonization of children. The Gibsons have now done the body of Christ worldwide an enormous favor in compiling their insights and wisdom in this book, *Deliver Our Children from the Evil One*.

This book is both preventative and therapeutic. Married couples who are not yet parents should read and absorb the contents of this book. It is not pleasant reading. But morning sickness and labor pains are not pleasant either. The desired result, however, can be a baby who is not only physically healthy, but who grows up with spiritual health because its parents have learned how to pray for him or her effectively, even from before conception. The results are well worth the effort.

Parents who are already experiencing difficulty with their children will need less urging to learn from the Gibsons. Many will be able to identify and root out footholds of the Enemy developed during pregnancy, unfortunate attitudes surrounding conception, or birth trauma. They will also be able to recognize strongholds of parents' disappointment with the sex of the child, lack of bonding with the mother at birth, or insecure feelings of a young mother. Once these are identified and dealt with, the invading demonic spirits can be dismissed quite readily. Healing is often dramatic.

The growing phenomenon of child abuse is abhorrent to most upright Christians. But it is an unfortunate fact of life, and we must know how to deal with it when necessary. The Gibsons have included several very instructive and revealing chapters on child abuse which are extremely helpful and liberating.

How can children become demonized? How can parents and others recognize the symptoms? Are any of these problems hereditary? How can parents defend their children against Satanic attacks? How should we pray for children? These and many other such questions are frankly and intelligently addressed by Noel and Phyl Gibson.

We have used this book as a training and instructional manual and found it highly effective. We believe you and your children will benefit greatly as you read and apply it. The Bible tells us to resist the devil, and the Gibsons show us how.

Peter and Doris Wagner
Fuller Theological Seminary
Pasadena, California, USA

Comments

When Noel and Phyl Gibson's married daughters heard that their parents were writing a book which included some of their own childhood experiences, Adrienne suggested that the three daughters should write the foreword. The others readily agreed.

Without speaking to one another, or knowing what each other had written, their unedited contributions are as follows:

From Adrienne, the favourite eldest daughter

'Well I am the experimental model – first off the production line. You might say now almost vintage, but maturing well!

How I thank God for giving me the most precious parents, who are my best friends. They say example is the greatest teacher. I remember so well, the tireless patience of my Mother, who always had time to correct my sewing, make a dress, or just to attend to my maths. Nothing was too much trouble. My Father though so busy, loved the Lord, and worked at it enthusiastically, as if Jesus was coming back that day.

The times of separation from our father was a faith building experience for me personally. To see God provide our daily food, replace a burnt out stove, and care for our daily needs, planted within me that seed of faith. The relationship I developed with my mother during his absences was so precious. Now as a mother of one teenager I find myself automatically repeating what I have learnt from childhood.

I am so excited about this book because I believe that we can as parents on a daily basis with God's power take our authority in the Name of Jesus – breaking, cleansing and releasing any problem before it has a chance to take root. Keeping them free from the EVIL ONE.'

Adrienne

From Aureole, the favourite middle daughter

'It was a shock to read Dad's confession of his shortcomings as a father during my childhood years. Our relationship is truly deep and enriched with great love, honour and respect. I can go to him with any problem and know that there will be acceptance, love and wisdom because he's not only my earthly father but my spiritual father as well. The hallmark of his life is that he has always been a man of the Word, and I thank God for his example which has taught me the importance of spending time with God in His word.

To have your mother as your best friend is the most wonderful experience. This has been built over the years by a mother who has always had time to listen, who has understood me, loved me, laughed with me and, yes, even cried with me. If that were not enough, she is a strong woman of God, full of faith, wisdom and prayer, who before my very eyes constantly demonstrated the fruit of a close living relationship with her God.

I owe my freedom to God but it was my parents whom He taught how to take His power and minister glorious release to me. And not only to me but also to my husband and three children, which has brought a new dimension into our relationship.

The Lord has given mother a special sensitivity to the needs of children. To see her praying with her grandchildren and setting them free from hereditary bondages and birth traumas that have plagued them, has brought tears to my eyes, for they are also my children.

Dad and Mother have now imparted to my husband and me the keys for setting our own children free and also helping other parents by ministering release to their children. I just know that as you read this book and take hold of the principles that, believe you me, have been tried and proved, you will have one terrific blueprint for your own freedom and your family's, and for your ministry.'

Aureole

From Yvonne, the favourite youngest daughter

'I speak with truth and authority when I say that I owe my life and the quality of my life to the co-authors – Noel and Phyl Gibson, as I have the great privilege of being their favourite youngest daughter.

12

My early memories of my mother were of a loving, kind, under-standing, fair person who was always there to supply all my needs and offer guidance. To this day she remains unchanged and still supplies all of the above, only now it is even more appreciated. My father whom I adored and missed dreadfully in his absences was a person I held in awe. However as I grew up his image of distant father changed and he came to represent and offer to me the same qualities that I found in my mother.

As a mother of four sons myself, I realise the magnificent upbringing my parents provided for me and indeed have drawn on this in raising my own family. Parents are not childhood figures only, my parents have continued to offer the same love, support and guidance through my adult monumental blunders and triumphs, never criticizing, always forgiving and accepting my own decisions and above all – always loving. This is why today we share the greatest God given parent-child relationship possible with the added bonus that they are both my very best life-long friends.

I urge all parents, potential parents and those who wish to reflect on their upbringing, to approach this book with an open heart and mind in order to receive the maximum blessing from the God-given wisdom contained within these pages.

Read this book and share the blessings that I have received through-out my life from this wonderful Spirit filled couple – my Parents.'

Yvonne

Quotes on
Deliver Our Children from the Evil One

For profiles of these specialist physicians see 'Acknowledgements' in the front of the book.

'In this book Noel and Phyl seek to distil the accumulated wisdom of many years of ministry to children. The result is a book which will be of great assistance to both parents and those more specifically involved in ministry to children. This book is written by a "layman" from a medical perspective but contains a combination of experience and revelation resulting from many years involvement in the freedom ministry. It provides insights which must be considered in any serious attempt to develop an integrated ministry to children based on a Biblical perspective of man. I have found it useful both as a father of five children, as a teacher and minister to the Body of Christ, and as a specialist physician.'

(Dr) Wade Brett MB, ChB, FRACP

'In the context of God's Word and His revealed wisdom these loving parents examine the "hidden agenda" influencing the growth and development of today's children. This distilled wisdom from a lifetime of counselling and personal ministry will be a blessing to all parents and parents to be!'

(Dr) Ernest J. Crocker BSc(Med), MB, BS, FRACP, DDU

'An important and very practical work, full of wisdom and witty anecdotes, firmly founded on Biblical principles. Highly recommended for every Christian parent who desires freedom, fulfillment and wholeness, both for themselves, and especially their children.'

(Dr) Martin E.A. Panter BSc, MB, BS, MRCS, LRCP, DObst, RCOG, FRACGP

Chapter 1

Love is Not Blind, but it Can Get a Little Out of Focus!

When I was married, no-one cared enough to warn me that I could face problems if and when I became a father. The marriage lights were green, and I was madly in love with my bride so I stepped on the pedal and entered the intersection where two lives became one, blissfully ignorant of red lights ahead. Had I been counselled I probably would have lightheartedly replied about love solving every problem. It surely has helped greatly, but it has not kept me from falling into some well-concealed traps which may have been avoided had some specialized information and mature advice been available.

Phyl, my beloved partner, on the other hand, was much more prepared. She was an excellent trained nurse and a lover of children. The transition was natural. Just like a duckling when it finds that floating and paddling are much easier and more natural than waddling.

In time, our combined love resulted in three precious daughters being born over a period of six years and three months. Each had special significance to us, and as they grew older I found I had a favourite eldest daughter, a favourite middle daughter, and a favourite youngest daughter. It never worried me that I had failed to produce sons. In fact my big mouth caused me a real problem on that subject. Before we were married Phyl said 'I'll have the first three children if you will have the next three.' And I agreed! Realising the impossibility of some biological transformation, I just hoped that some honourable way of 'saving face' would open up in due course, and it did. When I had officiated at the wedding ceremony of my third daughter, I triumphantly announced to Phyl – 'Darling, you have given me three daughters, and I have given you three sons!' Bless her, Phyl graciously accepted that as an honourable fulfilment!

TOO LATE – too late – too . . . ?

Unfortunately I cannot make up for my many blunders during those developing years of dad-daughter relationships. Each of them are now mothers with their own families. They have given us seven grandsons and two granddaughters who call us Papa and Bamma, (early child-hood names which have stuck). Being Grand-parents is both a delight and a special responsibility. To show how much I have changed, I even leave my study door open when they visit us so they can slip in and out as they want to. Our girls never could do that. So the old walls are crumbling at last!

Digging up the past

Praise God, not all my fatherly relationships were failures. I loved my girls and was proud of them in the right way. Phyl sewed beautifully and the four females of my household looked like a million dollars with very little financial outlay. We were living by faith when the girls were quite young so I became increasingly grateful for a partner who would have given the dollar a swelled head for all it could be stretched to do in sewing and entertainment.

Our girls were also obedient and well behaved. I saw to that. **I was a disciplinarian**. I knew no other way because that was how my father had treated me. I now know I didn't need to act like that because the Lord has shown me the hereditary causes of the 'like-father-like-son' syndrome. My father constantly disciplined me, so I followed his example. He did play a little cricket with me, and sometimes cycled miles along country roads with me perched awkwardly and painfully on the cross-bar to fish together for silver-belly eels. But he was not a good communicator, and in that aspect sadly fell short of being the 'dad' I needed as a growing boy. I believe I was able to communicate with my own girls, but the occasions were too few. Even so, the story of Goldilocks and the three bears did get into our family fun-times and I still have the legacy of being called 'Daddy-bear' by three adult daughters.

But there were other nasty habits. As an evangelist I was super-dedicated to the service of God by day and night, almost looking on days off as 'robbing God'. So **I was always busy**, and even now the girls speak about their early memories of my always being too busy to be available. I've repented of that too, but the regrets remain. There were, of course, some compensations. When Sunday afternoons were spent in beach evangelism, the girls often came and enjoyed playing nearby, as we conducted children's Gospel programmes. During our Christmas holiday beach and camping group missions, the girls also went along to help, and enjoy the relaxation. And then there were the camping holidays, when travelling, tenting, fishing, fun and relaxation brought great family unity. Even being squirted with tomato sauce by an over venturesome and not quite so favourite eldest daughter put pressures on dad's patience, but we all survived, with great memories.

Being an open air preacher also meant that we had to trust the Lord for finances. So there were times when the girls asked for things that were beyond our resources. We felt responsible for most needs, but at other times a wise mother would suggest that the children pray for their own needs. When Adrienne, (daughter number one), began music lessons with a friend, she felt she should have a music case so that people on the bus would know she was taking music lessons. So she said to her mother, 'Do you think Jesus would let me have a music case?' Mother said she felt sure that Jesus would like that. When the postie (mailman) came that morning there was a letter with an anonymous gift of ten shillings in it (pre-decimal currency worth one dollar). So Phyl boarded a bus for the city, and purchased the music case. When Adrienne returned home from school that afternoon, her eyes widened in astonishment when she saw what was waiting. She excitedly said 'I didn't think He would answer that quickly'. That incident laid a foundation of faith in her life which helped make her the woman of faith she is today.

On another occasion, the two older girls asked their mother for roller skates. Now that was a matter that only Jesus could answer, so the girls were encouraged to pray. Three days afterwards there was a knock on the front door. Phyl found a dear friend standing there, holding three pairs of little-used skates, with white boots attached to two pairs. 'Phyl', she said, 'I was cleaning out my children's wardrobes and I found these skates which may fit your girls'. They fitted perfectly; the Lord Jesus knew their individual sizes.

Another skeleton which shrinks from exposure is my **perfectionism**. It came from my attempts to overcome the rejection I had experienced in childhood. I was forced to play mostly alone in my own backyard; few friends were allowed past the front gate; I was denied the harmless comics my friends enjoyed; and was sent early to bed when my parents conducted weekly Bible studies for young Christians. Sundays were particularly miserable. Having no car, I was literally marched a mile to church, twice-a-day, always under a dire threat of punishment for the slightest misdemeanor. Shoes had to be cleaned on Saturdays, and Sunday reading and activities were very restricted. My punishment sessions infrequently resulted in being sent early to bed on an empty stomach.

I grew up with good values and aimed at high standards. However, my ego was deflated, so I got into the usual antics to counteract this – **pride, performance** and **perfectionism**. It was the latter which hurt our girls, because I always felt they could and should do better. I was picky, sometimes growling at their failure to reach my defined standard, and this must have been most discouraging to them. Of course I was proud of their performances because that made me feel good. But I know that my perfectionist attitude placed another unnecessary load on each of them.

I have an even more repulsive skeleton which I hate to uncover. It is well known that brothers habitually tease sisters, but far worse, **fathers often tease their daughters, and I did it in my lack of maturity**. There is probably nothing more discouraging to a daughter practising her singing scales than her father accompanying her in a falsetto voice. But Aureole, (daughter number two), has forgiven me and has overcome my discouragement. Now she sings beautifully for the glory of God.

But I could *not* help **the Freemasonry 'hand-me-downs'**. The full story of how my maternal grandfather passed on that curse to me is given in our previous book *Evicting Demonic Intruders and Breaking Bondages*. Coming through me, Phyl, our three daughters and nine grandchildren came under numerous bondages and dominations, particularly sicknesses and allergies. We have now prayed for them all and have seen them released and cleansed.

Each favourite daughter was of course unique. Adrienne was asked by her mother what lesson she had learned on her first day in Sunday School. She replied, 'It was about a man who gave another man a jig on his donkey'.

Aureole on one occasion came out to see me while I was cutting the edges of our front lawn. She opened her little fist and revealed a number of raisins. I was generously invited to help myself. I took one and ate it, making a fuss over it. Then she disappeared inside and the following conversation took place: Mother: 'What have you been doing darling?' Aureole: 'I'se been helping daddy.' 'How have you been helping daddy?' 'I'se been feeding him.' I might add she still feeds her 'Dad', she's a fabulous cook.

Yvonne was the one with the fertile imagination, and in no time she had made up nicknames for all family members, many of which exist to this day. She became the 'arty' type and her creations are increasingly excellent.

They all threw themselves wholeheartedly into supporting the work in which we were involved. Adrienne and Aureole used their musical and singing talents during our open air programmes, and took their turns with Yvonne helping their mother prepare for a smorgasbord meal for up to fifty voluntary workers at Sunday night teas.

Praise God, all my past mistakes are now forgiven and the love which flows among us all as a family is special. Dad's opinion is important and calls from various parts of the country are often made to ask for his advice on important matters. Only the memories are left, giving rise to these warning signs so that future generations who are verging on merging may be more enlightened than I was. There is a one-line gag often used at engagement parties: 'Love is blind and marriage is an eye-opener'. With me it was not marriage but the problems I caused as a parent controlled by my pride, weaknesses, inadequacies, and rejection. When disciplinarianism, workaholism, perfectionism, and teasing are added, the mixture is potentially lethal to relationships. But God, Phyl, and the girls have been most gracious to me.

And so I can truly say that I have become the most loving – understanding – impartial – encouraging – reasonable – and available dad – **forty four years too late!**

And yet in one way it is **never** too late. It has been our joy to pray for our girls, their husbands, and their children. Their bondages from heredity have been broken, and they have been freed from all oppressions which have been passed on. Other influences have been cleansed, and there is a constant and natural dialogue on every kind of subject, particularly the matters which concern the Kingdom of God. So the past is gone, the memories are muted, and we go on together.

On one occasion Phyl was being interviewed by the leader of a counselling school before we began our teaching programme. One question put to her went like this: 'Phyl, what was it that quickened your interest in working with children?' Her reply was, 'It commenced not long after we entered full-time Christian service. One night God told me through his Word, that he would give me *"the treasures of darkness"* (Isaiah 45:3 KJV). The very next day the International Director of the mission society Noel was serving invited him to visit American branches and share his speciality of industrial evangelism. I then realized what the Lord had prepared me for. During that six and a half month's separation I had to be mother, father, supplier, protector and adviser to our three young children without my partner's help.'

'It was then that I soon learned that the children were living out some of the same problems Noel and I had experienced in our younger years. I then realized that if it were possible to get children freed from hereditary problems their growth and developmental behaviour would be far less traumatic.'

That seed was sown in 1963, so it has had some time to develop and mature. And I believe that entering the grandparent era with some nine healthy growing children, we are having a refresher course from a more mature perspective.

Chapter 2

Read the Fine Print First!

When did you last read the fine print on the back of your airline ticket? I decided to check, and believe it or not, there are six pages dealing with luggage, liability limitations, baggage liability regulations, passenger compensation limitations, and lots of other items. If it ever comes to the crunch and you need to claim, you are judged to have read, understood and agreed to all the verbiage before boarding. It's legally airtight!

A flight lasts for only hours, but marriage and parenthood last a lifetime. So what are the fine print regulations which need to be read, understood and agreed to before those vows are taken before God and your guests?

God runs the best marriage bureau

God is best qualified to make the ideal choice of marriage partners because He alone knows what the future holds for each one. Call it mutual attraction, common interests, mutual vibes, love at first sight, body chemistry, the convergence of irresistible forces, or any other fancy name – unless God is actively involved, marriages can, and do fall apart.

God gave Phyl to me as my life's partner. We gave Him the right to confirm or break our mutual attraction and searched God's Word for seven months for guidance in black and white. When it came we were hundreds of kilometres apart, and the finger of God stopped at a verse we were both reading on the same day. Satan, sicknesses, separations and all manner of circumstances have not prised apart God's unity and love over our more than forty-four years together.

Boredom, unfaithfulness, lack of communication, lovelessness, meanness and selfishness are some of the white ants that are eating out the grouting of marriage unity these days, causing even the most solid looking families to fall apart. God should never be presumed to be the patron of good marriages simply because vows are exchanged in a place of worship. God hand-made the ideal partner for Adam, and from that moment they were Adam and M'adam. (Verses for reflection: Genesis 2:18, 20b, 21, 22).

God can do what super-glue cannot do – He makes two people, one

Divorce and mutual separation is greatly on the increase. It seems that marriages today frequently commence without that mutual respect and genuine love for one another which restrains both parties from engaging in premarital sex. Many who seek to be delivered from lust speak of the mutual stimulation and sexual activity before marriage which turned sour afterwards. Wives have felt shame, guilt, and even anger against their husbands for having taken advantage of them before marriage. The wife's subsequent frigidity has brought frustration and resentment, which in turn can lead to unfaithfulness.

When Phyl and I were planning marriage I felt too embarrassed to ask my father for advice, and in any case I was in the South Pacific war zone with the Royal New Zealand Air Force. So I turned to a Christian pilot friend of mine who was a great help in recommending a suitable book. But it wasn't the contents of the book, but the foreword which was the greatest help. It ran something like this; 'A woman is like a very beautiful harp. Any fool can strum and make a noise, but it takes the patience of a master to produce the best music.'

Love, patience, tenderness, and thoughfulness are the names of the fingers which play that harp. Physical union is but part of the beautiful melody which commences with marriage. We know! The discipline is more than worth it when the fruit of that partnership is the birth of a child whose life will be greatly blessed because of having been conceived in love, not lust.

Our marriage took place on a special day in the world's history: VE Day, the 9th May, 1945. While the world celebrated the end of the Second World War in the European zone, we commenced a married partnership which has been significantly free of even skirmishes of war. What God put together has stayed together; He holds us together. *'Houses and wealth are inherited from parents, but a prudent wife is from the LORD'* (Proverbs 19:14).

God's book of rules for successful marriage is never outdated

I was enjoying a meal in a pastor's home not long ago, when my eye caught a notice on the door of the refrigerator:

> TRUST IN GOD
> FAULT FINDING IS NOT ALLOWED IN OUR HOME
> REMEMBER – A PROMISE IS SACRED.

My host said it was reputed to have come from Dwight L. Moody's family home, put there by Dwight's mother.

Godly words, backed up by godly example, are indeed a priceless heritage. In retrospect, Phyl and I both thank God for this example in the families into which we were born. And I am sure, in due course we will have left some of the same with our children when we receive God's upward call in Christ Jesus.

Several years ago, I was asked to speak to the children of people attending a (YWAM) basic counselling school in Hawaii. There were only thirteen students between the ages of five and fifteen years, but the invitation raised a problem. I was used to speaking to non-Christian young people and sharing the Gospel, but I was unsure as to what this group needed to hear. I spent some time in prayer and the Lord gave me something entirely new.

The first day I spoke on what parents should give to their children, what this should mean to them, and how children generally react if they do not receive this.

The second day the subject was reversed, and we focused on what children should give to their parents, and their reactions.

On the third day I spoke about the ideal relationship young people could have with God, and what Jesus Christ wanted to do for them individually to make this possible. To conclude the mini-series I placed a small box with a slit in the top on one of the teacher's desks. I invited those who desired the freedom Jesus Christ promised to write their name on a slip of paper and to drop it into the box. I offered to spend time in praying with them individually on the following Saturday, with their parents being present if they wished this. Five students and two teachers turned up on the Saturday and around five and a half hours were spent in sharing the power of Jesus Christ with each one. The results were very confirming. Parents and children were reconciled, bondages were broken, children were freed to glorify Jesus Christ in their change of conduct.

Because the contents of that time with the children is so appropriate to ideal parenthood, the points have been expanded to form the following chapter.

Chapter 3

Keys to Ideal Parenthood

To reach this goal, the investment of selflessness and ten other vital spiritual and emotional values is more than worth the results which may be obtained.

1. Love blesses children

Children need love before anything else. Everything God has done for us parents or prospective parents has been possible because of his incredible love:

> *'Dear friends, since God so loved us, we ought also to love one another.'* (1 John 4:11)

> *'... if we love each other, God lives in us and his love is made complete in us.'* (1 John 4:12)

> *'... his command is that you walk in love.'* (2 John v.6)

When Christian parents channel God's love to their children, they keep them from feeling rejected, give them security, and a warm sense of being wanted which preserves them from lurking fears (1 John 4:18).

Some psychiatrists are now telling their patients to affirm themselves and others by hugging someone every day. If a genuine demonstration of affection had been practised in the childhood of these people, they probably would not have ended up being patients.

Phyl tells mothers never to give up hugging their sons. It is the greatest protection against a teenager becoming sexually aroused when he first comes into close contact with a female body.

It is said that 'love makes the world go around'. If love is genuine, it will apply to the world of marriage. But if 'love' means 'slushy sentiment', then the married lives of many people are doomed to failure. Nothing but genuine love which comes from God can propel a marriage into its proper orbit.

Love is said to have the same effect in family relationships as oil in the moving parts of a car engine. It helps prevent what we call 'wear and tear'. In inter-family relationships nothing produces emotional friction and heat more than the opposites of love (1 Corinthians 13:4–7):

Impatience
Unkindness
Envy
Boasting
Pride
Rudeness
Self-interest
Quick temper
Unforgiveness, resentfulness, resurrecting the past
Taking pleasure in evil things
Choosing to be untruthful and enjoying it
Never trusting
Always being negative
A defeatist attitude, and giving up easily

If we had been asked to list the family problems which make the greatest contribution to wrecking the emotional security of children, (and which continues to affect them adversely even in adulthood) we could not have put together a more complete list. The basis of spiritual problems in adults so often comes from these loveless attitudes and relationships. The damage caused can never be resolved by financial generosity or gifts.

Love assures children that they are wanted and that they are special to their parents. They will be secure, happy, and give of their best at home and at school. Lack of love will cause rejection, a sense of unimportance, loss of value, disobedience, anger and emotional hardness. These will cause them to withdraw.

2. Patience blesses children

'Fathers, do not exasperate your children; instead, bring them up in the training and instruction of the Lord.'

(Ephesians 6:4)

'But you, man of God ... pursue righteousness, godliness, faith, love, endurance (AV 'patience') *and gentleness.'*

(1 Timothy 6:11)

'For this reason, make every effort to add to your faith, goodness; and to goodness, knowledge; and to knowledge, self-control; and to self-control, perseverance (AV 'patience') *...'*

(2 Peter 1:5, 6)

One thing I always admired about Phyl was her patience with the girls. They were in the kitchen sink with her, in the mixing bowls, and always talking to her. But she was unruffled. She had always looked upon motherhood as the highest vocation, and gladly gave up nursing (which she greatly loved) to be a mother. She read endlessly to them, often the same books over and over again. She listened, talked, and listened some more, and constantly prayed over them. Then there was help with the homework, the things she sewed for them, and the woodwork items she made patiently with my tools! And where was I? I was a full-time servant of God, a part-time father, and an often impatient one at that.

God is also a God of patience:

'Or do you show contempt for the riches of his kindness, tolerance and patience, not realising that God's kindness leads you toward repentance?'   (Romans 2:4)

Patience is a fruit of the Spirit-filled and controlled life. The Holy Spirit has now taught me how to deal with my old flesh-life and to draw upon His abundant resources of grace. How my girls and I would have benefited from that understanding more than forty years ago!

We often say that patience wears thin. Of course it does if it is only a human resource. But the Christian should not be so limited. Time may

29

determine how long the listening ear may be available or the dialogue may continue, but patience should be constant.

Children shown patience will be confident, friendly, patient with one another, and have no trouble in communicating or improving their knowledge. Children who are not shown patience, will be frustrated, impatient, easily discouraged, may feel worthless and be disobedient and angry.

3. Fairness blesses children

In the parable of the prodigal son, the older brother obviously held a grudge against his father for what he thought was an injustice (which can be as effective as real injustice), so he became angry and refused to join the welcome-home party. So his father went out and pleaded with him. But he answered his father, *'Look! All these years I've been slaving for you and never disobeyed your orders. Yet you never gave me even a young goat so I could celebrate with my friends. But when this son of yours who has squandered your property with prostitutes comes home, you kill the fattened calf for him'* (Luke 15:28–30 emphasis added). The father quietly reminded the older brother that everything around him was his property. (The younger son had already received his share of the inheritance before his father's death). The father could not have been fairer. The elder brother had obviously treated his father badly, and justified himself in being angry. In reality he was also mean, because he could have had fun with his friends at any time he chose, but obviously he wasn't prepared to kill his own stock to celebrate.

It is said that if two children each want a half of an apple, or piece of cake, one should be asked to do the cutting, and the other then given first choice. One can guarantee there won't be an inequality.

Children have a strong sense of fair play, and can become incensed if they consider that they have been treated unjustly in punishment, rewards, food, payment, favours, jobs to be done, privileges, time allocation, and in fact anything in which some allocation is made.

Self-preservation starts early in a child's life. Just try taking a favourite toy away and the owner's alarm system sounds off, loudly and persistently. When other little ones come for a visit and toys have to be shared, selfishness mostly triumphs and the visitor has to be content with what can be snatched or handed over by the umpire of the peace-keeping force. Fairness is a learned behavioural pattern, and it starts with parents acting justly.

4. Giving children adequate time blesses them

Many years ago, I saw a TV programme which centred around a middle- to upper-class family. The father was a workaholic lawyer. His teenage daughter frequently went to his study to ask him to listen to her problems. Each time he said the same thing: 'Not now dear, can't you see that I'm very busy?', or 'Some other time please.' The mother was a socialite, and when the teenager wanted to talk with her she was usually speaking on the telephone and would refuse to interrupt her conversation. Other times it was 'I haven't got time now dear, can't you see I am going out?' What spare time the parents had was given to the 'light-of-their-lives', a two-year-old boy, an unexpected arrival, on whom they doted. The daughter became so lonely and frustrated that she 'kidnapped' her little brother, and cared for him in a run-down tenement. Of course, the police finally found the missing two, and there was a family reunion with the daughter who had been the victim of ill-conceived parental priorities.

Availability is the first step of the staircase to good family relationships. It gives security to a child to know that he or she has top priority when needed.

The next step is to have a **listening ear**. A frequent and accurate assessment of father-daughter communication is 'I can't talk to my father – he only lectures!' Personally, I am sure I have turned the ear 'off' and the tongue 'on' too frequently when I should have been listening to my teenage girls. Dads are naturally protective of their daughters, and bristle with good reasons for making decisions aimed at preventing unspoken fears from becoming facts. Listening fully to a child or teenager will prevent him or her from feeling frustrated, and the parent from making a wrong judgment based on incomplete information.

Step three is **knowing how long to listen**. The request may be made frequently, but quality time is always better than 'little and often', particularly when a parent looks intensely at a child while listening. If adults appreciate others giving them total attention, how much more satisfying will it be for children to be treated in the same way.

The 'right time' seldom means anything to a child, and with the male species, this weakness usually continues well into adulthood, if in fact it ever changes! Patience and careful time-planning may well be part of the female psyche, but the male usually wants to get everything off his chest as soon as he enters his security domain – home. If boys yell for mum and food after school, most men expect immediate attention from their wives as they drop their 'work-weary' bodies into their 'sacred' armchair. Then, without so much as an enquiry as to how their wives fared during the day, they pour out their problems and frustrations. Some children never grow up, they just look as if they have.

But there is another aspect of time which is as important as listening. It is **watching and encouraging**. All too frequently disgruntled adults have complained to us that their father or mother showed no interest in their schoolwork, or sports activities. This has produced resentment, bitterness and anger towards the parent concerned. One boy exploded and punched his father's nose because he had showed total disinterest in his son's sports achievements. Fathers generally deserve more blame than mothers. Few readers will not be able to recall the inner pleasure they had when a parent or grandparent was present at a time of personal triumph in the sports field, or at prize-giving.

There is also a three-letter word which demands attention. It can infuriate if repeated too frequently, but if handled correctly, may become a teaching point. It seems that after 'Mum' and 'Dad', 'Yes' and 'No', the most frequently used word is '**Why?**' The enquiring mind deserves to be informed, but the challenging mind sometimes needs discipline. Life-long quality relationships between parents and children often commence when children are given attention to their needs, rather than their wants.

When time together leads to right decisions being made, **wise parental judgements** will be the fourth step in ensuring parents and children have good family relationships.

It appears that some parents expunge the memory of their own childhood pranks, misbehaviour, and experimentation, with soothing words like 'socially acceptable habits' when dealing with them in their own children. Rigidity, legalism, even harsh attitudes and measures to preserve the family name, often exasperate the children and lead to frustration.

It is an unchangeable fact of life that when the parents most need wisdom to guide and train their children, they have the least resources to do so. But there are three important guidelines which should assist in making those all-important decisions:

FAITH IN GOD
PARENTAL FAIRMINDEDNESS
TRUST IN THE CHILD

The child who is allowed freedom within defined boundaries will be a secure child. Failure to define boundaries (which children often want but may verbally reject), will give them a false sense of freedom, but inevitably their choices will bring them into bondage. God condemned Eli the priest because *'his sons made themselves contemptible, and he failed to restrain them'* (1 Samuel 3:13).

The top step of the staircase to the most effective use of time is to recommend that **adequate explanations should be made as to why the decisions were reached**, rather than mere edicts with penalties for non-fulfilment. When children understand the basic principles upon which decisions are based, even the unpalatable ones are easier to receive.

Human-rights activists often undermine the authority of parents, school-teachers, and authority figures. It is therefore not uncommon for parents to be confronted when a child feels that his or her personal rights are being challenged. The Christian parent aiming to bring up children to respect God and His standards belongs to what is fast becoming a more and more oppressed minority. Satan will see to that!

5. Encouragement blesses children

Rejection is one of the greatest unrecognized dangers during child-hood. Imagination often contributes as much to a child feeling rejected, as what is actually said or done.

Encouragement is a sure antidote. But it must be genuine and reasonable. Anything that is flattering, therefore untruthful, may cause children to be deceived into believing they possess abilities which they don't really have. That bubble will burst sooner or later, disillusionment and self-rejection will result. When approval is exaggerated, and everything is 'fantastic', or 'marvellous', parents have no room to challenge their children to reach higher levels of achievement.

Genuine encouragement can dispel fears in a child, give fresh impetus to the desire to improve, and reward the diligence of self-effort. It is positive, stimulating, and a healer of inferiorities and low self-image.

Paul's reassurance to Timothy in Ephesus, and Titus in Crete, has left us three Epistles which demonstrate the value of this in direct, honest and forthright terms. The principles are just as valid in childhood.

A moment's reflection will remind us of people who have blessed our lives with a timely word which has encouraged us. It helped turn defeat into victory, inferiority into self-acceptance, or self-rejection into self-confidence. Encouragement is to the soul as physiotherapy is to the body.

6. Godly examples bless children

God promised Solomon abundant blessings on one condition:

> *'As for you, if you walk before me in integrity of heart and uprightness, as David your father did, and do all I command and observe my decrees and laws, I will establish your royal throne over Israel forever.'*   (1 Kings 9:4 emphasis added)

Paul reminded Timothy of the matriarchal example in his family:

> *'I have been reminded of your sincere faith, which first lived in your grandmother Lois and in your mother Eunice, and I am persuaded, now lives in you also.'*   (2 Timothy 1:5)

Children normally follow the examples of their parents when they grow up. Rudeness, gossip, bad language, criticism, infidelity, violence, dishonesty, stealing, smoking and alcoholism are some of the bad habit patterns that are learned from example. There may also be hereditary habits.

7. Instruction in Biblical principles blesses children

> *'These commandments that I give you today are to be on your hearts. Impress them on your children. Talk about them when you sit at home and when you walk along the road, when you lie down and when you get up. Tie them as symbols on your hands and bind them on your foreheads. Write them on the door-frames of your houses and on your gates.'*   (Deuteronomy 6:6–9)

Because God blessed Old Testament families who submitted to his commandments, could not the rejection of God's principles for family living be one key to such disintegration of the family unit seen today?

If parents are charged with the responsibility of teaching and demonstrating the truths of God's word to their children, each child then becomes personally responsible for obeying these teachings and following the example given. Those who choose to rebel against their godly heritage bear their own guilt. But the promise of God is

> *'Train a child in the way he should go, and when he is old he will not turn from it.'*   (Proverbs 22:6)

There are four spiritual experiences into which parents may guide their children:

(a) *Salvation, water baptism, and the filling and control of the Holy Spirit.*

The writer believes that from Pentecost onwards, there is Biblical evidence to show that these three experiences should take place at the time of new birth. Regrettably they have become separated by doctrine and time. For example, my father led me to a saving knowledge of Jesus Christ at seven years of age; I was baptized around twelve years of age, but not released in the Holy Spirit until thirty-two.

It appears to me that the Ethiopian eunuch (Acts 8:29–39), and the Philippian jailer with his household (Acts 16:25–34) had this triple experience at the one time. They were born from above, baptized in water, and filled with joy, which is an evidence of the control of the Holy Spirit.

Those responsible for physical birth are ideally the ones to lead their children into spiritual life.

(b) *The establishment of times of family worship.*

As the Jews celebrate the passover at the family meal table, so believing parents should have a similiar short time of worship when as many as possible can be present. When our girls were young, we had a variety of short readings or Bible stories, followed by one member of the family praying for the others and for their friends. Each one took their turn.

(c) Submission to Biblical principles of glorifying Jesus Christ in *daily life through Bible study and prayer*.
Psalm 119:9–11 says:

> '*How can a young man keep his way pure? By living according to your word. I seek you with all my heart; do not let me stray from your commands. I have hidden your word in my heart that I might not sin against you.*'

(See also verses 14–16, 97–100 and verse 130)

My earliest childhood memories of my father were of the priority time he gave to reading and studying God's word, and his early morning prayer in the kitchen. He used to pray aloud for his family, and missionaries around the world. He was a banker, but always a full-time witness for Jesus Christ. These habits were continued to his death in his eighty-ninth year. Childhood is the time to lay the foundation for a lifetime of witness to Jesus Christ.

(d) *Encouragement to worship and serve in the local church from the earliest age*.

Most churches have adequate teaching facilities for all age groups up to junior church, and this makes an ideal beginning for the children's church activities. If facilities are not available, no one seems to mind children playing quietly, colouring in, or sleeping on the floor during the service.

As our youngsters were growing up they also went with us when we conducted gospel programmes for young people. As they grew older they were able to help us in various ways. So their lives, like their parents', were deeply rooted in service for the kingdom of God.

One afternoon we watched an interesting scene outside our front gate. Aureole, our seven year-old 'special middle daughter' had gathered about a dozen friends of her own age and had them lined up facing her chalk board. We were intrigued as she began to sketch and tell a gospel story exactly as she had heard it. Her conclusion however was entirely her own: 'And if you don't believe in Jesus, you'll be flamed up in hell!' From what we could see, the children appeared unmoved. Our daughters grew up as soulwinners, and have never lost their zeal to win people to Jesus Christ. Lifelong habits commence in childhood. Children are indeed the future generation, but parents can strongly influence it.

8. Fair and appropriate discipline blesses children

With human rights activists crying 'brutality', 'violence', 'deprivation of human rights' and 'victimisation' against those who use physical means to punish children, it is not surprising that practical discipline is banned in most schools and avoided in many homes. Even Christian families are bowing to social pressures rather than submitting to the authority of God's word.

It takes the grace of God to know when to discipline a child, what method to use, and for how long it should last. Our three girls were basically different. With one, we only had to speak firmly; the eyes would fill with tears and the bottom lip quiver. With another firmness had to be combined with physical discipline. The third needed firmness, physical correction, and considerable reasoning to reach the desired result.

Because modern society has generally rejected the Bible and its ethical standards, it has become more and more permissive. This rebellious, permissive age has not caught the Bible reader unawares. Around AD 67 Paul wrote to Timothy in Ephesus saying:

> *'But mark this: There will be terrible times in the last days. People will be lovers of themselves, lovers of money, boastful, proud, abusive, **disobedient to their parents**, ungrateful, unholy, without love, unforgiving, slanderous, **without self-control**, brutal, not lovers of the good, treacherous, rash, conceited, lovers of pleasure rather than lovers of God.'*

> (2 Timothy 3:1–4 emphasis added)

When parents abandon their responsibility, or assign it to others for any reason, children become 'at risk'. The number of homeless children and teenagers in our large cities is alarming. They are exploited at every level, sexually active, and subject to diseases such as AIDS. Most are bitter towards their parents and the society which rejected them.

Solomon in his renowned wisdom talked about this in Proverbs 22:15 and 23:13, 14.

My father was the disciplinarian in his home, simply because I could run faster than my mother, and I could always make her laugh when she wanted to punish me. I learned that a laughing mother couldn't whack her boy! But those defences didn't seem appropriate with a disciplinarian for a father! His times of punishment were something else! They were always in our 'sitting-room' which was awesome in itself to a boy who was never allowed in there. There were Bible readings (which I soon knew by heart), and the usual remarks: 'Son, this hurts me more than it hurts you.' I could never understand that. I showed the welts from the thin leather strap, but my father never showed any physical discomfort.

Having survived these, and other 'post-graduate' incidents I recommend some disciplinary do's and dont's:

- Discipline should be appropriate to the seriousness of the misdemeanour, the personality of the child, and to whether it is the first occasion or a 're-run'.
- Punishment should never be administered in anger. If it is, the tendency is for the punishment to be more severe, and of longer duration than is just. I believe I have, at times, been guilty of that.
- Discipline should be administered as soon as possible after the need arises. Waiting time can amount to psychological torture. When my mother promised me paternal discipline, the rest of my day was ruined. When I heard my father's footsteps after work, I suffered some sort of emotional stomach rupture. I knew the procedure. Whisperings in the kitchen, then the grim invitation, 'Son, come with me', followed by the procession of father, Bible, leather strap, and son who had been suffering to some degree all day. So, on behalf of all boys and girls yet to receive discipline from a parent who reads this book – please make it short, just, and – relevant to what caused it.
- Beware double punishment. Because I was punished in a superspiritual atmosphere which included Bible reading and prayer, it became a 'heavy deal'. The punishment, I deserved. The repeated lecture bit, I resented. When the climax was added to a day of dread, I felt I was being a little over-punished!
- Make no empty threats of punishment. Carry it out if needed. Children will despise the word of parents who make empty threats. This may also cause insecurity, rebellion, and independence.

    Beware of causing a child to feel a sense of injustice because the punishment given is greater than that given to another sibling under similar circumstances.

- Discipline should be done in private where possible. Avoid shouting or using intimidating language in addition to the method of punishment. Words which should never be used include; 'I hate you'; 'I could kill you'; 'I never wanted you in the first place'; and 'what will other people think **of me** now because of what you did?'

- Never, never kick, or punch, or hit a child across the head. I used to have my ears 'boxed' but that can have adverse effects on eardrums and is a 'no-no'.

Children who are disciplined wisely in love will soon learn to respect their parents; later in life they will then accept the whole social system of order and justice, including respecting the property of others. They will feel secure in themselves, and will honour other people and their possessions.

Children who are undisciplined will do whatever they want, or are influenced to do. They will manipulate to get their own way, become deceitful, put on tantrums, and often become quite obnoxious to others.

Children who are over-disciplined may become insecure, lacking in self-confidence, fearful, have difficulty in sleeping, and struggle over schoolwork. They may also become anxious, bite their nails, and wet the bed.

9. Children are blessed for life when they are taught to exercise faith

Timothy's faith has already been mentioned. Hebrews chapter eleven is of course the Bible's honour roll of ordinary people whose faith was a way of life. So when it came to a crisis they simply acted normally. Faith is a lifestyle, not an emergency cord.

Our own children grew up knowing that what God did not supply, we would go without. Phyl and I believed we were responsible to trust God for basic necessities, but we encouraged the children to ask the Lord for special items. One trusted the Lord for the air fare for a holiday, and it was supplied. The Lord was always faithful. As God was then, so he is now. They continue to look to the Lord. Although each has passed through financial difficulties during marriage, the Lord has brought them through.

10. Children are blessed when their parents trust them

This is a double-edged blessing. Firstly, parents need to establish themselves as completely trustworthy and reliable in the eyes of their children. This means always keeping their word, and fulfilling promises. If this ever becomes impracticable adequate explanations need to be made, and alternatives carried out where possible.

Parents who deliberately or obliquely lie, ought not to punish their children who simply follow their example.

Secondly, the same standard of trust needs to be placed in children and teenagers so that they in turn will be encouraged to become reliable. Statements such as 'I trust you to come straight home', or 'I trust you to uphold Christian standards with your unsaved friends', will stimulate a sense of honour 'to make the grade.'

Trust is a deliberate choice and needs to be guarded carefully. It involves:

- avoiding subtle questions testing the degree of a child's truthfulness. This can undermine the child's feeling of being trusted;
- believing a child's explanation unless there is obvious evidence to the contrary;
- giving the child the benefit of any doubt which may arise in conflicting statements;
- making the punishment for untruthfulness such a deterrent that truthfulness will become the automatic choice; and
- showing your children that you will support them because you trust them.

Fathers and mothers come in many shapes and sizes, and in varying degrees of ability to fulfil the ideal requirements of parenthood. No one has been, nor is likely to be perfect. The wise will learn quickly, but be encouraged, even the slow ones can complete the course the second time around – with their grandchildren!

SUMMARY

1.   Only God is able to supply the best partner for marriage. Those who ask for his selection will always be grateful they did.

2.   God's rules for successful family relationships can never be outdated, or superseded. It is better to acknowledge and obey than to learn by the process of trial and error.

3.   The ten keys to ideal parent-child relationships are giving children: love, patience, fairness, adequate time, encouragement, godly

example, instruction in Biblical principles, fair and appropriate discipline, encouragement to walk by faith, and trust.

4. Lifetime habits commence in childhood. By obedience to Biblical principles parents will bless their children and influence the future generation for the glory of God.

Chapter 4

When 1 + 1 May Equal 3, or 4, or More

God has given all living creatures the capacity to mate sexually with their own kind, and to produce more of the same. The incredible range of methods of procreation used from the simplest life forms to the most developed and complicated vertebrates (in which life-mating is not unknown), is the greatest testimony to the versatile creativity of God.

It is in conception and the subsequent birth of a baby that we marvel most, as we see the climax of a process which blends two people into a new life form.

Very few people fail to discover their sexuality in childhood, but until sex education began in schools, sexual naivety was not uncommon. Many young ladies entered marriage as virgins, totally ignorant that sexual relationships were part of married life. Unless 'Mr Right' happened to be a thoughtful and gentle lover in every sense of the word, many a wife's romantic dream was shattered, and in the inevitable disillusionment, children became the victims of the mother's rejection and shattered emotions.

Because males generally are 'turned on' sexually by what they see, hear and think about, they often mistakenly believe that women react to the same stimuli. This is not so with the majority of women. They are affected by tenderness, thoughtfulness, respect, and genuine love for who they are, rather than for what they can give to a man sexually.

God obviously designed human sexuality for both procreation and recreation. Although the two systems were designed to function together, in the writer's opinion the enjoyment of recreation without procreation in the love and security of marriage is clearly sanctioned

(1 Corinthians 7:5). Sex outside marriage downgrades either or both parties by turning them into mere sexual beings for the gratification of lustful desires.

In the theistic creation of heterosexual partners (Genesis 1:27, 28), it is obvious that homosexuality and lesbianism were never in God's plan. It was Satan who caused this perversion (Romans 1:19–32). The sexual practices of homosexuals, and the deviant means used to gain acceptance are totally offensive to God, and will, with all sexual immorality, earn his wrath in the future judgement (Revelation 21:8).

The world's first man and woman were not born like us. They were made by God himself, according to the most credible eyewitness possible, Jesus Christ himself (Mark 10:6). He confirmed what God had told Moses (Genesis 1:26, 27) written thousands of years BC. This confirms the relevancy of the Maker's handbook with its rules and regulations for all generations of homo sapiens.

Adherence to those rules has since been challenged by Satan the usurper, who began his despotic rule over the nations of the earth by successfully tempting our first parents to reject God's sovereignty and follow him (Genesis 3:4, 5). Regrettably, most of today's generation still believe Satan's lies, and so reject God's book of rules for human behaviour as being outdated, repressive, and irrelevant to society's needs. So the Bible's sexual restrictions have become replaced by the humanistic philosophy, 'sex is OK as an expression of "love", or "help", or simply if desired by willing partners.' No wonder that babies born either pre-marriage, or to unmarried people feel unwanted and unimportant. Some are also unloved.

Human sexuality began with the mutual experience of togetherness and love reflecting the character of God.

God presented the first bride to her waiting partner in Genesis 2:22, and said that their sexual partnership would confirm their oneness (Genesis 2:24; Matthew 19:5). God's intentions for sexual relationships have never changed. The Lord Jesus sanctified marriage by his presence at a wedding (John 2:1–11).

The apostle Paul clearly confirms a New Testament marriage sexual partnership in 1 Corinthians 7:3–5.

God said that everything he had created was very good, and that included human sexuality in the context for which it was created (Genesis 1:31). He confirmed this principle by the way he spoke to Eve after the fall.

Firstly, childbirth was originally intended to be painless, but when sin caused spiritual death and a break in God-human relationships, pain in childbirth became part of Eve's judgement. *'I will greatly increase your pains in childbearing; in pain you will give birth to children'* (Genesis 3:16a).

Secondly, God made the woman subject to the authority of the man. *'Your desire will be for your husband, and he will rule over you'* (Genesis 3:16b). The Hebrew word translated *'desire'* is *'tshuwrah'* (Strong's Analytical Concordance 8669). It means *'stretching after, a longing, desire'*. The word comes from a primary root *'shuwq'* (Strong's – 7783) meaning *'to run after or over, i.e. overflow, water'*.

The word is used on only two other occasions in the Old Testament. The first is in the Song of Solomon 7:10, *'I belong to my beloved, and his desire is for me'*. The setting of the chapter is obviously one of sexual desire where the female body is poetically described and the fragrance of mandrakes (a well-known aphrodisiac) is mentioned. The only other use of this word 'desire' is when God speaks of the intensity of sinful desire to seduce Cain. *'But if you do not do what is right, sin is crouching at your door, it desires to have you, but you must master it'* (Genesis 4:7).

When God told Eve that her desire would be to her husband he was obviously restricting her to what we now know as the marriage relationship. But Satan, the world's king by popular acclaim, has opened a permissive floodgate for sexual freedom.

The tangible results of human sexuality

God's word is certainly not silent about what God will do in marriage and childbearing when he is honoured and obeyed:

- *'Sons are a heritage from the LORD, children a reward from him'* (Psalm 127:3). See also Jeremiah 1:5, Genesis 25:21, 1 Samuel 1:6, and Genesis 30:2.
- God put Onan to death for refusing to carry out inheritance laws with his deceased brother's wife, Tamar. Just before completing the sex act with his sister-in-law, he withdrew to avoid her conceiving and giving birth to a child who would be his brother's legal heir (Genesis 38:8–10).
- *'We should not commit sexual immorality as some of them did – and in one day twenty-three thousand of them died'* (1 Corinthians 10:8).

Although old-fashioned chastity and purity are not popular virtues in the 20th century, personal moral purity, the sanctity of marriage, and the honour of one another are certainly not an option for the born again, Spirit-filled and controlled believer. These are what Jesus Christ expected of those who follow him in laying the ground rules for discipleship (Matthew 16:24). He requires self-denial, submission to his standards, and perfect obedience. No one who knew Jesus ever doubted his personal purity despite every type of temptation (see Hebrews 2:17, 18; 7:26).

Where do the problems come from?

In order to understand the problems which newborn babies may face from their developmental years to adulthood, it is necessary to examine the three-phase development of how we came into being.

The forty weeks we remember least, but which have influenced us the most

One thing is certain, none of us is able to recall the igniting of our spark of existence, our lengthy preparation for life, or our arrival. Certainly none of us had any say as to whether we wished to be born, what our sex might be, what personality we would like, and to whom and where we would like to be born.

Yet most of these factors were determined for us, consciously or unconsciously, by two people whom we had never met, and whom we later took a long time to know. Most of us learned to love those two whom we learned to call 'Mummy' and 'Daddy'. But some individuals have struggled with accepting both their 'sponsors', and themselves.

In writing about the many problems we have seen in the lives of children and adults Phyl and I want to make it clearly understood that we are in no way claiming to be authorities in these areas. We have no professional expertise in specialist fields of medicine which cover conception, in utero growth and development, and the effects of the delivery processes.

Phyl is a registered general and maternity nurse with practical midwifery experience. I have had medical and hospital experience during World War 2, but nothing more. Our combined experience is certainly most helpful in counselling people with mental, physical, emotional, and spiritual problems, but the contents of this book have been learned through the teaching ministry of the Holy Spirit. The mistakes are genuinely ours!

Because the Lord has revealed the spiritual bases of the problems encountered, and shown how children (even adults) can be freed from them, we believe there is a great need to share these insights with pastors and counsellors. What the Lord has taught has been submitted to Spirit-filled, professional, and other much-used 'workers-together-with-God', and they have encouraged us to press forward with the spiritual work of release and healing which God has shown us.

Before dealing with problems encountered in the time span between conception and birth, we need to consider briefly the matter of conception itself.

The completed act of intercourse carries no guarantee of conception. Very obviously, preventative measures such as inter-uterine devices which cause failure of implantation of the fertilised ovum, (IUDs), condoms, birth control pills, and the rhythm timing method are designed to prevent fertilization. But so will low sperm counts, irregular ovulation, sterility, and other physical conditions. For couples who long for children, the inability to conceive is a cause of great sadness, and feelings of self-rejection and inferiority often follow. Some have sublimated their longings by the adoption process, and of these, a small percentage of women have subsequently been able to conceive, and bear their own children. Others have prayed fervently, and sought the highest medical assistance possible, but still have been unsuccessful. Their only consolation is the comfort their heavenly father gives, and he often does this by giving them opportunities to help children and young people who are naturally attracted to them.

But God still works miracles. Pastor Jack Hayford tells of exhorting Christians on one occasion to be spiritual reproducers, based on:

'Sing O barren woman, you who never bore a child; burst into song, shout for joy, you who were never in labour; because more are the children of the desolate woman than of her who has a husband, says the LORD.' (Isaiah 54:1)

While preaching, he said that while he did not have childless couples primarily in mind, he was sure that God would honour any who claimed the promise for that purpose. A young couple contacted him a little later saying that they had felt led to claim that blessing and that the Lord had honoured their faith, because the wife was expecting a baby. In due course a daughter was born to rejoicing parents.

SUMMARY

1.   Sex is God's gift for procreation and recreation for those he joins together.
2.   Those who follow God's Guidebook for rules for upright living are safeguarded from the devil's dirty delusions.
3.   God intends children to be the natural results of married life. They are a blessing from him. We are responsible for the timing and manner of their conception.

Chapter 5

The Beginning of the Most Important Forty Weeks of Our Lives

The most exciting news possible to couples who marry for love, is that a new family member is expected. The joy may be a little muted if the timing is not perfect, or if accommodation is already strained, but love and expectation soon turn up the volume of thankfulness.

Regrettably not all babies are welcome. And those who want them least, face many pressures when they fall pregnant. Some single women marry the person responsible, or find a partner willing to accept their unborn child. Those who are unwilling or unable to marry face three options. Firstly, to elect to go through with the pregnancy, and bring up the child with the support and help of family and friends. Secondly, to offer the child for adoption as soon as possible after birth. Thirdly, to have an abortion. This can be a 'no-win' situation as the removal of short-term responsibilities sometimes creates long-term problems for the prospective mother, and to any children she may bear in the future.

A brief look at the effects of a variety of pregnancy terminations may assist those who contemplate this, or have experienced it.

Termination of pregnancy on medical grounds

Historically, the medical profession has been ethically committed to support life. Some doctors still remain opposed to the termination of pregnancy, except for the very rare possibility of endangering the mother's health.

Present day medical investigatory procedures can diagnose the sex of the child and even unremedial foetal problems. Some parents elect to terminate on the medical evidence, or on their doctor's recommendation. Termination for the sole purpose of sex preference could only be classed as infanticide.

Miscarriages (involuntary abortions)

Dr Thomas Verny, writing with John Kelly in *The Secret Life of the Unborn Child* (Summit Books), says this:

> 'There is speculation that in the very first weeks – perhaps even hours – after conception, the fertilized ovum possesses enough self-awareness to sense rejection and enough will to act on it ... For now, as interesting as it is this theory is just that, a theory, not proven fact.'   (Page 19)

One wonders how such a theory could possibly be proved! What has become most evident to us through extensive counselling is that fertilized ova, although rejected by one or both parents, do survive the crucial forty weeks. In these cases, the evidences of rejection may be seen from the cradle to the grave.

But spontaneous miscarriages can occur up to the twenty-eighth week of pregnancy. Beyond that the death of a foetus is usually regarded as a stillbirth.

The modern legal tangles caused by the complications of in vitro fertilization and frozen fertilized female ova have certainly introduced a bio-ethical jungle in which medical, legal and theological experts have not yet emerged with acceptable definitions sustainable in a court of law. The creation of human life outside the womb (except for married couples in the opinion of many), and the genetic engineering for selective reproduction, are entirely outside of God's purpose in procreation. The Bible does not justify the methods used, or the results obtained. Much will be said and written in the name of God, but none of it will carry the divine imprimatur of 'so says the LORD'.

Abortion

'Abortion' is a very emotive word. Verbal, physical, and even property violence seem to mark the lines of demarcation between the

Right to Life Movements, and the proponents of abortion in some countries.

In the Old Testament the evil practice of sacrificing children to fire gods is well documented. Probably the best known of these was the Ammonite Molech, a hollow brass deity filled with fire. It had the head of a calf with human arms and hands outstretched to receive the offerings of babies and young children. They were immediately incinerated. The practice was utterly abominable to God, and was one of the causes of Israel being sent into captivity (2 Kings 17:17) in 721 BC, and Judah in 606 BC (2 Kings 21:6).

If God was grieved with the Hebrews for their wholesale slaughter of young life, how much more does the massacre of untold millions of unborn children in this evil age stir up the anger of God? He is not the God of abortion.

Men responsible for a young woman's pregnancy sometimes use inordinate pressures to force an abortion, and to such, embryo life has no sanctity. It is sacrificed on the altar of their own pride and convenience. But God holds the records, and justice will be done to those who plunder the womb.

A young lady who drank too much alcohol at a party, remembered being gang-raped, and became pregnant with twins. Enraged at what had happened, and ashamed to tell her parents, she arranged for an abortion. The legacy she carried for twenty-six years was bitterness, revenge, hatred of men, a deep sense of defilement, and an inability to respond sexually when she later married. We rejoiced to see the Lord free her entirely.

Another pregnant young lady was subject to strong pressure to abort by her mother who continually threatened to commit suicide because of the shame her daughter could bring to the family. Finally the girl won, gave birth to her baby, and the mother didn't carry out her threat. But the tension between mother and daughter was not resolved. Finally both mother and rejected child came to us, and the Lord released them both.

Many women have had pregnancies terminated by involuntary or deliberate means. When this is done by the medical profession for health reasons, no accusations of abortion should be levelled at the mother or the obstetricians involved. No matter how pregnancies are ended, children born subsequently are likely to have problems. Their 'forty-weeks' have been spent in the same womb in which life ended in death.

Some children have been brought for prayer because of excessive fears experienced since birth such as a fear of death; others have shown a spirit of death by being morbid, expressing a wish to die, and sometimes an excessive interest in death. It is also not uncommon for some to be gripped by a spirit of guilt passed on by their mothers.

Death and fear are spiritual partners, and Jesus Christ overcame them both. (See Hebrews 2:14–15, Revelation 1:18, 2 Timothy 1:6 and Romans 8:15).

Death and fear were unknown to humans until Satan deceived Eve and succeeded in tempting Adam to rebel against God. They both experienced spiritual death (Genesis 2:17), and both experienced the emotional pain of fear (Genesis 3:8–10). The death of Jesus Christ when he conquered all spirits of fear gives us delegated authority in his name to release children and adults bound by such spirits. Paul makes it clear that a 'spirit' is the root cause of the fears which can grip believers (Romans 8:15).

In the case of abortions, miscarriages, terminations, and stillbirths (when a dead foetus may have been in the womb for days, or even longer), either before or after marriage, we have found that those very spirits of death and fear can affect the next baby conceived. In childhood they may be retarded in emotional development, have bad dreams, nightmares, fears, be fascinated by death, and have thoughts of suicide. Suggestions as to how to minister to such children will be given in a later chapter.

We lovingly recommend that women who have suffered such traumas should seek release and healing from the past. The following list of relevant forces may help identify what needs to be cleansed and renewed. In this way if anyone desires to bear another child (children), the problems will have been resolved.

● *In the case of abortion:*
Spirits of murder and death in the womb; a spirit of unfulfilment, and if appropriate, rejection, unforgiveness, resentment, bitterness, anger, and hatred of men. Also spirits of lust, rape, fornication or adultery if appropriate.

● *In cases of miscarriage, medical termination, or stillbirth:*
Spirits of death in the womb, miscarriage or fear of miscarriage, rejection, grief.

A married mother with one child recently came for a session of deliverance and prayer. She told us that her mother had had three miscarriages and one stillbirth before she was conceived. When her mother found herself pregnant again, she pleaded with the 'Virgin Mary' for a daughter whom she could carry to full-term. She also offered frequent prayers to a statue of Mary in her home. When a daughter was born, the grateful mother named her 'Mary'. In due course Mary experienced new life in Jesus Christ, and was Spirit-filled. Eventually she married and became pregnant. She then experienced the same bleeding problem which had affected her mother. She rested in bed, trusted the Lord, and claimed His promise of fruitfulness from Malachi 3:9, 10, believing she had honoured God in tithes, offerings, and righteous living. God heard her prayer and a delightful baby daughter was born to her. Both were freed from hereditary spirits.

Another married woman who had been experiencing great difficulty in carrying to full-term, came for prayer. She had had three miscarriages, two at three months, and twins at six months. The Lord revealed that the causes were hereditary spirits of miscarriage and bitterness. Her mother had conceived her four months before being married, and had later confessed her bitterness. The daughter had grown up feeling rejected, and a failure.

In the next chapter we will examine problems which originate from the in-utero state. But before we reach that subject, we need to examine what commences at conception, and becomes evident after the child is born, or in early childhood.

Wrong motivation for parenthood

A bride of two weeks became deeply shocked when a brother committed suicide. Her marriage was already shaky, and she and her husband decided to have a baby as a means of holding them together. In due course a daughter was born, and when she was nine years of age, we were asked to pray for her. She obviously had every symptom of rejection, was shy, sucked her thumb, and was said to have shown a great fear of being abandoned when her mother had gone away for a two-day break. The girl was also insecure, and quite disinterested in spiritual matters despite living in a Christian community. A child always suffers when conceived for wrong reasons.

Conception, despite precautions

A mother was using an inter-uterine device (IUD) to prevent conception, when to her surprise, she conceived. Her in-laws strongly disapproved of the timing of the pregnancy, as it interfered with their family travel plans.

The child was brought to us at the age of seven, suffering deep rejection, hating herself, nervous, insecure, and wetting her bed. She showed inferiority, was self-destructive, and said that she wished she were dead. The Lord released her from those controlling spirits, particularly death, then we asked the Lord to cleanse and heal her.

The death of a twin

One of the most unusual cases we have had concerned a teenager who was one of twins. The mother told us that during her pregnancy she had miscarried, and that the doctor had given her an injection to cleanse the womb. Several weeks afterwards, during an examination he discovered to his astonishment that the woman was still pregnant. This was the first indication that there had been twins. A daughter was born in due course, and she seemed none the worse for the experience.

When she was around seventeen years of age, Phyl and I stayed with her parents. The teenager told us that she had always been conscious of a 'missing person' in her life. She always felt lonely, needed constant affection, felt as if she was 'two persons', and developed the habit of holding imaginary conversations with her missing 'other half'. She said she spent hours speaking aloud to herself. With a shrug of the shoulders she said, 'People probably think I'm nuts!' We certainly didn't, and asked the Lord to give her deep release and healing to her subconscious mind, which he did. The habit would have taken longer to break. This experience has been confirmed several times, and does not appear to be caused by auto-suggestion.

A mother's rejection of conception

The wife of a missionary wanted to have only one child so that her missionary work would not be hindered. When she became pregnant for the third time she began to hate the child within her, and did so throughout the pregnancy. When a daughter was born she was given no quality time by either parent. She slept in a room previously used by prostitutes and a witch, who left a curse on the room when forced to vacate it. As the child grew, she was sexually interfered with in that room, and finally raped, but the parents would never believe her. She tried to commit suicide three times and suffered from bulimia.

As an adult she had written to three pastors asking how she could get close to God but not one was able to help her. Every time she opened the Word of God she could see only negative Scriptures. Until the time she came to us, her parents had never shown her any affection.

Phyl ministered freedom to her from deep rejection, spirits of destruction, antichrist, prostitution, and many others. She left in peace.

The whole process of conception and pregnancy is indeed a master-piece of God's creative power. Medical science tells us that the male sperm contains genes, which according to the Concise Oxford Diction-ary are 'units of heredity in chromosomes, controlling particular inherited characteristics of an individual'. And so begins the first parental influence on the future child. These characteristics may of course be good, or bad. The whole principle of the hereditary transmission of sinful characteristics is examined in *Evicting Demonic Intruders and Breaking Bondages*. This process originates particularly from the father whose biological contribution to his future child is the blueprint contained in the sperm which affects the fertilisation process. As some paternal hereditary problems such as rejection and anger may manifest themselves very early in a child's life, they could have been transmitted only at conception. The two hereditary influ-ences a father transmits to his child are:

1. Conception passes on the spiritual curse of the fall

Through conception, the fertilised ovum (ova) receives from the father's genes an hereditary factor which ultimately causes physical death. Unlike a chromosome, it is invisible, and nothing yet dis-covered scientifically has been able to circumvent the inevitability of dying. '*A man is destined to die once ...*' (Hebrews 9:27). Even atheists and sceptics cannot deny the truth of that Bible statement '*Surely I have been a sinner from birth, sinful from the time my mother conceived me*' (Psalm 51:5). See also Romans 5:12.

The only exception

Jesus Christ is the only human not subject to this principle. God said that the seed (or child) **of the woman** would crush the serpent's (devil's) head (Genesis 3:15). Luke confirmed that Mary was **a virgin**, and that her child, who would be known as the Son of God, would be born through the power of the Holy Spirit (Luke 1:27–38).

Because no human father was involved in the incarnation, Jesus Christ received no curse of death, or hereditary sin. This is confirmed:

Firstly, the word of God clearly states that Jesus Christ was totally devoid of any manifestation of sin which would have been inevitable had his birth been caused by human conception. See Luke 1:35, Hebrews 7:26 and 9:14.

Secondly, God could never have accepted a sacrifice blemished by sin. No angel from heaven, nor a sinful human being, could have become a substitute for sinful mankind. Only a God of holiness could have provided an acceptable substitute by his mystical union with sinless humanity. John the Baptist said, '*Look, the Lamb of God, who takes away the sin of the world*' (John 1:29).

Thirdly, had Jesus Christ inherited sin and the physical death syndrome he could not have chosen the manner and timing of his own death. His death would have been natural and inevitable. But he not only chose to die (Psalm 40:6, 7); he also chose when to die (Matthew 27:50), and how to die (John 12:32). And when he rose from the dead, as conqueror, he took with him the very keys of death and Hades, the place of future punishment (Revelation 1:18).

2. Conception passes hereditary spirits on to the next generation

This subject has been examined in detail in the first volume of this series *Evicting Demonic Intruders and Breaking Bondages*. The following is a short list of what may pass into the new life which commences with the fertilization of a female ovum:

• Lust

When conception results from rape, incest, lust in pre-marital relationships, casual sex, or even lustful passion in marriage, the child to be born will grow up with inner pressures to fulfil sexual desires. When there a history of overtly sexual behaviour in the parents or grandparents of the growing embryo, hereditary spirits of lust (which may even have caused the conception itself), will add to the driving forces with which the child will later have to battle.

When very small children show an excessive curiosity in their own or other's genitals, or continually expose themselves, or stimulate themselves sexually, it can only be by the manipulation of the spirits which have been passed down. Desires for sexual fulfilment do not begin at such an early age.

We have prayed for a two-year old girl who would only go to sleep through stimulating herself sexually. Her parents said that if she woke in the night she would repeat the process. They could hear the satisfied little sounds she made, and knew what she was doing. No treatment seemed to be effective. In desperation and despite their scepticism, the parents asked for their daughter to be prayed for. The Lord released her, and the child started falling asleep immediately after being put to bed. The habit disappeared.

A three-year-old used to take off her panties and wander the neighbourhood, exposing herself to anyone she met. She had been conceived in a brief de facto relationship, and was controlled by a spirit of lust. She too was completely released.

• *Sexual deviations*
Spirits of homosexuality, lesbianism, and bestiality can be passed on to children, but may not manifest themselves until the following generation. In seeking the cause of an insatiable appetite for food in a thin adult, the Lord revealed that there was an hereditary spirit of homosexuality in the family. The counsellee was greatly shocked because there had been no indication of this.

• *Occultism and witchcraft*
A Christian grandfather was unwittingly controlled by a spirit of clairvoyance, believing it to be the enlightenment of the Holy Spirit. His daughter had the same gift, and as her son grew up she told him, 'You will never be able to do wrong without me knowing'. The teenager son told me it was incredible how often his mother would turn up while he was in the act of doing something wrong, and stop him. The Lord freed him that afternoon from his hereditary spirit. During the evening, 'a man' suddenly appeared 'out of the blue' explaining to the teenager that he was a clairvoyant, and telling him to forget all he had heard in the afternoon. He also told him to use his special family gift. The teenager stood in his freedom, and confessed the lordship of Jesus Christ. 'The man' left him in anger.

Children of those who have been involved in occult or witchcraft practices before they were born again, are often plagued with spirits which frighten them at night. Spirits of anti-Christ may also make them aggressively oppose Bible reading, prayer, or playing of Christian songs, particularly praise and worship. We frequently see the Lord release these little ones so that they are troubled no longer. More about this will appear in a later chapter.

● *Addictions of all kinds*

Obesity is an obvious problem in some families, particularly with women. So too are alcohol, cigarette smoking, and gambling. Many argue that the first two are family habits learned as children. Out of curiosity they drain a partially emptied glass, or puff at a discarded cigarette butt. But sociologists have proved that children of alcoholics are four times more liable to become alcoholics than children of non-alcoholics even though they are removed from the family influence, and are placed in the care of non-drinkers.

There are of course many reasons for these addictive habits commencing later in life, but when children between nine and twelve years of age have well-established addictions to alcohol and cigarettes, the cause can only be hereditary.

● *A variety of mental problems*

Anxiety, worry, depression and fears may begin to grip children before or after they commence primary school.

After a boy with this problem had received freedom and healing, the head teacher of his school sent for the mother and asked why such a remarkable change had taken place. He had noted also that his grades had suddenly improved. When told about prayer, he shrugged his shoulders (as most sceptics do), but admitted the change was real.

● *Rejection*

Parents who were rejected by their fathers or mothers will in turn, generally reject their own children. This seems to affect the children more strongly than other sources of rejection yet to be considered. The children are often emotionally retarded, slow learners, negative and dispirited. Freedom in Jesus Christ stops the process and enables the child to gradually recover from the influences which have retarded their development.

• *Anger, temper and violence*

These features of emotional volatility are inward driving forces which may begin to show themselves from babyhood. Unless God frees these children from the strongly aggressive spirits, some of them will regrettably give their parents many heartaches, and may well end up as wards of the State, or occupiers of jail cells.

Two brothers lived for fighting. If no one would fight them in a hotel bar they would dance on a table and fight the first person who objected. One went overseas during the 2nd World War. When he returned someone stole his jacket. He later found the thief, and challenged him about the jacket he was wearing. He replied, 'Are you a good enough man to take it from me?' The answer came in one smashing blow to his jaw. A portion of the thief's shattered bone pierced his brain, and he dropped to the footpath, dead. His assailant was charged with manslaughter and served only two years in prison as the judge took account of his good service record.

Meantime, the son of the convicted man grew up fighting and drinking, like his dad. The two used to visit hotel bars together, the father, now much older, deliberately caused fights for his son to finish. Three weeks after the boy came to know Jesus Christ as Saviour he went to a discipleship school where I was teaching. On the second day he asked for help. His anger and violence had become unbearable and I was (unknown to me), the 'target'. When the Lord set him free, he became my friend. His hereditary spirits of fighting and violence had gone. Of course if he subsequently deliberately disobeys God and goes back to his old ways, the spirit forces would be only too happy to take over again.

• *Sickness and allergies*

As rain water runs down drainpipes, so do sicknesses and allergies run in families. There seems to be too many spirits of these afflictions to name. It is as if these physically oppressive spirits agree amongst themselves to 'sponsor' certain families so that they will be assured of victims to afflict, for generations to come.

I had asthma as a child; so did one of my daughters. I had hay fever as a teenager and adult; so did another one of my daughters. I inherited them from my mother, and without being freed, naturally, passed them on in my genes.

I suggest that you, the reader, pause for a minute and ask yourself one simple question. 'What do I see in myself that I have either seen, or have been told, was also evident in my parents or grandparents?' It would be very surprising if some of the problems already listed do not come to mind. And what about other family problems of pride, apathy, manipulation, perfectionism, ethnic traits, bitterness, unforgiveness, resentment, religious attitudes and scepticism? Of course we need to be thankful for our hereditary blessings, and good points.

This chapter needs to conclude by attempting to answer one question: 'What can be done to prevent these things being passed on to our children?'

(1) Believers contemplating marriage and parenthood would be wise to seek deliverance from hereditary and any other spirits which may have dominated their lifestyles, before or after salvation. Unbelievers need to be born again, and set free.

(2) Couples who plan to have a family, or to add to it, need freedom from the causes of problems they have recognised, so that a child conceived after counselling and deliverance should be free from their own spiritual bondages or dominating spirits.

(3) Children who were born prior to their parents being delivered from such spirits need to be freed and cleansed so that they can grow up without demonic bondages and oppressions. Release is much quicker and easier in childhood before habits become established and spirit forces more strongly resist deliverance. By seeing that children are set free when they are young and tender, later struggles with rebellion, defiance, and self-assertiveness will be averted.

SUMMARY

1.　The news of an expected arrival may bring the greatest joy, or send the parents into depression.

2.　The motivation for, the timing of, and objectives of conception are more important to the child conceived than parents generally realise.

3.　A spirit of death may be present in a mother's womb. Abortion introduces spirits of murder and death. The Old Testament spirit of Molech continues to destroy life, and potential life, through abortive practices.

4.   Babies are beautiful, but the hereditary problems which are waiting to manifest themselves after birth, are ugly and destructive.

5.   Parents should seek freedom for their children from all controlling spirits of heredity as soon as they themselves become aware of these problems, or see them manifest in their children.

Chapter 6

Look Out World – Here We Come

Phase two of the human process is probably increasingly burdensome to the expectant mother. And here I can only speak from observation.

I took great delight in Phyl's three pregnancies, but I had to agree with her when she emphasized each time that we men have the easiest part of the process! I found it was the same after birth, as well. After all, I reasoned, 'Why should I get up early when it was feeding time? Phyl had all the endowments necessary!' But I must admit that after the babies had been topped up and tailed off, they were welcome in bed.

During pregnancy, not only does the foetus grow in size, but it is able to receive the intellectual, emotional and spiritual input of the mother. Specialists certainly encourage fathers to speak to their unborn children, so that their voices can be a source of comfort after birth, but that is not what I have in mind. The waiting role of the father is that of providing his wife with as much love, tenderness, assistance and security as she needs, so that the baby can receive the best input possible. That of course should spill over into lots of practical help in the home. The other children (if any) should practice this too.

There is no greater resource facility for revealing a pregnant woman's input into her unborn child than the Bible.

Jacob had two wives, Leah and Rachel. God prevented Rachel from conceiving, and allowed Leah to fall pregnant (Genesis 29:31).

What follows is the clearest evidence that parents either consciously, or unconsciously influence their unborn child. The emotional relationship between a husband and wife is expressed by the male in the act of intercourse, and by the female when she realises she is carrying a child.

Jacob's sexual relationship with Leah was anything but ideal. He made it obvious he did not love her. His sexual acts could only have been motivated by duty or lust, neither of which are ideal ways to commence a family.

Leah obviously felt a very rejected woman, and bitter at the way she had been treated. She made no secret of this in choosing names for her first sons. The details come from Genesis chapter 29.

From the record it is clear that Jacob kept on fathering her children, with little or no love and support as a father or husband. Leah obviously bore at least three children in a state of rejection, bitterness, resentment, hardness and frustration. It is patently obvious from the boys' subsequent behaviours that they were being motivated by some rather heavy hereditary influences.

No. 1 son, Reuben

When he was a young man, his father's spirit of lust stirred up his sexual awareness. He found some mandrake plants in the field and brought them to his mother to boost her sexual appeal to his father. The fruit of the mandrake is about the size of a small apple and supposedly has power to arouse sensual pleasure. (The Arabs call it 'the devil's apple'.)

It is no wonder that Reuben later became promiscuous. He despised his father, and dishonoured him by sleeping with one of his given 'wives' Bilhah (Genesis 35:22). Because of that he lost his birthright as the eldest son. It was given to the two sons of Joseph, Ephraim and Manasseh (1 Chronicles 5:1, 2).

Sons 2 and 3, Simeon, and Levi

Neither was conceived nor carried with love, and that was subsequently evident in manhood (Genesis chapter 34). When their sister Dinah was raped by Shechem, a Hivite ruler, all her brothers were furious and revengeful. Shechem obviously loved the girl and asked his family to arrange a marriage. Using deceit, the brothers imposed a condition of circumcision on Shechem and the other men of the city. *'Three days later, while all of them were still in pain, two of Jacob's sons, Simeon and Levi, Dinah's brothers, took their swords and attacked the unsuspecting city, killing every male'* (Genesis 34:25). All the brothers then got into the act, by looting the city and carrying away all the women, children and animals.

Where did Simeon and Levi learn deception, and where did that harsh, cruel, murderous spirit come from? Jacob was a deceiver by name and practice, and Leah's father was a master of the art; and nine months in-utero deprivation of love, plus the input of a mother's rejection and bitterness, certainly made a positive contribution.

Jacob was incensed by the Schechem slaughter. Probably, like some modern fathers, he wondered why his sons should turn out like that, after all, hadn't he been a model father? So it was with much anger and self-pity that he exploded (Genesis 34:30). The brothers stuck together claiming that Shechem had no right to treat their sister as a prostitute (verse 31).

No. 4 son, Judah

Judah also received his father's spirit of lust. After his wife died, he propositioned a woman by the roadside thinking she was a prostitute. He did not realise that she was in fact his widowed daughter-in-law, to whom he had broken his promise to provide another son. Tamar gave birth to twin boys, Perez and Zerah (Genesis 38:12–30).

So the record of the first four sons born to Jacob whose sexual partnership was loveless, and to Leah who felt bitter about being rejected in love, does not bring credit to either of them. For forty weeks those boys were being prepared for life in a somewhat emotionally confused atmosphere. The result became obvious in later life.

Tensions between the twelve children of the four women in Jacob's life were often high, and boiled over when they thought that Joseph, Rachel's first son, (and the second youngest), might gain prominence over them all. The frustrations, jealousy, insecurity, rejection, anger and deception, so evident in the parents, were so deeply entrenched in the children, that the events which marred the relationships in later life were almost predictable.

In the foreword to *The Secret Life of the Unborn Child* by Thomas Verny MD with John Kelly (Summit Books), these statements are included (pages 12, 13):

'The foetus can see, hear, experience, taste, and on a primitive level, even learn in-utero (that is, in the uterus – before birth).

Most importantly, he can feel – not with an adult's sophistication, but feel nevertheless.'

'A corollary to this discovery is that what a child feels and perceives begins shaping his attitudes and expectations about himself. Whether he ultimately sees himself and, hence, acts as a happy or sad, aggressive or meek, secure or anxiety-ridden person, depends, in part, on messages he gets about himself in the womb.'

'The chief source of these shaping messages is the child's mother. **This does not mean that every fleeting worry, doubt, or anxiety a woman has rebounds on her child**. Chronic anxiety or a wrenching ambivalence about motherhood can leave a deep scar on the unborn child's personality. On the other hand, such life-enhancing emotions as joy, elation and anticipation can contribute significantly to the emotional development of a healthy child.'

A pregnant married woman was informed by her gynaecologist that she would have an abnormal child, either with Down's Syndrome or other physical abnormalities. Throughout the rest of her pregnancy, she was torn between her great desire to have a child and the temptation to abort. After birth the child appeared to be normal in every way, but as she grew up she was double-minded. She had the greatest difficulty in making decisions and sticking by them. She was twenty-six years of age before she learned that she could be released from in-utero influences, and when she came to us for help, the Lord totally freed her.

About two or three weeks before Aureole, our second child, was born, Phyl went outside to place some garbage in the bin by the back door. As she returned to the kitchen, she noticed to her horror, that a weta (a very large wingless horned grasshopper) was clinging to her dress. She was terrified, and the baby went rigid with fear within her causing her considerable pain. She managed to knock the weta off, and trod on it. From her earliest days, Aureole showed an abnormal fear of all insects, spiders, or 'creepy-crawlies', and would yell for help when she saw even the smallest 'daddy-long-legs' within ten feet of her. The Lord has freed her of that terror, but she has never made friends with them. In fact her children think they have a brave mother because she kills any spiders that upset them!

A woman suffering from a thyroid condition was told by her doctor that her baby could either be physically or mentally disabled. Because of her religious beliefs, she refused abortion, and continued the pregnancy full of fear. The child grew up to have the 'two-person-syndrome', and in adulthood she asked for prayer for freedom. There is no doubt that this was the will of God for her life, so she was freed.

A man who was over forty years of age asked for help. His mother had been a foundling (deserted child of unknown parents), and she was brought up in an orphanage. From birth he had known hereditary rejection, but conquered it sufficiently to take a leading position in the work force, even when it required opposing strong union officials. In due course he married, and daughters were born. He found he just could not demonstrate his love to them. When two fellow executives opposed him, and some youth workers at church failed to respond to his leadership, a sense of rejection began to dominate him. He could no longer handle threatening situations, withdrew, became negative, introverted, full of fears, passive, excessively tired, and wept without provocation. He stopped working around the house, and spent more and more time alone, reading. He was dominated by the hereditary rejection received in-utero. The Lord set him free.

These case histories confirm the need for potential parents to be freed from dominating spirits received from heredity, or from deliberate sin, so that they are not passed on to their children.

It would of course be unfair to consider the negative side of in-utero life only. The Scriptures throw light on the blessedness of those who are born to mothers who are filled and controlled by the Holy Spirit:

The conditions of motherhood imposed on Samson's mother
(Judges chapter 13)

Manoah and his wife (whose name is not mentioned) were childless. The angel of the LORD appeared to Mrs Manoah and said,

> *'You are sterile and childless, but you are going to conceive and have a son. Now see to it that you drink no wine or other fermented drink and that you do not eat anything unclean, because you will conceive and give birth to a son. No razor may be used on his head, because the boy is to be a Nazarite, **set apart to God from birth**, and he will begin the deliverance of Israel from the hands of the Philistines.'*
> (verse 3–5, emphasis added)

Here is the clearest evidence of positive blessings of in-utero influences upon an unborn child. It was by God's grace that the child was to be born; by God's will that he was to be his agent of deliverance; and by God's command the mother had to refrain from alcohol which modern medical research shows predisposes to abortion. Such abstinences would also prevent the child in adulthood from yielding to temptation to defile the conditions of his order (Numbers 6:1–21).

The in-utero response of John the Baptist (Luke 1:39–56)

Elizabeth, the priest Zechariah's wife, had a special visitor when she was six months pregnant. It was Mary, a relative from Nazareth, and her greeting from the doorway had a most unusual effect upon Elizabeth and the child she was carrying. Elizabeth was consciously filled with the Holy Spirit, and her unborn child literally jumped for joy within her. Discerning the good news about Mary, she blessed her, and spoke of the child to be born to Mary as 'my Lord' (verse 43).

Luke had already described the priest and his wife as *upright in the sight of God, observing all the Lord's commandments and regulations blamelessly* (Luke 1:6). They both had ideal qualities of character for parenthood. Their son John was certainly unique. Hundreds of years before he was conceived, his ministry was spelled out (Isaiah 40), and God gave his name. Before he was able to speak, it was revealed that his ministry would be in the spirit and power of Elijah, and unlike any before him, he was to be filled with the Holy Spirit from the moment of birth. Actually the NIV suggests it may have been *from his mother's womb*, (*even from before his birth* The Living Bible) (Luke 1:62–66). When Zechariah was filled with the Holy Spirit, he announced publicly that God's call upon the life of his son was greater than any claim he might have as a parent (Luke 1:67, 68).

John the Baptist illustrates the greatest blessing an unborn child might receive. In every generation, dedicated, upright, and praying parents have sought the help and blessing of God in conception and childbirth, and have been blessed. God always has a special claim on those children, and a special work for them to do.

The climax to it all

In the days of Phyl's childbearing, fathers were not allowed in the delivery theatre. So I missed out on seeing the final traumatic climax of the forty weeks of my own girls. I was not in that small percentage of husbands who physically go through sympathetic labour pains! As much as I tried to appreciate Phyl's discomfort and pain through which our children came into the world, I am sure I failed. Even when I lined up with other doting fathers and relatives to gaze through the nursery window at 'Baby Gibson', I didn't understand the magnitude of the birth trauma each daughter experienced.

Fortunately, none of us remember the feeling of alarm when the amniotic fluid drained away leaving us literally high and dry; the relentless pressures of being expelled from our position of comfort and rest; perhaps the pain of extracting forceps; the succession of terrifying sounds, lights, feelings of being pulled into unusual shapes; and finally an utterly new sound coming from ourselves as we breathed for the first time and heard our own voices. Yet in no time at all, most of us were sleeping without a care in the world.

Over many years of praying for children, we have found that the manner of delivery and after-care may considerably affect the child.

Protracted labour

In our experience, babies born after very protracted labour are often drowsy, and develop a spirit of apathy as they grow up. They generally show a lack of enthusiasm and little self-motivation. Sometimes they are slow learners at school and care little for sports activities. These children will also show symptoms of rejection, including low self-image, insecurity, inferiority, and sometimes anger or anxiety.

Overdue births

The apathy associated with prolonged pregnancies may develop into impassiveness in later years. A young lady came to us who had been one month overdue at the time of birth. She had no desire to live, and appeared to be devoid of emotion.

Fast deliveries

Some children are born in a remarkably short time, even before their mothers reach hospital. This often causes the child to suffer from shock, fear, and insecurity. Because some babies have to be placed in a humidi-crib the bonding process with the mother is delayed and this will commence the rejection process. Adults may be dominated by fears which commenced through a fast delivery.

Unexpected births

As unlikely as it may appear, women occasionally give birth to children without having been aware that they were pregnant. Such children have rejection symptoms, and usually have difficulty in experiencing normal emotions.

A married woman who already had seven children lived next to us early in our marriage. She noticed she was putting on weight, and despite her past pre-natal experiences, totally rejected any idea of being pregnant again. She convinced herself that she was just getting fat, after having had children. Finally, her doctor convinced her that she was seven months pregnant. The shock to the mother and her rejection of the child, which we noticed, were considerable.

A young man shared with me the most unusual circumstances of his birth. His mother (who already had three daughters) told him that she had no indication that she was pregnant until, to her astonishment, she gave birth to a one and a half-pound boy during a regular visit to the toilet. She placed him in a shoe-box and took him to the nearest hospital where he lived in a humidi-crib for three months. In all my ministry I have never met such an emotionless person as that young man. As he grew up in an otherwise female household his sisters often teased him, so it was not surprising that he had turned to homosexuality for male comfort. He came to see me when he was in his twenties. He was no longer indulging in a homosexual life-style, but was emotionally 'dead', and lived his Christian life by will power, without feelings. I was sorry not to have been able to help him more than I did.

Caesarian births

There are of course many medical reasons for a child to be born by Caesarian section. However, after speaking with women who had a child, or children delivered in this way, we have concluded that when a baby is not subjected to the normal head-moulding muscular pressures of the mother's pelvic region, some unusual problems often occur as the child grows up.

Firstly, they mostly seem to suffer from emotional insecurity, need encouragement and more physical love than other children.

Secondly, they frequently fail to be able to gauge distances between themselves and objects, resulting in frequent collisions. They are usually blamed for carelessness or for being clumsy.

Zachary, one of our grandsons, was born by Caesarian section. As a growing boy, he constantly wanted assurance of being loved, but more constantly ran into the poles, posts and uprights that his older brother had no problem avoiding. After many visits to the hospital for sutures to head injuries, the Lord showed that a spiritual helmet of salvation needed to be put on daily for his preservation. The recurring problem then ceased.

Sometimes when we have been teaching deliverance, grandmothers have confirmed seeing these symptoms in their own families.

Instrumental births

Not only do some children suffer temporary or longer-lasting physical problems from forceps deliveries, but the emotional scars may remain after physical injuries have healed.

Some children show the results of that trauma as they grow, making a great deal of fuss over the slightest pain. They may grow up with a fear of injury and pain, and grow into hypochondriacs.

Births to mothers with serious health problems

When women with ill-health fall pregnant, or when ill-health occurs during pregnancy, the emotional well-being of the child may well become endangered, especially when the mother's health deteriorates, and there is a fear that the process of giving birth could be fatal to the mother.

A friend of ours who has university degrees in two different professions, shared with us when in her early seventies that her mother had not been expected to survive her birth. Her father was very upset at the possibility of losing his wife through childbirth. Her mother did not die as expected, but those in-utero influences affected her from earliest childhood. She said she could never remember a time when she had not wished she were dead, but had always lacked the courage to take her own life.

When children are brought for prayer, Phyl normally asks each mother about the circumstances of the child's birth. If there was a difficult birth this trauma becomes the first item requiring prayer. By listening to the problems the mother has experienced with the child, and listening to the family background, a list is soon compiled of bondages to be broken, or dominant spirits to be released; and for which cleansing and healing needs to be ministered.

Why should our children become victims of spiritual forces which will continue to trouble them sometimes throughout life, when the healing touch of Jesus Christ can bring them release while they are still young?

Children who have had difficulties at birth need release from the individual trauma, fear, rejection, and other problems mentioned.

SUMMARY

1.   The emotional relationship between parents at the time of conception can affect not only the unborn child, but its life after birth.

2.   The mother's in-utero influences on her child are considerable, both negatively and positively.

3.   The manner of birth may affect the child in childhood and in adult life.

4.   Jesus Christ is able to free children and adults from emotional and spiritual traumas through conception, during the time in-utero, and at birth.

Chapter 7

Whatever Has Gone Wrong?

Almost everyone loves babies. But there are exceptions. Fathers who get broken sleep at night because the baby cries a lot; the cranky neighbour next door; the young brother or sister who forfeits first place in time and attention for the newcomer without being asked to do so; and sometimes a teenage daughter who is rather reluctantly pressed into being nursemaid at some loss of her personal freedom.

Babies look innocent, but soon prove they are not; sound frail, but can summon a household by simply raising their voices; and appear so placid and mild-mannered, until they are crossed, or get hold of your hair. Despite their many beautiful features they have the potential of growing into such 'monsters'! I mean they tear, break and smash the things we hold dear, and soon show anger, hatred, selfishness and self-protectiveness. Later, they learn to swear, lie, steal, cheat, and do all the things of which the family is ashamed.

'What has gone wrong?' is indeed a valid question. There is no simple answer, because there are often many causes. Of course it is popular and customary to blame the parents, but most of them would strenuously deny responsibility. So all possible causes need to be carefully looked at so that we can see how past wrongs may be remedied, and future wrongs avoided.

Some causes of child problems encountered

The baby's sex is deeply disappointing to the parents
A girl is born when they were so 'sure' it was going to be a boy (or vice-versa). Christians are sometimes more susceptible to this if they have been relying on some 'word of the Lord' on what the sex of the child

will be. So they become disappointed with possible resentment, bitterness, and rejection of the child. So the baby, so warm, secure and wanted before birth, senses the emotional disturbance in the mother and fails to receive the love and security it so desperately needs. By the time the parents readjust, irreparable damage may have been done to the child's emotional nature, and the symptoms of rejection may be evident. The baby may cry frequently, be difficult to feed, and be a restless sleeper. Other symptoms of low self-image, insecurity, inferiority, anxiety and fears will follow in childhood. Deeply embedded in that child's personality will be a desire to please others to avoid rejection, even to pretending to be the sex the parents originally wanted. And so girls become 'Tom-boys', or boys show feminine leanings in clothes and lifestyle. They may even become lesbians or homosexuals. But praise God for the changes we have seen in some mature adults who were rejected at birth. Jesus Christ gives freedom then healing from the past, and enables people to accept themselves and their true sexuality. Ideally, freedom should be sought as soon as a mother recognizes the symptoms of a sex-rejection trauma manifesting in the child.

One adult woman seeking help liked to wear overalls, drive trucks and appear to be tough. She was masculine in appearance and speech. She even wore a man's watch, and rejected feminine jewellery of any kind. After being set free, she wore feminine clothes, make up and lots of female accessories. She was gentle, loving, and glad to be a woman.

A baby's separation from its mother for any cause usually commences the rejection syndrome

Examples include:

(1) Premature babies being placed in an incubator (humidi-crib).

(2) Long delays in the bonding process because of a need to stabilize a baby's vital functions, or because of the mother's impaired state of health. Recently, we met two fathers who became bonded to their daughters by holding them in their arms for up to one hour in the delivery room while their wives were receiving post-natal care. One was a baby whom the father doted on. The other became a toddler whose daddy could do more with her than her mother.

(3) Hospitalization of a baby.

A mother's insecurity, or fears of not being able to cope with motherhood may be passed on to her daughter

Women who are emotionally immature, or who do not have a strong maternal instinct, sometimes become overwhelmed by the sudden and demanding responsibilities of motherhood. Babies who cry incessantly when they are taken home, interrupting normal sleep patterns, will sometimes cause their mothers to be fearful and tearful. From experience, I believe the best antidote to these problems is an experienced and patient grandmother. Phyl always tried to spend the first two weeks with each of our three daughters after they were discharged from hospital – either by bringing them to our home, or by going to theirs. This facilitated bonding, rested the mothers, and because Phyl loves babies so much she also became bonded to them. As the grandchildren have grown up, that love-bond and loyalty to their grandmother remains strong.

Should mother-baby relationships not be normalized quickly, the child will suffer emotionally, and the roots of rejection will commence to grow.

The manner in which parents treat their children

Just as a bud needs rain and sunlight to unfold and grow to its maximum size, colour, and perfume, so does a baby need loving care to maximize its human potential. Should that loving care not be given, or be stopped or withdrawn for any reason, emotional growth does not keep pace with physical development. As a result, children may be well built, but show signs of emotional retardation. They may be unsure of themselves, have no confidence in trying new things, excessively strive to please people in order to gain acceptance, and continually seek approval and demonstrations of affection. Whatever a parent may do for the child will never satisfy the deep longing for physical affection and closeness. Love is an intangible spiritual warmth which flows from one soul to another, normally accompanied by some physical demonstration. That flow needs to be maintained throughout childhood and teenage years.

A child who does not receive love does not sit down to reason why a mother or father is withholding love, or is unable to express it. Children are controlled by their feelings. Consequently, a child may feel rejected, or imagine that he or she has been rejected without parents being aware of what is happening. In fact they may become

mystified when their children show symptoms of rejection. To counteract this possibility we offer this advice:

(1) *Children need constant assurances of love*, with the physical
cuddles and kisses that children associate with love. They live in a
personal, real world, not in the unexpressed thoughts and emotions of
parents.

(2) *Parents should carefully guard their tongues when angry with their
little ones*. Through busyness, frustration or anger, it is so easy for
hasty words to demolish fragile bridges of relationship. If this should
happen, apologies should be made and a warm caring attitude re-
established. The fallout could be bitterly regretted in later years if
thoughtless words were taken seriously and caused alienation.

(3) *Parents who were not given physical love during their childhood*
should ask the Lord for his help to show love to their babies and
children. Commence with a commitment to love and the feelings will
follow. When married couples have a child to 'hold their marriage
together', this places a very unfair responsibility on the child. Unless
true love develops and binds the parents together with the child, that
child could manipulate competing loyalties and split the marriage
instead of healing it. The proposed healing agent has become the
hurting victim.

(4) *Growing children find security in their mother's presence*. When a
boy comes home from school, his mother is expected to fill an empty
stomach; be a 'nurse' for cuts and scratches, and a 'judge' for
determining rights from wrongs. She is expected to know more than
school teachers on all subjects; console a broken heart; and be an
advisor on emotional matters. All of this has to be done again and
again with no reward other than a deep inner satisfaction of being a
good mum. To express these requirements in two words, they would
surely be – **constant availability**.

(5) *Parents need to avoid general criticism of their children*. Of course
it is necessary to point out, and correct obvious problems. But how
easy it is for us parents to forget the faltering and often painstaking
steps by which our own characters developed. Just as a dog cowers and
cringes through overmuch discipline, so a child's confidence and well
being can be eroded by non-specific criticism or correction. A different
approach is needed to help the child reach the expected standards.

(6) *Unfairness is especially hurtful to children*. Although fairness was
listed in chapter two as a means of a parent blessing a child, it needs to

be reinforced. Just give one boy a small piece of cake and his brother a larger piece, and it almost commences an international incident! Punish one child a little more severely than his brother for the same offence, committed even months earlier, and the offended party will yell louder and longer about the imagined injustice than about the discipline itself.

Children are specially sensitive to fairness and justice, even if it is subjective! The common saying that 'Justice must not only be done, but must also appear to be done', is particularly appropriate to children. To prove it, just give one child one more sweet than the rest, then stand by for the protests!

A spirit of injustice may cause a child to become selfish, self-protective, and sometimes, revengeful. In fact, many adults receiving counselling, have retained vivid memories of injustices in the home, or at school, and continue to show evidence of what commenced many years previously.

(7) *Spoiling children is bad for them*, and for everyone who has anything to do with them. Few of us have not reacted negatively against spoilt children. We have either felt 'on edge', or had the strongest desire to personally 'hand out' discipline to some loud-voiced whiner, or screaming, yelling, tantrum child who specializes in performances in supermarkets and public places. Then there is the 'sullen type', intent on teasing, or reaping revenge on a brother or sister behind their parent's back; or the 'cherub' who grabs everything 'sacred' in your home. His mother's only reaction is to smile and say indulgently, 'You really shouldn't, Murgatroyd'. And who hasn't secretly wished to forcibly restrain the boisterous human tornado who demolishes everything in its path, and terrorizes other children, and animals in the process? Spoilt children are manipulative, self-centred, and unpopular. Unless they are 're-educated', they will grow into self-assertive and demanding adults who will wreck good relationships, particularly in marriage.

(8) *Too much discipline* will give a child a spirit of rejection, and cause other unpleasant fallout symptoms. These include fear of a parent, hatred towards a father or mother, fear of authority figures, a low self-image, sometimes worthlessness, and an inability to give or receive love. Unless release is obtained, an authoritarian spirit will be passed to the next generation, and when these children become parents they will treat their own children as they themselves were treated.

(9) *Favouritism* in a family can cause feelings of rejection, and break family unity. The non-favoured child, or children, can also become jealous and resentful towards the 'apple' of the parent's eye. Some of the ways this may occur are:

- When parents constantly challenge one child to achieve better results by eulogizing an older brother or sister's achievements in education, sport, art, music, or in making friends.
- When a father obviously favours one child, and the mother favours another. The children will respond with competitiveness, performance, manipulation, and even telling tales on one another.
- When parents overlook the achievements of one child, and praise the same results in another child.

Regardless of the method used, the results in the child who has become victimized can be most severe.

(10) *The unfair use of rewards or threats* to encourage a child to produce better results can destroy initiative. Rewarding honest efforts to improve performance by reasonable rewards does not create problems. But the use of rewards like fertilizer to stimulate greater achievement is immoral manipulation which may set false standards that will continue through to adulthood.

Threats to penalize non-performance should never be used in a Christian family. When family pride or social standing over-rules a parent's responsibility to love, protect, and assist a child to develop within his or her ability, it is an act of parental delinquency.

Parental example in the home or community

Recently a lady came to measure our lounge for vertical blinds. She was a friendly, warm person, and was soon chatting freely about herself. 'I'm a cleanliness fanatic' she gushed. 'If I get home at ten o'clock at night, I have to start sweeping and cleaning. I'm all the time cleaning the blinds and the refrigerator, just as my mother taught me. I hate her for it,' she said with a chuckle, 'but I don't change.'

If you pause a moment to reflect on the things you learned by example from your parents, you may be surprised by the number you have adopted. I asked Phyl what she had learned and retained from her parents. She quickly came up with this:

'My mother's example caused me to be a hard worker; to always have food on hand for unexpected guests, to be orderly in all I did, to be sure I welcomed my husband each night looking as fresh and attractive as I was able, to assist neighbours where possible, and minister to the sick. My father's constant positive attitude and cheerfulness, particularly during the times of financial stringency in the Great Depression, greatly impressed me. He would rattle a few coins in his cash box when the business accounts came in and despite never having enough cash to meet all needs, would say cheerily, "There's corn in Egypt yet!" Dad's attitude gave me faith to trust God when we entered full-time Christian work.' So our family continues to be blessed by the example of godly parents now in glory.

Regrettably, all examples are not as positive. Here are a few of the negative ones:

(1) *Criticising other people*. When parents find fault with others in front of the children criticism gains some sort of endorsement. The term, 'roast preacher at Sunday dinner' was probably coined last century, but it is still meaningful. Criticism damages the person doing the criticising more than the victim, and often commences when a rejected person tries to build his own image by demolishing others. It is a learned syndrome which is habit-forming, and can keep family feuds alive for generations.

(2) *Meanness*. Poverty is often unavoidable, and children may become self-protective as a result, but a niggardly spirit comes from a miserly nature, and is associated with covetousness, greed and materialism. When parents are mean, their children are often embarrassed in front of their peers, and may turn to stealing as a cover up. A generous spirit will be a blessing to both giver and receiver; believers with limited resources can still give to others and trust the Lord to supply their needs. By being open and honest with children great lessons of faith may be shared and learned.

(3) *Parental dishonesty* teaches children to be dishonest. Examples:

- 'It fell off the back of a lorry' is a well-known synonym for stealing. A Christian father recently found himself unable to pray effectively for his son who was developing a stealing habit; his whole family had been 'respectable' thieves.

- To avoid spending time on the telephone, a child is told to tell a caller, 'Mummy has gone out'. So the child grows up using deception when convenient, because of a parent's example.

- A father boasted to his family that he was given more change in a certain shop than he was entitled to, but claimed it was their bad luck. He was in fact, a common thief, but would have denied it strenuously if accused. Little ears heard, and when the opportunity came, the process was repeated because 'That was what my Dad used to do'.

- Fathers sometimes instruct a child to tell an untruth to shield another family member. So the child reasons 'If daddy does it, it must be OK', and will deliberately lie when convenient, particularly if it is 'for a good cause', such as to help a relative, or friend. Thus another bad life-time habit commences.

(4) *Immoral conduct* by either parent can have a devastating effect on children.

Firstly when parents fail to teach and live out the principles of moral purity and faithfulness to one another, the children cannot be blamed for believing that promiscuity is allowable for adults. When they grow up they will feel quite justified in doing the same thing.

Secondly a mother's promiscuity can become so embarrassing to a daughter, that she will reject her mother and grow up resenting both her mother and her own femininity. The next steps are withdrawal, hatred of men, then emotional and sexual frigidity. A number of married women have been released from this syndrome.

Similarly, a promiscuous father will also be rejected and despised. Should a father have any sexual involvement with a friend of his daughter, anger, hatred, and even physical revenge may be added to the daughter's sense of rejection and outrage.

(5) *Pride* is an offence to God (1 Peter 5:5), and usually offensive to others. Pleasure in one's family and in its accomplishments, or self-esteem with dignity is not what is in mind. Rather the vanity, egoism, conceit and self-glorification which ostentatiously swaggers through families. It is our experience that almost every adult who has a problem with pride speaks of it as being a family problem.

(6) *Argumentativeness* between a husband and wife may cause a child to become verbally aggressive right through to adulthood and married life. No marriage is ever so perfect that disagreements do not occur. But there is one rule which should not be broken. Disagree in private if you have to, but **never** in front of the children.

Frank and open discussions are healthy signs of marriage partners feeling free to converse. If tolerance and grace are practised, anger, aggressiveness, accusations, blame, recalling the supposedly forgiven past, arguing, shouting and threats will be avoided. If not, children will become insecure, fearful, and perhaps show physical evidences such as disturbed sleep patterns and bed-wetting.

(7) *Inconsistent ethical or religious standards*. When parents expect (or instruct) a child to keep high ethical standards and don't do so themselves, confusion and questioning will arise in the child's mind. Unless this is remedied, children will themselves develop double standards and probably become rebellious and defiant. Simple examples include:

- Parents who do not keep their word. Unless a child accepts that there are justifiable reasons for a promise not being kept, the credibility of the parent will suffer, and 'optional truthfulness' could become a way of life. A child can certainly feel rejected and become oppressed by a spirit of injustice when a parent's promise only means 'maybe'.
- Parents who insist that their children attend some place of religious instruction, but who never enter a church door themselves, can cause them to reject 'religion' when old enough to make their own choices. Meantime they often rebel and cause disturbances amongst others at church or Sunday school.
- Other inconsistencies include parents who swear, but punish their children for swearing; parents who espouse morality but watch blue movies and parents who boast about their own past misdeeds while punishing their children for similar conduct.

(8) *Shouting at children* may release the volcano within 'mum', but it has a considerable fallout on junior. In lecturing, Phyl often refers to 5 p.m. as a 'young mother's zero hour'. It is a kind of 'time log-jam'. The toys have to be put away, the children bathed and fed, the evening meal prepared, quiet restored, and mother renewed before dad walks in! Mothers will know that this short list is only basic. It is no wonder that patience becomes a commodity in short supply, and mothers sometimes have to raise their voices to be heard above the din. The older and bolder ones of course may rebel, and yell back. Whichever way a child responds, he or she is the one who is most affected. Phyl sometimes passes on something she remembers reading: A boy said to his mother, 'Hey mum, how come that when you shout, you always say it is because of your nerves, but when I shout, you always say it's my temper?'

(9) *The power of good example*. When fathers and mothers are courteous and demonstrably affectionate to one another, the children

will grow up ready to give, and expecting to receive a similar courtesy and love. Regrettably, those who have not seen this in their parents will not know how to bless their partners.

Cleanliness and tidiness are habit patterns learned from parental example. The lack of these qualities in married life can become a disruptive factor. There is some truth in the statement that 'the condition of one's accommodation is a reflection of the condition of one's mind'.

Sibling relationships may cause problems

Children born to the same mother and father soon show considerable personality differences, even in the case of identical twins. Early rivalry, and even fighting is normal in sibling relationships, but lifelong bonds of love, and hatred, may also commence in childhood.

Jealousy, personal rivalry, and competition may precipitate an undeclared 'state of war'. Acts of discrimination, cruelty or sexual abuse by other siblings may cause a victim to develop a life-long hatred for the brother or sister responsible.

When hatred is added to injustice, an explosive emotional condition develops within the aggrieved child. This may surface as a personality change, and may induce physical problems.

Problems in the school system

There are two sources:

(1) *Teacher-child relationships*. Thank God for schoolteachers! But thank God I'm not a schoolteacher! They surely are special people, to be able to manage so many different personalities, all clamouring for attention, in one room, for so many hours a day.

Most of us quickly form likes and dislikes and schoolteachers are no exception. But because of their liking (or love) for children, and their professionalism, children are generally treated in a very even-handed manner. Of course there will always be exceptions. Some boys and girls have felt rejected by a teacher's tone of voice, or by being constantly picked on. These children may show their rejection both outwardly and inwardly by defiance or withdrawal. Regrettably, it may be long term.

The other side of that coin, is the over-sensitive child who imagines he or she is being rejected. The signs are just as real, despite the lack of a genuine cause. Injustice, either real or imagined, can also trigger numerous symptoms in children which often prompt parents to talk to the head-teacher about their child's 'plight'.

(2) *Peer pressures*. Every child in the educational system is subject to pressures with which they learn to cope. But coping with what fellow students do and say to one another is a pressure which some children find most difficult to handle.

Children are 'experts' at hurtful nicknames, snide remarks, 'ganging up' on the innocent, and cutting one another out of friendships. They use bribes and threats, often with reckless abandon, and 'send one another to Coventry' very effectively. Some of it is only playful, but nasty little hereditary problems can begin to appear.

Some of the hurt ones can become quite emotionally disturbed, insecure, rejected, and develop a low self-image. Nervous symptoms may also appear. Cases of intimidation or harmful conduct may need to be drawn to the attention of school authorities, but major attention should be given to teaching the child how to handle such pressures. A week in the life of a child may seem a very long time, but things can often change dramatically and quickly in that time.

Children may reject themselves

Unless children are able to do what others do, particularly physically, they often reject themselves. Types who experience this are:
- those who have been born blind, deaf, or with limb deformities which means they can never play games or enjoy sports activities.
- those who have suffered long illnesses, or been hospitalized, causing them to fall behind in schooling or physical activities associated with their age group.
- children who, having been healthy and active, suffer accidents, or contract diseases which permanently impair them.

Specialized care given these afflicted ones, whether the conditions were present at birth or resulted from other circumstances, can be very successful in preserving them from falling into the trap of self-rejection.

There are other causes of self-rejection which deserve mention.

Firstly, there is the child who feels neglected because the parents are forced to spend time, attention, and money on another family member suffering illness, or having a condition which necessitates prolonged bed-rest or personal care. A number of adults who have sought our help trace their rejection back to this kind of childhood situation.

On the lighter side, a teenager came to us on one occasion, obviously very cross with his brother for getting more attention than himself. 'I wish I was sick and had to say in bed' he grumbled, 'then I would get eggs for breakfast too.'

Secondly, as children develop, they become very sensitive to their physical appearance. Especially girls. Long noses, freckles, pimply faces, big ears, disproportionate body shapes and hair colour have all contributed to teenagers rejecting themselves, and later coming to us as adults to be freed from their ongoing self-rejection and obsessions.

Personal tragedy

The worst thing possible is to be sexually abused. This often causes life-changing attitudes and behaviour in boys, girls and teenagers. This subject is too important to receive only a brief mention. It will be dealt with more fully in a later chapter.

A trauma in relationships causes severe stress, e.g.

- the death of a parent.
- the death of both parents resulting in the child being bought up by relatives or friends.
- the divorce or separation of parents in which a father or mother leaves the family home.
- the remarriage of a solo parent, leading to rejection or emotional and physical abuse of a child by the new step-parent.
- the death of a child's close personal friend or even a pet animal.

In such cases what follows is a sense of rejection, a feeling of being abandoned, loneliness, grief, and emotional distress.

Hereditary factors

Considerable attention was given to the origin and power of hereditary spirits in *Evicting Demonic Intruders and Breaking Bondages*. Further treatment will be given in later chapters of this book dealing with the biblical evidence upon which the concept of deliverance (freedom in Christ), is based.

This present list of children's problems would be incomplete without a thumbnail outline describing some effects of heredity.

Parents tend to punish their children for doing the very same things they were ashamed of having committed in childhood, or for continuing the habits they hate so much in themselves. The tendency is to punish the child for parental guilt, rather than to help them overcome the problem.

Here is a brief list of hereditary problems which affect children deeply:

- The rejection syndrome which includes low self image, withdrawal, anger, etc.
- Deception, lies and stealing.
- The rebellion-anger-temper syndrome.
- Nervous and mental problems, including anxiety, worry and depression.
- The curse of Freemasonry, and the sicknesses, infirmities and allergies which frequently afflict the children and grandchildren of Freemasons.
- Promptings to commit suicide.
- Domination by spirits of fear and hereditary mental problems.
- Spirits of anti-Christ coming from family involvement in occultism and witchcraft.
- Addictions to drugs, alcohol, nicotine, food, gambling, excessive physical exercise and excessive spending.
- Sexual promiscuity.

The ways in which parents and counsellors can bless children by setting them free from these troublesome problems are outlined in later chapters.

SUMMARY

Causes and effects of problems which affect children and teenagers

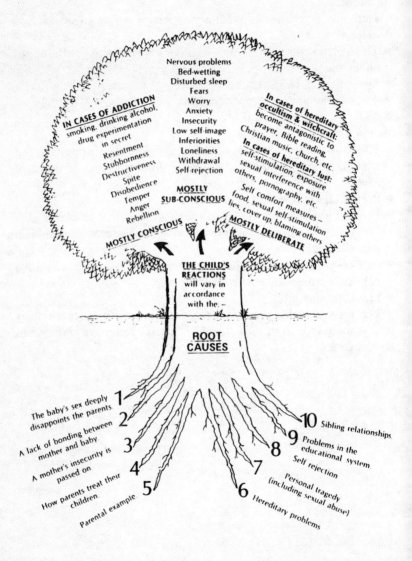

Nervous problems
Bed-wetting
Disturbed sleep
Fears
Worry
Anxiety
Insecurity
Low self-image
Inferiorities
Loneliness
Withdrawal
Self-rejection

MOSTLY SUB-CONSCIOUS

IN CASES OF ADDICTION
smoking, drinking alcohol, drug experimentation in secret
Resentment
Stubbornness
Destructiveness
Spite
Disobedience
Temper
Anger
Rebellion

MOSTLY CONSCIOUS

In cases of hereditary occultism & witchcraft:
become antagonistic to prayer, Bible reading, Christian music, church, etc.
In cases of hereditary lust:
self-stimulation, exposure sexual interference with others, pornography, etc.

Self comfort measures –
food, sexual self-stimulation lies, cover up, blaming others

MOSTLY DELIBERATE

THE CHILD'S REACTIONS will vary in accordance with the –

ROOT CAUSES

1 The baby's sex deeply disappoints the parents.
2 A lack of bonding between mother and baby.
3 A mother's insecurity is passed on
4 How parents treat their children.
5 Parental example.
6 Hereditary problems.
7 Personal tragedy (including sexual abuse)
8 Self rejection
9 Problems in the educational system.
10 Sibling relationships.

Chapter 8

Digging Out More Roots

In the previous chapter we suggested some causes of the more common problems parents see in their children. In this chapter the reverse process will be adopted. Some children's problems for which parents have sought help will be stated. Some suggestions will then be made as to possible root-causes for which freedom may be claimed in the name of Jesus Christ.

The authors wish to make it very clear that the suggested diagnoses and recommendations are in no way intended to be taken as depreciating the expertise of the professions dedicated to helping young people, mentally, emotionally, physically, educationally and socially. They are intended to assist those helping children by using spiritual principles that are often unknown, overlooked, or even despised. We have not yet addressed the issue of remedying the problems. This will be done in chapters 16, 22 and 23.

Some of the problems with suggested root causes are:

Problem No. 1: An obsession with death

Suggested causes:

(1) A loved one or close friend may have died. The whole matter of death needs to be talked out. Children often have a more realistic attitude to death than adults.

(2) The reading matter of the child and stories read at school may be responsible.

(3) Some children born with the umbilical cord wrapped around their neck have been found to grow up with a fear of death, or of being choked.

(4) When a child is the next one born after a miscarriage, still-birth, or an abortion, he or she will frequently be disturbed by a spirit of death.

(5) When a pregnant mother's health has so deteriorated that it is feared that childbirth could cause her death, the baby is often born with a spirit of death.

In our experience, these problems may be resolved through prayer for release and healing.

Problem No. 2: A child who is normally happy at school, develops a sudden fear, and refuses to attend

Suggested causes:

(1) The child has been threatened or bullied, and is fearful of it happening again.

(2) There has been some form of sexual intimidation, or abuse, and the child is terrified to speak out, fearing punishment. Careful examination by a gentle medical practitioner is advisable as a precaution. This can then be a basis, if the circumstances warrant it, for taking the matter up with school authorities, or the police. The child must be treated lovingly, and certainly needs to be spiritually released and cleansed from fears, insecurity, and spirits of lust and sexual abuse which will have entered if the sexual experience did in fact happen.

(3) The child may have been wrongly blamed for the actions of another and is suffering from spirits of injustice, and fear of punishment. The cause of the problem needs to be discovered. The child also should be released through prayer.

Problem No. 3: Sudden changes in a child's personality

Suggested causes:

(1) *Jealousy*. This can be caused by:

(a) the real or imagined favouritism towards another family member. This may be as simple as one child getting new clothes while another gets hand-downs.

(b) failure to adhere to an agreed system of privileges.

(c) disproportionate helpings of food.

(d) unfair allocation of jobs between children so that one child feels he or she is given only the dirty or heavy work.

Jealousy can be followed by resentment, self-pity, anger, unforgiveness, and a host of other nasty little attitudes.

(e) Jealousy may result from a baby taking prime time and attention away from the youngest brother or sister. A variety of outcomes may be expected including displays of temper, grizzling and crying for attention, claims of tummy pains and other non-visible symptoms. Guard the new baby from attempts to hurt it by the younger children. Some have been physically abusive, and others throw heavy objects onto the baby or into its cot or pram.

(f) Believe it or not, family dogs sometimes become jealous of a new baby. Tragically, some babies have been mauled by jealous pets, and a few have even died.

(2) *A guilty conscience* over some wrong doing may cause a child to withdraw and become secretive. This could be caused by the pressure of others to participate in, say, the vandalising of a classroom, or school. The child becomes fearful of being caught, and of what their parents may say and do; others may be bribed to keep quiet.

(3) *Shame and guilt* usually follow forced sexual activities, particularly incest or homosexual acts. The child usually withdraws, refuses to communicate, and often shows changes of eating and sleep patterns. Sensitive and wise investigation is needed to obtain the truth, reverse the process, and release the defiling spirits. Pray for healing and wholeness.

(4) *The use of drugs should never be discounted* when teenagers unaccountably go through personality changes. Although they may vigorously deny this when questioned tell-tale signs should be carefully noted. These include small pupils, a tell-tale smell on the breath, sudden requests for money, unexplained lengthy absences, needle marks or bruising of the skin, and excessive mood changes.

Problem No. 4: Habits (such as over-eating, thumb-sucking, bed-wetting and nail biting)

Suggested causes:

It is not possible to put these problems into one category and supply a pat answer. In fact, suggestions for handling them will fall far short of the number of medical and psychological treatments which are available. However, from our ministry to boys, girls, and teenagers, we know that God blesses and releases children.

(1) *Over eating*

(a) The cause is often hereditary. It is not uncommon to see an overweight parent with an overweight child. The child gets a head-start when the spirit of gluttony is both inherited, and encouraged by example.

(b) It may also be caused by a desire for comfort because of rejection, or as a result of some trauma. Unless the appetite is curbed, a spirit of gluttony will take over, which soon becomes an addiction; and in due course will be passed down the family.

(c) On occasions obese women have confessed that they had deliberately made themselves unattractive to men by over-eating; the cause: guilt or shame caused by incest or sexual abuse.

(d) Boredom will often cause a child to eat excessively. Children normally use up their food energy in physical exercise, but a lonely child usually just sits around, watches TV and eats. Television advertisements encourage this. Spiritual ministry and parental co-operation can break the habit of over-eating.

(e) Hereditary spirits of alcohol or gambling may cause a child's food addiction. Anorexia nervosa, or bulimia can occur before children are old enough to be trapped into the adult habits, and have been found to have been hereditary to the third generation.

(2) *Thumb-sucking*. It may surprise some readers to learn that this habit is not confined to children. Adults sometimes seek help in this, they are ashamed because non-family members have seen them sucking a thumb in bed.

Thumb-sucking is a habit which is often maintained by a dominating spirit, from which it is possible to be released. A nine year old boy in a house where Phyl and I were guests had an unbreakable habit of sucking his thumb. he shrugged off the ribbing he got from school mates. At the meal table he would take his thumb out of his mouth only to eat food. As soon as he had swallowed, back went the thumb.

We asked the Lord to free him, and he did. Completely. As a matter of habit he brought his thumb up to his mouth for a short time afterwards, but then his arm would lock and he found he just couldn't put his thumb in his mouth. In a short time that habit too was broken and has not returned. The boy's father, a pastor, has testified to this during a deliverance seminar.

(3) *Bed-wetting*. This is also a problem which does not respect age. It is quite natural for babies, but embarrassing when it continues.

Teenagers have sought deliverance because they were too ashamed to sleep at their friends' homes. Even a married man came for help because he had no bladder control at night.

The sleep of some children is at a very deep level and they simply do not respond to the normal nerve stimuli which alerts sleepers to get up and relieve themselves. Waterproof sheets with alarm systems are available for hire and these sometimes help the problem.

One of our difficulties in writing about the results of praying for many children and teenagers afflicted with this complaint, is that we move on and do not hear how effective the prayer ministry has been. From those in our own locality, we have found that after dealing with basic fears, traumas, or insecurity, the habit can be broken even if we need to pray a couple of times. Parents also need to help by limiting the child's fluid intake after 5 p.m., and in waking them for a toilet visit, before they retire.

A comment which some may find interesting is that young bed-wetters sometimes are very attached to soft cuddly frogs. Have you ever met a frog that was not more at home in water than any other environment?

(4) *Nail-biting*. This habit often starts through feelings of rejection, loneliness, insecurity, or nervousness. When basic causes are identified and dealt with the habit needs to be broken. Painting the fingers with bitter compounds may help, and of course personal discipline is needed. We have found that prayer for release is of considerable benefit.

Problem No. 5: Controlling fears

Suggested causes:

(1) *Heredity*. During the nine months of pregnancy there is ample opportunity for fears to be passed on to the unborn child. Should an expectant mother be suddenly overcome by fear, the babe in-utero often goes rigid, and may cause considerable pain to its mother. After birth the child will be troubled by that spirit of fear. Counselling may help control these effects, but deliverance is needed for total freedom. The sources of fear are many and varied, for example – spiders, animals, the dark, or simply being alone.

(2) *Accidents*. When Adrienne, our eldest, was only a child, I was towing her on a water toboggan behind a speed boat. In the short time

it took me to check speed and direction during a turn, the toboggan and rider were dragged under the surface of the water for probably three or four metres. I was upset, Adrienne was terrified. Although she was good at swimming and water-skiing, that fear remained with her, and after she was married, it surfaced strongly in her firstborn, a daughter. It was her grandmother who finally released her by prayer, and encouragement in the water. She now loves being in and under the water. Other accidents which open the door for spirits of fear are those caused by motor vehicles, bicycles, horses, roller blades or skateboards.

(3) *Shock*. Violence, house fires, death, and sudden loud noises can all cause fears to commence in a child.

(4) *TV Programmes*. Violent or scary movies can terrify children, cause disturbed sleep patterns, and instil fears. If adults do not supervise viewing times or programme content children may be affected.

Another danger which parents often overlook, and may need to check out, is that their children may be watching violent, or other X-rated videos in the homes of their friends after school, or at weekends.

(5) *Threats by other children*. The Mafia has no copyright on standover tactics. Bullies get what they want from other children by threats of many kinds; fears may be the only sign that this is happening.

Problem No. 6: Comprehension difficulties

Suggested causes:

(1) *Mental confusion*. Children, and grandchildren of Freemasons regularly suffer from this problem which often affects their learning ability. The only remedy we have found is to free the child from the twelve groups of spirits associated with this blasphemous false religion (see *Evicting Demonic Intruders and Breaking Bondages*).

(2) *Hereditary spirits of occultism and witchcraft*. These strong family spirits will trouble children in both their school and church activities, particularly the latter. Spirits of anti-Christ need to be made to leave in the name of Jesus Christ.

(3) *Disinterest, or apathy*. Some children live for the day when they will no longer be forced to go to school, and the outdoor types endure

education for the least time possible. Children of large or neglected families often feel dispirited and have no zeal for schooling. Day-dreaming is a pleasant form of escapism.

Problem No. 7: Sleeping problems

As well as fears, here are some other possible causes:

(1) *Anxiety*. Children often pick up snippets of their parents' conversation and commence worrying about matters they do not understand, or need not be concerned about. They imagine the worst, feel insecure, and worry. You may recognise the scenario. Sleepless eyes wandering around the bedroom, followed by the patter of little feet, and the 'I-want-a-drink-of-water' syndrome commences. Sensitive parents will satisfy a real thirst, and patiently search for causes of imaginary thirst, before 'reading the riot-act'.

(2) *A highly developed sense of imagination*. A street light, wind in the trees, a moving blind, and everything between a monster and a 'bogey man' will be in that room. A time of explanation and prayer will do wonders.

(3) *Oppression by hereditary spirits of occultism and witchcraft*. These can really frighten children, particularly if they have inherited spirits which give them psychic sight of the para-normal. Only deliverance will rid them of these troublesome spirits and induce sleep. Medication is only a palliative for problems of a spirit nature.

(4) *Bad dreams and nightmares*. Books, films, traumas, fears, and spirits of occultism and witchcraft can all disturb sleep. Prayer for release will be effective.

Problem No. 8: Suicidal thoughts, and attempts to commit suicide

Suggested causes:

(1) *Hereditary spirits*. We have prayed with many young people who have had a parent and/or grandparent who has committed suicide. Each one has either contemplated suicide, or has actually attempted to take his or her own life. These spirits are very strong, and will continue to oppress during adulthood unless driven out by the power of God.

(2) *The example of a close friend*. A high school student whose close friend had committed suicide, came for ministry after the funeral. He admitted he had been giving serious thought to the idea of following his friend's example.

(3) *The influence of rock-and-roll music*. There are many examples of pressure put on teenagers by rock-and-roll lyrics.

(4) *Depression about a hopeless future*. Suicide has a real appeal to children and teenagers who are underprivileged, thrown out of their homes, disowned by parents, or hopelessly ensnared by the drug habit. Regrettably too many take the exit ramp before help is effective. This destructive spirit of death may be totally defeated in the name of Jesus Christ.

(5) *Family honour and pacts*. In Japan, suicide is preferable to disgrace. Some children and teenagers commit suicide because they cannot stand the family pressures driving them to excel at school or college. Children will also join their parents in a family suicide pact.

Finally, some miscellaneous problems:

(1) *Rebellion*. A boy may receive an hereditary spirit of rebellion from a strong, manipulative mother or father.

(2) *Hyper-activity*. Doctors have not yet agreed on what causes this condition, but we know that there is a spirit of hyper-activity which can be released in the name of Jesus Christ. Many children have shown a complete change after prayer.

(3) *Hypoglycemia* (which is distinct from true diabetes), in one child was caused by a troublesome spirit. He had been close to death on several occasions in early childhood. His doctor agreed, after he was set free, that his healing was 'miraculous'.

(4) *Attention seeking*, even to the point of a child injuring himself or herself, may be the manipulation of a spirit of performance or rejection.

Some parents may have been searching for the answer to a problem whch has not been included in this list. Please rest assured that each and every behavioural problem which hinders a child from normal growth and development can be prayed over in the name of Jesus Christ.

SUMMARY

1.   Causes need to be determined and dealt with on a spiritual basis before problems can be resolved.

2.   There are many indicators which will assist counsellors to reach this goal.

Chapter 9

How Parents May Cause Their Children's School Teachers to Have Problems

The daily crowd of mothers and children outside school gates each weekday morning is always a fascinating sight. Especially at the beginning of a school term. There are shouts of greeting, tears of parting, the dragging of reluctant feet, stern or appealing words, and even threats or promises.

After the mothers leave, it's the turn of the teachers. Try and imagine what's happening now inside. Tommy is teasing and Susan is crying. George has used a naughty word and someone has taken Mary's biscuits. Two boys are fighting while things are being thrown around the room. Audrey has brought her teacher a bunch of flowers, while Harry is calling out that he needs to leave the room.

The scene is not an orchestrated anti-teacher demonstration, but simply an accumulation of incidents normally seen at home.

Although professionally prepared, teachers find that they also are expected to act as parent, adjudicate, reward or punish, solve problems, and above everything else, co-ordinate and harmonise the diverse and often manipulative personalities of their charges, capable of many nasty little habits.

It would seem that school teachers are expected to be a very special class of people, capable of doing what parents sometimes have been unable to do, and usually with perfect fairness and patience. That, however, places an unfair responsibility on teachers, who are there primarily to impart knowledge.

Regrettably, many people have little idea of what it means to bring

97

up children. Some believe that by supplying basic necessities such as accommodation, food and clothing, and adding a few luxuries like toys, bicycles and television, they are good parents. But what about the spiritual qualities of love, affection, fairness, justice and security? A listening ear, effective conversation, wise advice, quality time, periods of entertainment and relaxation, backed up by good example, are needed by every child. Children of Christian parents also have the advantage of being taught God's standards for right living.

There may also be understandable (but not necessarily justifiable) reasons why children are disadvantaged. Some are conceived pre-nuptially, or are unwanted, while others are the tail-end of large families. Other problems may include inadequate or overcrowded living accommodation, poverty, and parental health problems. Both parents can also be working full time in order to purchase the family home. And regrettably, some women either do not have a natural aptitude for motherhood, or regard their social life as more important than bringing up children.

Each student is virtually a human barometer of the prevailing relationships and atmosphere of the family home. For example:

- A child's security or insecurity may reflect their parents' marriage relationships.
- The emotional relationships prevailing at home are often reflected in a child's nervousness and stress, or relaxation and tranquillity.
- Children are quick to continue their home loyalty or hatred to one another while at school.
- When children are particularly angry, vengeful, rebellious, stubborn, lustful, talkative or fearful, these may be just re-runs of what they see and hear in their parents.
- Standards of home discipline can affect a child's school behaviour. For example, if there is little or no discipline bad habits will continue. If there is too much discipline, the children may be subdued or fearful. When children are taught to obey their parents, school discipline should be no problem, except under provocation.
- Parents' ethical standards can also be reflected in their children's responses of honesty, fairness, and respect for the property of others.
- If children have been abused physically, emotionally, or sexually at home they may show signs of physical or emotional disturbance at school. But usually they will not reveal the true cause, out of loyalty

to their parents, or because they have been threatened. In addition to, or even in the absence of evident signs, there may well be a general lack of concentration, tearfulness without apparent cause, or fearfulness.

- The victimisation of a child at home by parents may cause a brother or sister to 'pick on' that particular brother or sister at school, or tell tales to the teachers so that the child's life may become thoroughly miserable.

- Children who constantly strive for their teacher's physical love and approval are usually very much rejected at home, and are just longing for human affection. Children of single, deserted, separated, or divorced mothers will often look to a male teacher for the approval, guidance and affection they lack in the absence of a father.

- Sometimes children show the strong religious, or cultish beliefs of their parents, long before they have the maturity to decide for themselves what they want to believe.

- Financial problems in the family home may result in sub-standard clothing, skimpy lunches, or petty stealing.

- With marriage relationships under strain, the children will often show insecurity, anxiety, fears, and lack of concentration. This is particularly so when one parent has ill-health, when there is physical and verbal abuse towards each other or when either partner is an alcoholic.

There are other variables which make an already complex teaching situation even more difficult. These include:

- The way by which children relate to one another. The first signs of social snobbery are often visible in early childhood. An answer to a simple question such as, 'What does your father do?' may include or exclude a child from a peer group. The class of family-home and car, and where the family spends its holidays can all make or break childhood friendships on the basis of parental social attitudes.

- The differences of ethnic background, colour of skin, religion, and physical size also tend to separate children into groups.

- Variable learning attitudes and abilities to receive, retain, apply and communicate knowledge must also frustrate many teachers, and cause them to categorize students. The brighter ones tend to rise in the teacher's approval rating, while the rest stabilize at their own levels.

- Student personality differences, likes and dislikes for the subjects being taught, the attitudes of parents, the pressures to excel, and the popularity of each teacher, all contribute to the general class atmosphere, and test the skills of the educator.

In practical terms, behind the facade of clean faces and brushed hair, there is virtually a Pandora's box of hereditary and personal problems just waiting to be loosed on teacher and fellow students alike. The events of each day may indeed be the keys which open and spill the contents of individual boxes.

The evidence of reality removes the possibility of writer's fantasy

Some readers may consider that the problems outlined so far come more from a writer's speculative imagination than from a real-life classroom situation. The following practical experience should remove any concern. Some time ago, Phyl and I were invited to pray for some needy pupils in a Christian school. Phyl had been invited to do so previously, but had declined to do so without the permission of their parents.

On this occasion the parents had not only given their permission, but one or both parents were present while each child was being prayed over. In addition, we had the teacher's written comments on the child's behaviour in class, academic standard, and specific problems which the teacher asked us to pray about. The school principal had most efficiently co-ordinated information, parents, children and ministry times.

In this way, we were able to talk to parents about each child's problems, and find background causes before praying for the children in the parent('s) presence. Over three afternoons we prayed for around thirty-six boys and girls. The teachers expressed gratitude for the evident changes they saw in the attitudes, behaviour, learning ability and relationships of the children prayed for. The principal was delighted with the results, and both Christian and non-Christian parents were very helpful. Some of them even asked for spiritual help afterwards. After co-ordinating the teachers' and parents' comments with my personal notes, it is possible to tabulate some of the problems stated, with case histories:

Case history 1: A ten year old stepson

(1) *Teacher's comments*: 'This boy has never been released from hurts arising from his father's death, and shows anger and temper at school.'

(2) *Mother's comments*: 'His father died when he was six months old. I remarried when he was one year old, but the boy has shown constant sadness over his father's death and has grown up with rebellion, anger, temper and resentment towards his step-father. He is afraid that I might die, or leave him; he shows an attitude of rejection and is generally fearful.' The boy had a multi-cultural heritage.

(3) *Ministry*: Having asked the Lord to free the boy from the root cause of the listed problems, and after praying for cleansing and healing, I felt the Lord wanted me to bind the boy emotionally to his step-father. So I asked him to sit on his dad's knee. He balked. 'I'm too heavy', he said to begin with, but then gave way. I asked them to put their arms around one another, then laying one hand on each, prayed for their emotional bonding. Then I said to the boy, 'When did you last sit on your dad's knee?' He replied 'I can't remember ever having done that before'. So I asked them to do it again, and prayed the second time. By then the step-father's eyes were brimming with tears, and he whispered in the boy's ear as they hugged each other, 'I love you'. The reply was prompt and warm, 'I love you too'. Ten years of rejection, loneliness and fear were gone.

Case history 2: A fourteen year old girl

(1) *Teacher's comments*: 'This girl is very intelligent but is defiant, disgruntled, rebellious, sloppy, disrespectful, lazy and selfish.'

(2) *The mother's comment*: She explained that she and the child's father had been hippies, and that after the child was born they had lived in a motor car for one whole year. The girl had a slow birth and was an only child. The mother's background was of mixed European parentage.

(3) *Ministry*: The girl was released from her rejection – the self-protective and self-defensive syndrome – also anger, temper, defiance, stubbornness, anxiety, worry, depression, daydreaming and laziness. There were also hereditary spirits of anti-social behaviour, occultism, witchcraft, Hinduism, Buddhism, drugs, smoking, gambling and lust. What a load that child was able to leave behind after prayer for cleansing and inner healing.

Case history 3: Two brothers aged 12 and 13

(1) *Teacher's comments*: 'The older boy needs God's friendship in a greater way; needs some kind of breakthrough from past mental and relationship blocks. He avoids homework, is rejected by others, and has a low self-image.'

'The younger boy needs affirmation about who he is in Christ. He is bull-headed and needs paddling. He is quiet and often sick.'

(2) *Parents' comments*: Both parents (Christians) were present.

(a) *Of the older boy*. 'He feels very rejected and is introverted. He is performance-orientated and champions the under-dog. He is passive, anxious, depressive, and shows signs of schizophrenia. There is suicide in the family and we think a 'hex' (curse) may have been placed on the boy by a disgruntled employee of my husband. We also think he has a problem with lust.' The Lord released him.

(b) *Of the younger boy*. 'He screamed for six weeks from the time he was born, disturbing everyone.' His mother said she had asked God for understanding, and then remembered she had visited a psychiatrist about the time of conception. The mother had also been bitten by savage dogs two weeks after his birth when she had gone to the rescue of the older boy. I was also asked to pray about hereditary insanity and anger. The boy was also stubborn, argumentative, challenged authority, aggressive, restless, and walked in his sleep.

(3) *Ministry*: After prayer, the lad willingly accepted being emotionally bonded to his mother.

Case history 4: A nine year old boy

(1) *Teacher's comments*: '... can't sit still, and can't keep his books and stationery in order.'

(2) *Parent's comments*: The mother told me she had divorced the father when the boy was four years of age, and had not remarried. She was a school teacher, and admitted her intolerance by saying, 'I can't stand him'.

The boy had been diagnosed as 'having significant learning disability', and was struggling at school. He had *five ethnic backgrounds*, was hyper-active, had a disorganized mind, and was confused. There were also hereditary spirits of Freemasonry, asthma, allergies, alcoholism, lust, psychic abilities. The mother, a nominal Christian, had clairvoyant abilities and was able to foretell the future.

(3) *Ministry*: Each of the above problems and rejection were prayed over in order to break bondages and release dominating spirits. We then prayed for the boy's cleansing and healing.

Case history 5: An eleven year old boy

(1) *Teacher's comments*: 'This boy has no organisation; gets F's in everything; has a tremendous spirit of rejection; is sloppy; his mind and hands do not co-ordinate; he also steals and lies.'

(2) *Parent's comments*: The mother told me she was a trained social counsellor employed by local authorities. Regrettably she showed little wisdom or a true maternal instinct. She claimed her three children were constantly sick, and that her de facto partner had some mental problems.

(3) *Ministry*: We asked the Lord to release the spirits of rejection, mental confusion, stealing, lying and insecurity. After praying for healing, mother and son were emotionally bonded together.

Case history 6: A twelve year old boy of Asian background

(1) *Teacher's comments*: 'He is disruptive in behaviour, fidgets constantly, and is a slow learner.'

(2) *Parent's comments*: His mother confirmed the teacher's remarks saying he was also hyper-active, angry, lustful, and resisted physical love. She explained she had many fears while carrying the boy. There was also a family history of mental illness, occultism, and witchcraft practices.

(3) *Ministry*: All of the problems outlined were prayed over, plus the rejection syndrome. I then asked the boy how he said goodnight to his parents. He replied, 'By shaking hands with them'. It was obvious that mother and son needed bonding together, so I asked the boy to sit on his mother's knee. At first he protested, saying he was too dirty. Finally he sat on her knee and I prayed for them both. When the prayer finished, the mother kissed him on the cheek. He jumped up, and spontaneously brushed 'the kiss' off his cheek.

Case history 7: An eleven year old boy

(1) *Teacher's comments*: 'Assumes unnecessary burdens. Needs to know a greater security in his heavenly Father. He is very artistic and smart, but does not receive instruction well.'

(2) *Parent's comments*: (Both parents present.) The mother had a multi-cultural background, including a spirit of indigenous spirit worship which caused her to have clairvoyant abilities. They admitted the marriage had been shaky at times, and that during the pregnancy the mother had suffered from many fears. Both parents felt their son had the ability to reach his goal of becoming a film producer, although he was small and sometimes bullied by bigger boys. Although he was quiet by nature he used to act as a rebellious punk in order to gain acceptance amongst his peers. The boy himself told me that in his dreams he often cried, because he felt like a baby.

(3) *Ministry*: After praying with the boy over his sense of rejection, low self-image, inferiorities, insecurity, fears and the controlling spirits from heredity, I felt he needed bonding to both of his parents. At first he protested, but then submitted. The Lord broke barriers between the parents, and their relationship with their son. He began to receive and to respond to their love.

Case history 8: An eleven year old boy

(1) *Teacher's comments*: '... is very rebellious and critical. He constantly blames others for his problems. He is defiant. A straight 'A' pupil.'

(2) *Parent's comments*: 'He is rebellious, sullen, stubborn, non-communicative and closed emotionally. He also challenges those who are in authority over him. He dominates other kids, and has a deep sense of injustice. He will lie, steal, and covet what others have.'

(3) *Other information*: Both parents were obviously suffering from a deep rejection syndrome when they married. Because of the husband's apathy, anxiety state, and outbursts of anger, the marriage was very unstable. Drugs and adultery featured in the early years.

Because of the boy's deep sense of rejection, I asked the parents to prayerfully consider possible causes. The father then confessed that when his wife was pregnant he had a fixation that the baby was going to be a girl. When the nurse invited him to go and look at his new son he was angry and disbelieving. He sat sullenly in the waiting room for twenty minutes without moving or speaking. Finally the nurse got impatient with him so he casually walked over and looked at the baby, then muttering to himself, walked away and vented his disappointment and anger on his wife in the recovery room.

It would be difficult to imagine a more overt act of rejection. It was no wonder that the teacher was having so much difficulty with the boy. No warmth of emotion was ever expressed between parents and son, and any kisses were from a sense of duty.

(4) *Ministry*: I suggested the parents ask their son's forgiveness for what they had done to him, and they willingly responded. They had both become Christians since the boy's birth, and their marriage had become more stable. Phyl and I had previously prayed for the parents to be released from hereditary problems and the dominating spirits caused by their conduct before being born again. They obviously deeply regretted having rejected their son.

Meantime the lad was showing evident signs of deep emotion as his father confessed to his past attitude, and expressed genuine sorrow for what had happened. He expressed forgiveness to them both.

The boy was prayed over and released from very deep rejection, hereditary rejection, self-rejection, and the fear of rejection together with all the problems they cause. He was also released from hereditary problems of addictions, lust, occultism and witchcraft. We prayed for cleansing, wholeness and healing to each part of his personality. Finally, mother, father, and son were bound together and the family left showing warmth to one another.

It is obvious that if these problems can occur within a Christian school where many parents are born again, how much greater must be the problems in State Schools? It would seem that there are three options open to teachers:

1. Take a strictly professional approach to avoid emotional involvement with the students

When formality replaces personal warmth, discipline may seem to be without mercy. This may cause problems to smaller children.

Firstly, those who receive no love or encouragement at home will feel more rejected, and may withdraw further. When deprived of personal warmth in the major alternative environment to the home, children sometimes become emotionally hard, even vindictive, and develop habits of cruelty, particularly to household pets.

Secondly, children can be punished without the teacher taking into account home factors or contributory schoolroom influences. When punishment comes by a pre-determined formula, or by a 'knee-jerk' reaction, it deals only with the fruit, not the root of the problem.

A simple illustration would be 'Frank' who is a shy boy subjected to teasing, and the occasional rough handling by other boys in his class. He bcomes hesitant about going to school, and his dad encourages him to stand up for himself and fight back. The less he does so, the more his father pushes him. Finally he summons up his courage in the class-room where he feels secure, and when the boy behind pulls his hair, he hits back. The teacher only sees Frank's response, and punishes him for aggression. No questions asked. The boy is more deeply hurt than ever, and his tormentors step up their tactics. So Frank's self-image hits basement level, he becomes tearful, fearful and withdrawn. Finally, the teacher may recommend that his parents take him to a psychologist, or psychiatrist. Because we have seen a number of children released from emotional problems and able to fully cope with the ups and downs of school life, we know the power of prayer with children.

Little people have sensitive personalities. They need, and rightly deserve, sensitive, warm, discerning and understanding teachers.

2. Teachers take the children's problems so much to heart that the emotional pressures upset them

Many a teacher has found he or she has been unable to cope with these pressures. This is particularly so if the teacher has been rejected in childhood, and cannot handle the personal memories that the child stirs up. He or she either asks for a transfer, or leaves the profession. This is certainly to the loss of all concerned, as children need sensitive, warm, loving and understanding hearts.

3. Taking spiritual authority over the forces controlling the lives of children

Two lines of action are possible:

(1) *In Christian Schools*. Although many parents of children attending Christian schools are true believers, the remainder would probably

be good living church attenders. This gives a Christian school teacher an opening to discuss with parents possible root causes of any attitudinal or behavioural problems evident in the classroom. If needed, recommendations may also be made to both parents and children aimed at removing family spiritual bondages and dominations revealed in classroom behaviour so that the children's healing and wholeness may be prayed for.

Of course this will never remove the need for discipline in the classroom, or at home. Children also need to be taught how to control those natural desires which are part and parcel of physical growth and development. Sinful human nature (which the Scriptures also call *'the flesh'*), (Galatians 5:17 KJV), will always be part of the human experience. This is controlled by self-discipline, **not** deliverance.

Christian parents who give school teachers authority to pray over their children seeking release from their bondages and dominations, will bless the teachers and themselves.

(2) *Secular schools where believers are teachers*. Some time ago a high school teacher phoned asking for practical advice on how to deal with difficult students. He, and his wife and family, had all been set free by Jesus Christ, and he was convinced of the effectiveness of children being set free. His three year old son had been terrified of loud noises, and always hid when an aeroplane flew overhead, or when his father mowed the lawns. The day after prayer for release, the child's mother phoned Phyl, so excited because the little fellow was following his father around as he cut the lawns, and pointing to every aeroplane he saw.

The particular pupil who gave this man concern, was rebellious, disruptive, and inattentive. Phyl advised him to ask the Lord to cleanse the room each morning from adverse spiritual forces before lessons began, and every time he passed the boy's desk to quietly bind the spirits causing the unruly behaviour. In one week the boy had changed, and positively responded by showing a friendly attitude to his teacher. From then on he would wave and greet him from a distance.

That same high school teacher attended a deliverance seminar some time afterwards. He not only publically confirmed the events just recounted, but added a further testimony to the power of God in the classroom.

A white girl with aboriginal blood in another high school to which he had been transferred, was causing him problems. She had a particularly filthy tongue and was aggressive towards the males in her class. The teacher said he just applied the power of prayer silently, and the girl quietened down totally. One day she came with her hair attractively done and became very coy when the teacher commented on how nice she looked. A day or so later, one of the boys publicly called her a very uncomplimentary name, denigrating her cultural background. The teacher said he had expected an emotional and verbal outburst, but she simply sat there, and shrugged her shoulders.

The born again, Spirit filled and controlled believer, always has the power and authority of Jesus Christ against all the might of the enemy (Luke 10:19; Mark 16:17; Colossians 2:15). Whether used quietly, or openly, the power of the name of Jesus Christ and the effectiveness of His shed blood are always effective.

Christian school teachers need to stand against the wiles of the devil by using the principles of spiritual warfare. Since we have been released from the works of the devil at Calvary (1 John 3:8), victories need to be claimed, and children reclaimed from the enemy's grip. It is not automatic.

SUMMARY

1. Children at school are human barometers of the relationships and atmospheres of their homes.
2. Children deserve to be treated as persons in the classroom. Teachers should not leave their emotions at home.
3. Spiritual power and authority is available to every born-again, Spirit-filled and controlled teacher. The power of Satan in the classroom may be overcome through spiritual warfare.

Chapter 10

Stop Them Playing Russian Roulette

During the reign of the Russian Czars, army officers sometimes played a deadly game during their drinking bouts. One of a group would place a single bullet in the revolving chamber of a pistol, spin the chamber, point the muzzle to his own forehead, then pull the trigger. If chance favoured him, there would be only the click of the hammer. He would breathe a sigh of relief, and pass the weapon to the next player in the circle. When chance dealt a fateful combination of trigger, hammer and bullet, funeral arrangements were made.

Of course no parent with a sound mind would allow their child to play with a loaded firearm. But that same caring parent may very well be exposing his or her child to a Satanic onslaught capable of bringing death to the soul. How? By not carefully supervising what a child reads, watches or does.

Enter fantasy

The thin edges of occultism and witchcraft are introduced by 'Hansel and Gretel'; giants, dungeons, and fears of supernatural powers through 'Jack and his Magic Beanstalk'. Although disguised, 'Little Red Riding Hood and the Big Bad Wolf' involves violence, even murder; hatred, jealousy and individualism are normal living in 'Snow White and the Seven Dwarfs'.

Add to these the legend of the toy-making Santa Claus and his world-travelling reindeer, the Easter bunny nonsense with chocolate eggs; the Tooth Fairy and her host of relatives including elves, gnomes, smurfs and trolls, and the evil potion thickens. Some schools have cauldrons of 'witch's brew' during Halloween; while many toys and games feature unimaginable out-of-space fantasy creatures which all have some effect on the conscious or subconscious mind. Satan often uses those memories as tools in later life.

Fantasy fascinates the young. When one realizes how the Concise Oxford Dictionary defines the word 'fascinate', the danger is obvious. 'Fascinate – (Esp. of serpent); deprive (victim) of power of escape or resistance by look or presence; attract irresistibly, enchant, charm.'

Imagination is a creative gift from God. It enables us to invent, to discover marvels of science, and to produce artistic works which bring pleasure to the eye and ear. But when out of control, imaginations may result in fears, sicknesses, and mental problems. They can also stimulate jealousy, anger and murder, at any age.

Children who are suffering a sense of rejection (real or imaginary), may withdraw and spend countless hours in worlds of escapism, grandeur, and make-believe. One man spoke of spending hours amongst the bushes as a child playing battles with armies made of leaves and flowers. He became so engrossed that when other boys came to play he sent them away.

Unless the imaginations are controlled, children can grow to adult-hood justifying their excessive appetite for reading fantasy. One young man read two hundred space-fantasy books per year for ten years, and wondered why he was 'spaced-out'.

Children who day-dream excessively, gaze into space, show inatten-tion, who have learning difficulties, or who cannot concentrate, all need to be investigated. Possible physical problems need to be elimi-nated first, so that demonic root causes of mental or emotional problems can be released, then healing and wholeness claimed.

The films they watch

The term, 'The **force** be with you' is frequently used in space films. Most adults shrug it off with a chuckle, but children haven't the same discernment. In the realm of outer space, it is the devil's none-too-subtle substitute for the power of God.

We have found that some children have become antagonistic to Bible reading, family devotions, prayer, and even Christian music through watching the wrong kind of film on TV. This is particularly so if they have an occultic 'headstart' through an hereditary spirit.

Out-of-space visitations are now both totally acceptable and highly credible through realistic space films, and the subtlety of films such as 'ET' or the highly popular TV programme 'Alf'. The number of films with para-normal content (including the humorous 'Bewitched') is rapidly increasing and opening the souls of the next generation to the manipulation of the evil one.

It is better for parents to be called 'mean' and a 'spoilsport' for restricting child viewing than to be judged irresponsible on the day of reckoning.

Rock and Roll (or screaming and stomping mania)

Maybe I'm showing my age, but nothing can be said in favour of this most popular sound manipulation of the souls of listeners. The ear-shattering volume level; the morbid, disgusting and mind-manipulating lyrics; the backward masking, (Satanic eulogies recorded backwards and dubbed into the sound track), the use of witchcraft in marketing techniques; and the African jungle drum-beat rhythm, contain nothing worthy of commendation.

Rather than cover ground others have ably dealt with, I believe parents need to know a little about the private lives of the band members who produce such musical and lyrical garbage. The following is written testimony given to us, (and used by permission), by a man who organized rock concerts. As tour manager for bands such as 'The Police', 'Duran Duran', 'Hall & Oates', and many more, he writes:

'On all these tours and "gigs", the same old backstage setting was there – of sex, drugs and egos. Sex to build up the egos, and drugs to keep them there. I saw the biggest names in the rock industry grovelling to get one more line of coke, or one more hit of smack (cocaine and heroin); and they would go to any means to get them, from throwing tantrums to refusing to perform. An endless line of groupies, hangers-on, and drug dealers circulated in and out of the back rooms, toilets, and any hidden place. These were the idols of thousands of young people aspiring to be just like their wonderful on-stage heroes. The industry is full of manic-depressants. I know. I was one.

This is truly 'Satan's world', where morals just don't exist. Now I'm a Christian, I look back at the spiritual oppression that controls the whole industry as pure Satanism. It is full of lust, power, aggression, jealousy and total deception.

My first look at rock 'n roll was when I lived in a house with six other guys, one being from a band which is now world famous. He was totally demon-possessed, his room was full of demonic drawings and devil worship. He had two skulls on his mantlepiece and used twice as much drugs and alcohol as the rest of us. This later showed in his music 'Highway to Hell', and 'Satan loves me', both best sellers. He died in his own vomit in his mid-twenties.

Working in recording studios over the last eight years with major bands convinced me that as the Holy Spirit anoints Gospel music, so Satan's spirit is placed on rock records. I saw records hit the number one spot and maintain that position because of backward masking urgings to buy more records.

The largest single market segment in record sales are young girls between thirteen and nineteen. They account for approximately sixty per cent of sales. Seductive tones, frequencies and the pitch of certain notes are put subliminally into the songs to stimulate sales. These sensual tones can be traced right back to the jungle beat of primitive tribes.

Satan's trump card is rock 'n roll. It is a deception to control the minds of youth. Sex, drugs, rock 'n roll are all bedmates. This rotten industry almost cost me my wife, family, respectability, conscience, and my health as it was a direct path to hell. But praise the Lord, His mercy endures forever.'

To the glory of God, this man, together with his wife and step-daughter were triumphantly freed from all the spirits involved in the rock industry.

What can be said after such an exposure from the very heart of the business?

The dangers that come through customs inherited from ethnic backgrounds

Whether children grow up in the country of their parents' birth or in an adopted country, racial traditions affect them. When these customs are rooted in spirit practices, children become oppressed. Examples:

(1) The Scandinavian Light Festival (Lucia), involves children participating in symbolic sacrifices to the gods, and the scaring away of evil spirits. Girls sometimes carry three lighted candles on a head-piece.

(2) Chinese and Japanese children freely participate in spirit festivals, wear lucky charms, are brought up to be superstitious, and to fear displeasing spirits.

(3) Most children in the United States of America are involved in 'trick or treat' door-knocking at Hallowe'en – a thinly disguised witchcraft celebration. The increasing Christian groundswell to change this custom is well justified.

(4) Many indigenous dances and customs rooted in spirit worship are being taught to western school children; this exposes them to the same spirit oppression. Maori hakas are an example. Even the Welsh Eisteddfod is steeped in Druid mystical symbolism.

Children should be freed and cleansed from ill effects which arise from participating in spirit-based rituals; they produce a spirit bondage, domination, or fear.

A teenage niece of ours, became oppressed by a Maori spirit through painting traditional anti-spirit emblems on a Maori meeting house at a New Zealand high school. When visiting us in Sydney one evening, we were horrified to see her suddenly pitched into a sliding glass door near her, which exploded in broken glass. She received deep cuts to one leg requiring seventeen stitches. Falling glass slivers also cut hair from her head. It was a miracle she did not impale herself on the jagged pieces of glass remaining in the door. She told us that she knew the door was closed and was intending to walk to her bedroom in the opposite direction but was slammed into the door by a force she could feel. She was later released from a Maori spirit; which caused her to shudder from head to foot as it left.

This warning of the dangers of cultural spirits is therefore not mere speculative imagination, but comes from practical experience.

Toybox trouble

Parlour games are now being used to introduce dangerous spirits of witchcraft into the family home. A recent Australian TV advertisement was for a game named 'The Fortune Teller'. It had been put together by a clairvoyant using actual readings she had made for people. The Ouija board is sometimes found in Christian homes. Indulgent parents often take the attitude 'Well it's only a game; what harm can it do?' Playing with these demonic toys **opens the door to spirit forces**. Read Deuteronomy 18:10–12 and Galatians 5:19–21.

There was a time when these warnings would only have applied to adults, but this is no longer so.

A very talented ten year-old boy who wrote and illustrated his own comic strip adventures with an outer-space theme, featured a being to which he had given an occultic name. This had either been prompted by an hereditary spirit, or by occultic reading. We prayed over this boy in his mother's presence, and by the time we had finished, his mind had come up with a benign name which changed the whole tone of his adventure series.

Modern transformer toys are certainly ingenious; cars, aeroplanes, trucks and other four-wheeled vehicles can be quickly twisted into menacing outer-space monsters. The very concept of giving a child a sense of power with a flick or two of the wrist – turning reality into unreality – is, in the writer's opinion, not explained only by inventive genius. The mechanics of the toy certainly are, but the whole idea has occultic overtones. It is a well-publicised fact that many of the unbelievable humanoid creatures which appear in out-of-space movies came to mind as a result of spiritistic trances. If the truth were known, transformer toys could well have had a similar origin.

Many out-of-space characters can cause children to become fearful, and some children become frightened of the toys themselves. We have prayed over some boys and girls, asking the Lord to release them from spirits of occultism and witchcraft; afterwards, they have handed the offending toys to their parents, saying that they didn't want them anymore. Previously, they had refused to part with them.

Unsupervised toy closets may contain some nasty little suprises which could be dangers in disguise. Children, like adults, are usually bargain hunters, and will either barter with friends, or rummage through garage sales to get hold of the unusual.

Further information on the dangers to children of other parlour games and the demonic overtones associated with toy snakes, dragons, owls, unicorns and frogs, are referred to in the first volume of this series, *Evicting Demonic Intruders and Breaking Bondages*.

The poisons that young people may be encouraged to try

Peer pressure can be irresistible. The less secure children and teen-agers feel, the less resistance they will probably offer to the false comfort of drugs, alcohol, and tobacco. Each is a poison to the human system.

The most serious of these three poisons is of course the hard drugs which are often introduced through smoking marijuana, falsely alleged to be harmless. The possible consequences of using marijuana are frightening. Here are some of them:

(1) We may find ourselves living with a generation of young people many of whom are suffering from irreversible brain damage.

(2) There is a growing body of evidence that the use of marijuana leads to indulgence in other drugs.

(3) We may be taken over by a 'marijuana culture' – a culture lacking moral backbone, motivated by a desire to escape from reality and by a consuming lust for self-gratification.

Children sucked into the vortex of drug or alcohol addiction need to be freed from the dominating spirits which control them. Counselling is not sufficient by itself, but when it is linked with the experience of deliverance, victory is possible.

The dangers of some reading materials

It has been said that 'a man is known by the books he reads'. Tragically some boys and girls have found their father's pornography, X-rated videos and blue movies, either hidden or lying around. As adults, many have spoken of the habits of masturbation or promiscuity, which they could not overcome, which commenced when they read or viewed such materials. Impurity and lust are a spreading forest fire which destroy everything in its path.

Parents should taken an unobtrusive interest in all their children's reading matter. Teenage mental and moral pollution has not only been caused but even justified by some educators through the ridiculous claim that the materials had 'literary merit'. If the law requires that poisons must be adequately marked, and that cigarette packets must display sizeable health hazard warnings, how can those same law-makers permit such deliberate moral pollution without adequate warning?

The standards set by the apostle Paul may be regarded as out-moded, narrow-minded, and too restrictive for modern youth, but they are God's requirements nonetheless:

> *'Finally brothers,*
> *whatever is **true**,*
> *whatever is **noble**,*
> *whatever is **right**,*
> *whatever is **pure**,*
> *whatever is **lovely**,*
> *whatever is **admirable**,*
> *if anything is **excellent or praiseworthy**,*
> *think about such things.'*

(Philippians 4:8 emphasis added)

SUMMARY

1.   The minds and emotions of children are prime targets for demonic infiltration and captivity.

2.   Cultural customs, parlour games, music, reading and films may all have concealed demonic traps.

3.   Parents who do not exercise careful supervision of their children's leisure activities will, in part, be responsible for what happens to them.

4.   Some of the dangerous recording artists and Rock and Roll bands include – Kiss, Michael Jackson, Jimmy Hendrix, Bruce Springsteen, Billy Idol, Sex Pistols, The Damned, Twisted Sister, Ozzy Osborne, Dio, Black Sabbath, AC/DC, John Cougar Mellancamp, Jimmy Barnes, Devo, Iron Maiden, Madonna, Blue Oyster Cult, John Denver, David Bowie, Pink Floyd, Mick Jagger, The Who. (This list was supplied by a Rock and Roll addict who used to fall asleep while listening to their music. The Lord released him from the dominant spirits of Rock and Roll and cleansed him from his previous desires.)

Chapter 11

Concrete Boots – the Appropriate Penalty for Sexually Defiling Children

'At that time the disciples came to Jesus and asked, "Who is the greatest in the kingdom of heaven?" He called a little child and had him stand among them. And he said: "I tell you the truth, unless you change and become like little children, you will never enter the kingdom of heaven. Therefore whoever humbles himself like this child is the greatest in the kingdom of heaven. And whoever welcomes a child like this in my name welcomes me.'

'BUT if anyone causes one of these little ones who believe in me to sin, it would be better for him to have a large millstone hung around his neck and to be drowned in the depth of the sea. Woe to the world because of the things that cause people to sin! Such things must come, but woe to the man through whom they come.'

(Matthew 18:1–7, emphasis added)

There are some very clear inferences from these direct statements:

(1) Humility and simple trust are the basic qualifications for adults to enter the kingdom of heaven (vv.3, 4).

(2) Those who bless children bless Jesus Christ himself (v. 5).

(3) The worst punishment imaginable is given to anyone who leads children into deliberate sin. Jesus said it would have been preferable for the guilty party to have been drowned with a millstone around his neck than to suffer the penalty God would hand down.

(The 20th century equivalent of the millstone is the well-known criminal practice of encasing a victim's feet in concrete, known as 'concrete boots', before throwing them into deep water.)

(4) Jesus said that the ultimate destiny for these offenders would be hell with its eternal fire (vv.8, 9). He also said that it would be better to

117

avoid eternal punishment by physically destroying the part of the body used for such an offence.

Clearly, Jesus Christ is speaking about deliberately leading a child into the practice of sin. Parents, family members, school teachers and friends who intentionally or unconsciously sin against a child by words, action or example, will be judged in a day to come. However the writer does not believe this is only what Jesus Christ had in mind. The word *'offend'* is used in the King James version, and the NIV translates it *'... if anyone causes one of these little ones who believe in me to sin.'* The Greek word used is 'skandalizo' meaning to put a trap or a stumbling block in a person's path with the intention of causing a fall. The English word 'scandalous' is defined as 'disgraceful, shameful, disreputable, highly improper, offensive, shocking, outrageous, reprehensible' (Reader's Digest Word Finder).

Many sins against children illustrate one of these words, but the sexual abuse of a child can only be adequately described by using all of the nine words just quoted. This is not personal prejudice, but an honest evaluation of the devastating effects childhood sexual abuse may continue to have upon adults of both sexes, particularly women folk. We have prayed for many and seen them set free.

In order to understand the causes, effects, and results of sexual exploitation, we need to define our terms:

Sexual assault or abuse

This includes the manipulation of children or teenagers by any means, including force, to submit to, or gratify the sexual desires of others. Offenders may use their age, size, relationship, threats, bribes or betray trust to indulge their own lust. Examples include:

(1) Fathers, grandfathers, brothers and other male relatives incestuously fondling, stimulating, penetrating, or attempting to penetrate young female family members. When full intercourse takes place, even over a period of years, some girls have become pregnant and have faced pressures to abort, or have the child adopted to protect the relative responsible.

(2) Homosexual acts of sodomy or lesbian stimulation have a particularly degrading effect on children. Regrettably, sexually deviant life styles have often developed from these offensive acts.

(3) Relatives exposing their genitals to young ones, or making

pointed remarks about a child's or teenager's sexuality and developing body, causing shame, withdrawal and rejection.

(4) Mothers excessively touching or drawing attention to their children's genitalia while bathing; or allowing their children to handle their own sexually sensitive areas while taking a bath with them.

(5) Fathers sensuously kissing their daughters, arousing or shocking them to the point of fear and withdrawal.

(6) Neighbours, baby-sitters, or visitors to the home making children submit to a range of defiling acts, or forcing them to do sexual acts upon themselves.

Sexual defilement

This may be caused when:

(1) children have either witnessed, or participated in mutual masturbation, oral stimulation, or bestiality.

(2) parents who, without permission, have regularly invaded their teenagers' privacy while they were dressing, undressing, showering or bathing, causing shame, resentment and rejection.

(3) parents have encouraged, or shamelessly allowed children to watch them love making. Others have had children burst into the bedroom during love play, or intercourse. Either way, the sexual awareness of the children is considerably increased and often leads to sexual experimentation on themselves, or others.

(4) grandparents or parents who have practised nudity of varying degrees in the family home cause children to become more sexually aware and active than normal.

The list is neither exhaustive nor descriptive. It simply states facts. Professionally produced materials are readily available. The objective of this chapter lies in what follows.

Behavioural indicators which can alert a parent or counsellor to the existence of a sexually based problem

(1) *Withdrawal*. The child withdraws, spends time alone and may live in a world of imagination, become vague and not hear what is said to them.

(It may take much patience and gentleness over a number of sessions before the truth will come out. Care must be taken to avoid a judgmental attitude.)

119

Silence may also be caused by:

- fear of punishment.
- a threat made by the seducer if he or she is exposed.
- the child being bribed to keep silent.
- loyalty to a guilty father, particularly when he tells his daughter that she will break up her parents' marriage if she tells her mother.
- fear of not being believed. Daughters have been both blamed and punished by mothers who refused to believe them. Some have accused their daughters of wickedly enticing their husbands. One mother even said 'Get your own man, leave mine alone'.
- the sense of defilement and worthlessness. This can be so great, that a child may vow never to reveal it to anyone.
- a child feeling agitation and nervousness in the presence of an offending party.

(2) *Unhealthy sexual activities*.

- A child showing an unhealthy interest in sexual organs, or the subject of sex.
- When a child develops a habit of pulling down underwear, self-exposure, self-stimulation, and/or the stimulation of others it may indicate there has been sexual interference. This may also come from heredity if experienced at an early age.
- Some girls have actually offered or tried to masturbate men whom they want to like them, because their fathers have taught them to do this. Acting out of fear of rejection, these abused children want to please those from whom they least want rejection.
- Children who suddenly become physically aggressive and hurt family members or friends may be redirecting their anger at having been sexually outraged. The trauma releases emotional pressures either outwardly to others (usually the ones loved most), or inwardly by self-hatred, anxiety, worry, depression, and worthlessness.

(3) *Eating problems*. Sexual trauma, amongst other causes, may cause a change of eating habits; this should be investigated. While girls are affected much more than boys, concern has recently been expressed that the percentage of boys becoming anorexic around thirteen years of age is on the increase. Anorexia nervosa is often referred to as a 'killer disease'. When a child becomes a 'finicky eater', then eats less and less to the point of not wanting to eat at all, these may be anorexic indications.

The other swing of the 'eating pendulum' is to bulimia, when enormous quantities of food are eaten in binges. An attempt to control weight is made by forcing vomiting and taking laxatives.

We have previously mentioned children or teenagers who deliberately overeat so that they will look as unattractive physically and sexually as they feel emotionally because of sexual abuse.

But there is good news for sufferers of these three classes of eating disorders. We have seen adults who were sexually traumatised as children or teenagers set free by the power of Jesus Christ. Before healing can be prayed for, they need to be released from the particular spirit of lust causing the sexual trauma, together with rejection, guilt, shame, worthlessness, resentment, anger and bitterness. Spirits of masturbation, sexual fantasy, frigidity, unforgiveness to themselves and the person who caused the offence, will also need to be dealt with before the spirits of anorexia nervosa, and/or bulimia can be released. Eating habits need also to be broken.

(4) *Sexual activities*.

- Sexual trauma may become fuel to a flickering flame of hereditary lust. A child or teenager may become sexually aggressive with their peers, or with adults, particularly if the sexual trauma was caused by an adult or adults.

- Some women have told us that because of extreme rejection in childhood, they have become sexually abusive towards themselves to dishonour their femininity. They have deliberately injured their breasts and genital areas as a type of self-imposed penance. In such cases worthlessness rather than sexual trauma has been the cause of aggressive sexual behaviour.

- There is a staggering demand for pornographic materials featuring adults' sexual activities with children or teenagers. The enticement of drugs and money becomes so irresistible to children and teenagers who feel too worthless to care, that they are unable to resist the enticements, or to stop the inner drive of hereditary lust. What is so sickening are the brazen paedophiles who attempt to justify their degraded sexual appetites for children by flowery words like 'love', and 'meaningful' or 'fulfilling experiences'.

Two persons who have received freedom have told us that at least eighty per cent of prostitutes in the USA and Holland were victims of incest in childhood. The first person was a trained social worker from Los Angeles. The other was a qualified medical practitioner from the Continent.

(5) *Fears*. Fear is a major sign of a child or teenager having suffered sexual trauma. This may be widespread. Examples:

- Fear of going to school, or to wherever the sexual trauma occurred, or fear of being left with someone whom the child distrusts.
- Fear of being left alone in the house, of going out alone, or sleeping alone.
- A child who wants to live with other people, get away from home at an unusually young age, doesn't want to come home, or even runs away may be indicating a problem associated with someone in the home.

Most parents are reluctant to suspect that a partner or family member would ever sexually defile one they love. But it has happened, and regrettably will continue.

(6) *Other indications*:

(a) When a normally open and carefree child wants to withdraw from sports or swimming activities where they have to change clothes in front of others, this may indicate a sexual aberration. Other signs may be unusual modesty in taking a bath, or using the toilet, where previously there had been no indication of embarrassment. Fear of going to a public toilet alone may also be an indication of sexual trauma.

(b) When children accumulate gifts without adequate explanation, or seem to have more money than normal, discreet enquiries need to be made. The possibility of a pay-off should not be overlooked.

(c) When suicidal thoughts and attempts happen, they may be indications of a deeply disturbing sexual event if there is no history of hereditary suicide.

(d) When children or teenagers develop unusual emotional or physical symptoms. Pregnancy is probably the last condition an unsuspecting parent would expect to find, but the possibility should not be ignored.

(e) Physical symptoms such as sleeplessness, or difficulties in eating, may also arise from guilt and shame coming from sexual interference.

Physical signs

Parents or guardians should be sensitive to certain observable physical symptoms, and if necessary arrange for medical investigation.

Examples include:

(a) Unusual scratches or bruises near the genital, anal, or breast area. If the child has been tied up there may be marks or rope burns on the wrists and ankles.

(b) Itching, or frequently rubbing of the genital or anal areas, may indicate inflammation caused by sexual assault or abuse. (The usual cause for this is threadworms.)

(c) Unpleasant odours coming from lower body openings may indicate an infection received through sexual penetration.

(d) The presence of fresh or dry semen on a child's body or underwear.

(e) If a brother's and sister's normal relationship goes through subtle changes so that they appear to be more boyfriend and girlfriend than siblings, a sexual relationship may have developed between them.

Some further aspects of this sin against children will be looked at in the next chapter.

SUMMARY

1.   Forcing, encouraging, or enticing a child to sin sexually is a sin punishable by hell-fire according to Jesus Christ. Drowning would be preferable to the judgment to follow, but is not an option.

2.   Parents and guardians should be aware of a range of behaviour indicators which indicate that a sexual trauma may have been suffered by a child or teenager.

3.   Jesus Christ is able to release, cleanse, and re-sanctify victims so that they can live wholesome and fulfilling lives including marriage and parenthood.

Chapter 12

The Tragic Long-Term Results of Childhood Sexual Abuse

One of the saddest recorded cases of incestuous sexual abuse is to be found in 2 Samuel 13:1–22. Amnon, King David's eldest son, became lustfully infatuated with his beautiful half-sister Tamar, and deceived his father into sending Tamar to prepare food for him, on the pretext that he was so ill, only the fair hand of his sister could prepare the food he needed.

When Tamar arrived, Amnon dismissed his servants, and proceeded to rape the young lady despite her pleas not to disgrace her. To make matters worse, Amnon afterwards called his servant and had the girl thrown out and the door locked.

Having been brutally raped, and utterly humiliated, Tamar tore her princess's ornamental robe (a sign of virginity), threw ashes over her head, and set out for the house where she lived with her brother, crying loudly and bitterly all the way.

From then on she stayed at home '... *a desolate woman*' (v. 20).

What had been to Amnon just an experience of sexual self-gratification became to Tamar a life-sentence of defilement, misery, the bitterness of rejection, and the shameful blight she would carry to the grave. There are many women today who could identify with Tamar.

Some general emotional problems of rejection, low self-image, self-hatred, guilt, and worthlessness caused by sexual trauma have already been listed but some of these cause specific problems in adulthood:

1. A life of singleness caused through fear of marriage

In the event of childhood sexual trauma the emotional deprivation suffered does cause some young ladies to so fear sexual relationships that any thoughts and desires of marriage are rejected and offers declined.

2. Emotional frigidity

It is clear from Scripture that sexual partnerships within marriage are expected to take place in the atmosphere of mutual love (Ephesians 5:2). But sexual acts against children and teenagers are not motivated by love but by lust. Where a girl has not been a willing partner, severe damage is usually done to her emotional nature by the violation of her person. She becomes confused as to the true meaning of love, and then reasons that love and lust must both motivate sexual intercourse which for her has caused only pain, grief, and guilt. She then withdraws emotionally and determines never to be hurt again by any expression of love; she may even develop defensive or aggressive tactics for self-protection. Unless released by Jesus Christ, that attitude may remain.

3. The substitution of false love

Some daughters whose fathers have sexually molested them have subsequently been unable to receive any male affection. Some have said they used to go rigid with fear whenever their fathers, or any male put a hand on them, or when they were embraced.

Subsequently, as they grow to maturity, the fear of men causes some to seek the affection and company of other females. Most of these relationships begin with the mutual sharing of emotional comfort, but very often develop sexual interplay. Many of them end in full de facto lesbian partnerships. Many prostitutes are said to become lesbians to satisfy their need for love; because the men who pay for their services are only motivated by lust.

Boys or teenagers who have been sexually molested usually commence to masturbate (if they have not already done so). Despite their hatred for what had been done to them, they often find themselves irresistibly drawn to the male figure (particularly the genital area). Some never go any further and seek prayer for their guilt and shame, while others become practising homosexuals. Praise God some of them have also sought and received freedom.

The love of God which is so freely available in Jesus Christ is truly a wonderful source of deep comfort to those who have been defiled by false love.

4. Lighting the fire of promiscuity

Grandfathers and fathers who molest their own family members may provide the spark needed to ignite the fuel of generational lustful desires which Jesus Christ alone can fully extinguish. Teenage girls have been known to go on to have such an insatiable sexual appetite that they will not go to bed without a male companion. After being freed, wholesome marriages and parenthood have resulted.

5. A bride turns out to be sexually frigid

The fear of the sexual act is not always overcome by a romantic Romeo and a beautiful wedding. The moment of reality arrives on the honeymoon when the bridegroom expects the marriage to be consummated. The bride is now alone with her man and her fears, with no mother to call upon for help! If his love and gentleness win, the fears may be gradually conquered. If the fears win, she becomes tense, maybe rigid, and unyielding. Marriages have been annulled, and others have been ruined because of this attitude.

Some wives submit sexually in order to have the number of children they planned, then refuse to have sex again. It is no wonder that some husbands turn to other women for their sexual fulfilment; many of these marriages end in divorce.

6. Marriage, an opportunity for sweet revenge

One unfortunate result of childhood sexual pollution is that girls may develop a bitter and long-lasting hatred for males. This may become so obsessive that a woman may enter marriage for the purpose of punishing a male for what was done to her in childhood. Others have even confessed during counselling to wanting to get married so that they could punish a man for what their fathers had supposedly done to their mothers. One single young lady who fell pregnant aborted the baby and would not tell the young man responsible, so as to keep him from having the satisfaction of knowing that he had made her pregnant. She hated men, but used them to satisfy her sexual desires.

7. Some fear having children

Some women have such a vivid memory of their forced sexual defilement as a child that they determine they will never have children who could be exposed to the same trauma. Even if they do marry, they will take every precaution against conception, and if they do conceive, will terminate the pregnancy.

A close friend once told us that her mother did not mind having boys, but did not want a daughter, who would eventually become a 'sex object' for men.

Some men who were interfered with in childhood have told us that they lived in constant fear of sexually assaulting their own children. The Lord has freed them from their desire with the associated guilt and shame.

8. An unsubstantiated possibility

Numbers of adults have shared with us that they had strong desires to commit suicide after having been molested, raped, or the victims of incest as children or teenagers. It would be impossible to estimate how many have committed suicide, but there must have been a considerable number.

The fact that those who sexually defile the young never suffer to the same extent as their victims, is often bitterly resented by those who have suffered. Even if the offenders are caught and sentenced, a few years of imprisonment is often little comfort for those who have been condemned to singleness, childlessness, or the guilt of lustful habits which to them is a lifetime sentence. Some have become so obsessed with revenge that they have murdered those responsible.

The fall-out is long, perhaps even a lifetime. The effects are life-changing, often crippling. The heartache, grief, deprivation, and rejection which generally follow are heart-breaking.

Consolation and help are available from a variety of soures, but no one is able to release, cleanse, and renew like Jesus Christ. Whether in childhood or later life, wholeness and healing may be received. Only in Jesus Christ can the future be freed from the past.

SUMMARY

1. The effects of childhood sexual trauma may well extend into adulthood, even lasting for a lifetime.

2.   Childhood or teenage sexual abuse may cause marital problems, difficulty in receiving love, sexual frigidity, and fears of having children.

3.   Bitter wives may seek to revenge their previous sexual traumas on their husbands.

4.   Release, cleansing, wholeness and victory in Jesus Christ may be received at any age.

Chapter 13

Many of Our Children's Problems are Caused by the Evil One

An open and friendly boy, no more than five years of age (who said he loved Jesus), was brought by his mother to be released from spirits of rebellion, anger, defiance and stubbornness. (This is not an uncommon problem with boys of all ages!) We asked him why he acted like he did, and his reply was quite revealing. He said, 'I asked Jesus that question, and he told me that Satan's helpers were making me do these things'.

In order to understand just how much Satan can do to children, we need to look at several factors:

The evidence of Scripture

Amongst the many Gospel accounts of deliverance the two which involve children give us considerable understanding on the subject.

The first account involves a little Greek girl, recorded in Matthew 15:21–28 and Mark 7:24–30.

Mark tells us the girl was *'young'* (KJV) or *'little'* (NIV). Strong's Concordance describes her picturesquely as *'daughterling'*. So obviously she was very young. Mark records the girl as being *'possessed of an evil (unclean) spirit'* (v. 25), which the mother describes as *'a demon'*. Because the Lord Jesus also referred to a *'demon'*, it is clear that evil (unclean) spirits are also called demons. It does appear however that the Scriptural use of the words *'evil (unclean) spirits'*, (Greek *'akathartos pneuma'*), refers to a specific kind of demonic spirit whose nature is unclean or impure. Those two words are used only nineteen times in the New Testament, while the most common words used for 'demon' or 'demonisation' (people acting under demon control), are used seventy-five times.

This means that this little girl's demon was an impure, dirty spirit. The question naturally arises 'What could this little girl have done at that early age to have become demon possessed'? The answer is simple – 'Obviously nothing'. The source could only have been from heredity. It is not the source of the girl's problem we are addressing but the fact that a child so small desperately needed deliverance. Quite obviously, some conclusions may be drawn from this story:

(1) Demons who can dominate children from infancy, respect neither age nor sex.

(2) Children may become demon oppressed through circumstances beyond their control.

(3) A child may have a demon of impurity and uncleanness long before he or she is capable of knowingly committing an indecent act by choice.

(4) Deliverance by the power and authority of Jesus Christ is the only way to freedom. The Syrophenician mother had to break through rigid ethnic and cultural barriers to have her daughter set free. Obviously she had not found help in her own country.

The second story concerns a Jewish boy whom the disciples were unable to free. He was brought to Jesus Christ by his father, with a desperate plea for help. The synoptic Gospel writers all include the story (Matthew 17:14–20); Mark 9:14–29; Luke 9:37–42). As Mark gives the incident the greatest coverage, we will concentrate on his account.

When Jesus Christ asked the father how long the boy had suffered from the demon possession, the father replied that it had been since childhood (NIV). The Amplified Bible puts it this way – *'from the time he was a little boy'* (v. 21). Strong translates the words *'from infancy'*. Like the little girl, the boy's problems also began in infancy, which means he was in no way to blame for his plight.

Throughout the story the demon is named *'a spirit' (pneuma)*. Although it produced epileptic symptoms, had obviously injured the child, and even tried to kill him, Jesus rebuked an *'evil'* (impure) spirit, and called it a *'deaf and dumb spirit'* (v. 25). When ordered out, the demon left protesting, and the child appeared to be dead. Jesus Christ took the little fellow by the hand, and fully healed him. Like the little

Greek girl, the Jewish boy also was possessed of an unclean spirit, but this one also had the power to produce sickness, destruction and death.

Eight aspects of demon-domination in children may be clearly seen in this story:

(a) *Demons may afflict children with physical sicknesses*. The boy's father told Jesus that his son was an epileptic (Matthew 17:15). Certainly the symptoms of *'teeth-gnashing'*, *'rigidity'* and *'convulsion'*, *'falling to the ground'*, *'rolling around'*, and *'foaming at the mouth'* (Mark 9:18) would appear to confirm such diagnosis. However Jesus showed that a spirit of epilepsy was not the basic cause, but an unclean deaf and dumb spirit (Mark 9:25). Right causes need to be discerned to obtain right results.

(b) *Demons can prevent children from being able to control their own actions*. (References from Mark 9.) The father said the demon had robbed his boy of speech (v. 17). The boy was also incapable of stopping himself from falling into fire or water (v. 22).

(c) *Demons may physically harm children*. The very presence of Jesus Christ caused the demon to make the boy convulse and fall to the ground, rolling and foaming at the mouth (v. 20). The father also said the demon had often tried to kill the boy, either by throwing him into fire or water (v. 22). No wonder the father was so desperate for the Teacher to have pity on him (v. 22).

(d) *Demons may defy the person trying to free a child from their control*. The disciples were unable to release the boy (v. 18) obviously because their faith didn't stretch that far (v. 19). They, and the boy's father then learned a lesson which every generation needs to learn: *'Everything is possible for him who believes'* (v. 23).

(e) *Demons defile children by satisfying their own evil natures through them*. The demon was a dumb and deaf spirit which would not say a word to Jesus Christ as most other demons did. (See Mark 1:24, 34; 5:9; Luke 4:41.) Therefore the boy was unable to speak.

The demon also had the power to cause sickness, and death. As a result the boy was constantly harassed by epileptic fits and attempts to kill him. Even when leaving, the spirit was violent (Mark 9:26).

(f) *Demons can also make children perform, or show off*. As soon as the boy was brought to Jesus, the demon put on such a show that the crowd came running (vv. 20, 25). Jesus interrupted his teaching on faith, and ordered the spirit to leave. This abruptly terminated the demon's domination of the child.

(g) *Demons may continue to control a child until someone with discernment and faith in the authority of Christ drives them out*. When commanded to leave and never re-enter, the evil spirit resisted no longer. To this point all other attempts at deliverance had failed, and the child was becoming worse. Jesus Christ alone is sovereign over spirit beings.

(h) *Demons may induce symptoms of death when forced to leave*. *'The spirit shrieked, convulsed him violently and came out. The boy looked so much like a corpse that many said, "He's dead". But Jesus took him by the hand and lifted him to his feet, and he stood up'* (vv. 26, 27).

When we combine the separate accounts of what demons actually did to these two little children, we are confronted with a distinctly frightening possibility. It is that some at least of our children's and teenager's problems (even more than we dare to imagine), are actually caused by evil spirits.

Such a conclusion may stir the opposition of conservative Christians and even offend those to whom psychological explanations are more rational. But Biblical facts never yield the right of way when confronted by non-Biblical theories.

Twentieth century deliverance experiences confirm the same demonic tactics and the continuing power and authority of the teachings and ministry of Jesus Christ

(1) *Children may give manifestation of demons received through heredity without personally having done anything to cause their oppression*. The term 'age of understanding' varies in each child according to their mental alertness and maturity. So when children under five years of age, not having reached that stage of development, are rebellious, very disobedient, quick to show anger, refuse to love, show strong fears, are resistant to spiritual matters, or show an excessive interest in sex, it is a fair deduction that their conduct can be caused only by hereditary spirits.

One three-year-old boy was extremely angry, and woke up screaming frequently at night. He had strong hereditary spirits of anger from his father, and witchcraft and occultism from his mother. After prayer he slept all night without waking.

(2) *Demons may dominate children from babyhood*. A mother brought an eighteen month old child for prayer because she had cried

day and night since birth. We used our authority over a 'crying spirit' and asked the Lord to break the habit and heal the child. From that night onwards the little one slept soundly.

Then about two months afterwards, the mother awoke one night to sounds of a child crying. She went into the room where her three children slept, and each one was fast asleep, so she returned to bed. One hour later the same crying sounds awakened her, so she went back to check out the youngest again, but all the children were sleeping soundly. Puzzled, she opened the bedroom window and listened for the sounds of a neighbour's child crying, but heard nothing. Once again the now tiring mother returned to bed, but could still hear the sounds of crying. She quietly returned to the children's bedroom and stood by the bed of her youngest child. To her amazement she could hear the sounds of a child's cries actually moving around the dark room. Realizing the crying spirit from which her daughter was freed was wanting to oppress her again, the mother opened the window and simply said, 'In the name of Jesus Christ get out'. She then closed the window, and returned to bed and sleep. No crying sounds have been heard since.

Phyl once prayed over a one-year-old boy in New Zealand who used to wake up terrified at night, but he soon developed many fears. Because he was unable to explain what the problem was, Phyl enquired if the parents had been involved with occultism and witchcraft prior to becoming Christians. They had. The boy was prayed for again and released from hereditary spirits; the problems disappeared entirely.

(3) *Children may be taken over by a demon through circumstances beyond their control*. This is particularly so when a child is forced to submit to sexual molestation. One girl was first molested by a baby sitter, then by her father. Following this, her mother stimulated her sexually for two years, forcing the daughter to do the same thing to her. As the girl grew up, she could not resist fornication, lesbian relationships, and pornography.

A teenage Christian was babysitting in a Christian's home when she found four rock-and-roll records among the general collection. She told us that as she listened to them, 'something' had entered into her, filling her with fear. Later, as she was showering one night, a 'brown shape' came over the shower screen and grabbed her. She was terrified and screamed for help. The Lord freed her from all the spirits which began to oppress her through listening to these records.

(4) *A child may have a demon of impurity and uncleanness long before he or she understands the consequences of wrong choices*. We were once asked to pray for a three year old boy who was making his penis red and sore by constant handling. Neither parent had apparently had problems with lust or masturbation. The boy's spirit of lust was released by prayer. On one or two occasions afterwards when he went to school, he again handled himself when under emotional stress, but after further prayer, he stopped entirely.

(5) *Deliverance by the power and authority of Jesus Christ is the only way to freedom*. During a church camp a number of parents brought their children for prayer. One girl told us that she got frightened when the light was put out at night. She was prayed for. That evening she told her mother to put out the light when she went to bed and leave her in the dark. After a short time she called out: 'Mother it works'. When her mother asked her what worked, the girl simply replied, 'Prayer'.

A boy of eight years of age was devastated when his father unexpectedly died. For the next twenty-eight years he could not mention his father without breaking down and weeping. He had unsuccessfully tried everything to break the habit. Then he came to a seminar Phyl and I were conducting. His problem became evident when talking with us, and he wept as usual at the mention of his father. We asked the Lord to set him free from the spirits of grief, mourning, loneliness, abandonment, and rejection. The weeping ceased, and that was the end of his embarrassment.

(6) *Demons afflict children with physical sickness*. Probably the most outstanding experience we have had was with a boy who suffered extreme lactose intolerance, and who had nearly died in his early years. His mother brought him for prayer when he was seven years of age. We asked the Lord to free him from hereditary spirits of alcoholism and violence, then spirits of infirmity, particularly hypoglycaemia. About three hours after the Lord had set him free his mother decided to run her own check on just how effective prayer was for children. She gave her son a chocolate Mars bar, and waited. His normal reaction would have been diarrhoea and vomiting, but this time nothing happened. But she wasn't convinced, so she gave him a second Mars bar, and still nothing happened. When six and a half hours had passed and there had been no adverse reaction, the mother was finally convinced that God had indeed healed her boy. She was soon knocking on our door, face shining, excitedly sharing the good

news. We have seen the family twice per year for a number of years, and that boy is growing well. His doctor admits that something out of the ordinary has happened to him, as he shows no sign of his previous sickness. And what do you think that he likes most for a treat? Chocolates of course!

Many children are brought to us for physical healing when other treatments have failed. We take authority over the appropriate spirit causing the physical affliction, then pray for cleansing and wholeness. Occasionally those who were not totally freed are brought back for further prayer.

(7) *Demons may prevent children from controlling their physical actions*. Most children respond positively to discipline and wise counselling for habits of anger, temper or violence. Of course there may be protests, but they feel secure when firm guide-lines are established.

Unfortunately, some of them just cannot respond because they are being relentlessly oppressed by evil spirits. Unless this is understood by counsellors, some children or teenagers may end up by being put out of the family home or taken over as State wards, because traditional methods have failed.

A small adopted boy was brought to Phyl because he was aggressive with other children in a crèche and constantly smashed sturdy toys. Phyl asked the Lord for wisdom and prayed against hereditary cultural spirits of anger and violence, received from his natural parents who came from two different SE Asian cultures.

The following Sunday the mother was approached by the crèche supervisor who thought her little boy was sick. The reason? The boy hadn't punched anyone or broken a toy. He just played quietly by himself. The mother simply said, 'Oh, he has been prayed for'.

If demonic powers do not control the physical actions and reactions of children, then what other explanation can there be when:

(a) Placid babies, some even asleep, become extremely restless or cry when hands are laid upon them to release them from hereditary bondages and dominations?

(b) Children as young as two years of age become disturbed when told that someone is going to pray for them? Some even cry out 'No prayer, no prayer!'

(c) Small children physically resist prayer with the laying on of hands, by twisting their heads vigorously from side to side? Some will aggressively punch, kick, and try to bite. But in each case, after prayer for deliverance and healing is over, the child usually is warm, friendly, even loving, showing no animosity.

(8) *Demons may cause death, or injury*. A child of six told his mother that he was going to commit suicide. The mother didn't believe him and casually said, 'Go ahead'. Some two hours later, the mother found his little body lying on the laundry floor. A plastic bag was over his head. Spirits of suicide and death often trouble children and teenagers.

Some children, (like adults), are accident prone. Cuts, bruises, broken bones and other misadventures seem never-ending. It can become distressing and very frustrating especially when they are constantly deprived of playing sport. Believing that a continuity of accident (and continuous sicknesses) is an indication of the activity of troublesome family spirits, we have prayed over many and seen them released.

(9) *Demons still defy spiritual challenges to leave the children they dominate*. Sometimes our spiritual authority is challenged by children brought for help. Some will refuse to be prayed for, or strongly object to prayer. We do not believe in violating the free-will of a child but prefer to talk to them so that they become willing to co-operate. In some cases where children have been particularly belligerent, parents have asked us to ignore protests and begin to pray as they well know that the child is controlled by a power they have been unable to conquer.

Spirits will even speak through a child receiving ministry by saying 'No I won't go, and you can't make me go!' When King Jesus asserts his authority they do go!

(10) *Demons defile children by satisfying the habits of their defiled natures, through them*. From experience it has been found that demonic spirits may:

(a) cause a child to develop attitudes and habits which dishonour family standards, and which cannot be controlled.

Children have been brought for deliverance because they are dominated by fears, unable to stop eating, have a fixation about death, are convinced they are failures, have an obsessive interest in occultism, excessively fantasize or have some of the sexual problems already mentioned. Such features are not natural in children, and they often do not respond to counselling. From time to time parents ask for urgent consultations with us because school counsellors have suggested that they take their child to a psychiatrist.

(b) cause a child to manifest a problem which is known to have been in the family for generations.

This may include stealing, deceit, lying, anger, mental problems, passivity, occultic powers such as being able to move objects by mental power, perfectionism, as well as ethnic and cultural characteristics. Addictive problems may also become evident in childhood, such as abnormal desires for drugs, alcohol, nicotine, or food.

(11) *Demons make some children perform, or show off*. Demonic powers are expert in distraction, deceit, and cover-up. They have fooled 'experts' for centuries so that those who discern and expose their true natures and activities, are looked upon as 'kinky', and to be avoided. Very few people would seriously believe that children who constantly entertain people by their antics could be doing so under the control of demons. But it happens. Of course some children have natural gifts which cause laughter, and pleasure. The difference between the naturally gifted child, and those under demonic pressure, is often a matter of timing, intensity and duration. The child with natural gifts remains in control, and will stop when spoken to. The child with the demonic problem will usually perform at the most untimely opportunity with excessive zeal, even to the point of embarrassment, and will often have other uncontrollable habits. Unless such a child is set free, this conduct will continue into adulthood.

(12) *Demons continue to control children until someone with special discernment and faith in the name of Jesus Christ overcomes them*. Demons differ from one another in rank, and authority. Some are more powerful than others. The disciples had neither the faith nor power to set the little boy free (Mark 9:18).

Phyl and I see this same principle in today's deliverance scene. Sometimes we are asked to pray for children others have prayed for; some children have to be prayed for several times. There are also both children and adults whom we have not been able to see freed. Some because they are unwilling, others because we have insufficient discernment and knowledge.

One major deliverance in the writer's experience concerned a woman whose demonic domination began with her great-grandmother who dedicated her grandchildren to Satan after bizarre demonic sexual experiences.

As a child, this woman would be awakened in the night and carried outside by spirit beings who passed her from one to another as they danced around a fire. Her grandmother would become very angry the next morning when she found the living room furniture totally re-arranged, or some of the girl's bedding in the kitchen sink with the tap on. She was also very puzzled by footprints in ashes outside the back door.

During deliverance, the demons interrupted me saying, 'You have no right to her, we have. Her great grand-mother sold her to the devil'. While ministering peace, they said, 'We promised her peace as we danced around the fire with her when she was a child'. The spirit-control which began in childhood was still evident in adulthood. The Lord gloriously freed her, and everyone could see that she was obviously a changed woman. Unfortunately, I later heard that after going well for some time, she and her husband returned to their old ways. The problem was not in the deliverance but in the woman's unwillingness to continue to glorify Jesus Christ as Lord of her life.

Another teenager receiving help was physically and verbally obstructive. The demons spoke through her telling us that her grand-mother had made a pact with Satan that if he would grant her request he could claim a granddaughter for his use. The demons claimed that we had no authority over the girl we were praying for as Satan had chosen her as his own. Fortunately, Jesus Christ had a prior claim, paid for in blood, and the teenager was completely and permanently set free. The writer has seen the evidence of this years afterwards.

(13) *Demons still induce symptoms of death when forced to leave*. On two occasions, Phyl has seen a child receiving help become deathly white and go totally limp. When she took authority over a spirit of death, both colour and vitality returned. The same has happened while ministering to adults. Unless the scriptural precedent is known and the spirit of death is defeated, it could be quite an unnerving experience.

Before moving to the third proposition, what is already obvious needs to be re-stated. Demons have not changed their tactics in the last nineteen centuries. There has been no need to as their success rate has been so high.

Children themselves are very aware of spirit activities

While this chapter was being written, the writers held a deliverance seminar. Participants were invited to share with us any experiences they had had with evil spirts during childhood, or any features they had encountered while ministering to children. Here are two edited versions of what was submitted in writing:

- 'A four year old boy disliked and feared a glass bulge in the front door of his house. He called it "the lion in the window". One night he screamed and continued crying loudly. His father rushed to him, and was told that a lion was in his room trying to get him. The father prayed over his son, taking spiritual authority over the spirit of fear in the imaginary lion, telling it to go. The boy then said to his dad, "It's all right now, the lion went out my bedroom window" (which was open). When the parents later enquired about the lion in the glass bulge, their son replied that he no longer saw the lion there, and was not afraid of that part of the house.'

- 'From as early as I can remember I've always felt as if somone was walking behind me, or standing at the bedroom door. I've had evil nightmares. I lived in a house visited by poltergeist spirits and often heard my name being called during the night. I had an incredible fear of the dark. My sister and one brother used to talk to imaginary friends (one was a horse). My parents wouldn't believe me. But now that I'm older, I've found out that all my family members have experienced strange happenings such as unusual smells, lights going on and off, moving shadows, winds, and feeling the presence of people they couldn't see. I have since learned why my friends would never stay overnight. They were afraid of the strange things which happened.'

- 'A six year old claimed to have seen a horrible face at his bedroom window. He said the face then started to come through the window in the form of a brown blob like plasticine which crept up the walls, over the ceiling and across the floor. He screamed; and when his mother rushed in he told her that the blob was coming closer to his bed. The mother commanded it to stop and to go in the name of Jesus. The child could still see it advancing, so again she commanded it to stop, claiming the cleansing of the blood of Jesus Christ in the room. According to the child the blob vanished immediately.'

- An ex-warlock whc came for deliverance told me his para-normal experiences began as a child. His parents told him he was a reincarnation of a grandparent, a Freemason. His grandmother, mother and aunt taught him astral travel, and as a child he used to go into a trance for up to eight hours at a time. He found he was able to move objects with his eyes. This led him into the grossest witchcraft practices. But God had mercy on him, saving him and setting him free from what began in his childhood.

Mothers have testified to demonic influence over their children

Another written testimony from the seminar was:

- 'Our son never wanted to sleep in his own room from a very early age. We prayed over him and had a pastor come and pray in his room, but the boy remained frightened. He told us that dark shadows were still there but we were unsure whether it was not just attention-seeking. One night he didn't come to our bedroom upstairs, and I told him the next morning that he was a good boy to have slept in his room all night. He said, "I was on my way up to your room, and an angel on the stairs told me to go back to bed and that everything would be alright – he would look after me". He was four years old at the time. He spent some nights in his room, but then continued the habit of coming up to our bedroom.

  When he was seven years old we decided to sell our home, so renovated his room which had been papered with animal-decorated paper when he was only a baby. The paper was removed and the walls painted white. From that time onwards he slept alone in his own room in both the old house, and the new one. He has said he never wants to have anything but white walls again. We then knew that it was something on the wallpaper which had disturbed him, but we still didn't know why. At this week's seminar you mentioned the use of the goat by Satan as one of his symbols. Then we realized that the main animal on the wallpaper in our son's room was a goat.'

- Some time ago a mother recounted a similar story during a time of deliverance. She lay down to rest in a room where her children slept. The curtains had been handed down in the family over many years and were covered with animals featured in the children's fable, 'Old MacDonald had a farm'. With a start she suddenly realized that the fork in the farmer's hand was not a hay fork, but a trident. But worse was to come. Under the cat, was the word 'Lucifer'. It was then that she remembered that the children had always been restless in that room and had often come into her bed in the middle of the night.

  So down came the curtains. They were packed in a box and put away in a cupboard under the stairs. The next night, her daughter had a dream about a cat which spoke to her saying 'You're stupid'.

Another seminar contribution was this:

'In January 1987, my eldest daughter was severely ill with meningoencephalitis, a complication of chicken pox. She had been deteriorating for several days and had reached a point when as well as being in severe pain, she had lost partial use of her arms and legs. That night I woke suddenly in the early hours of the morning with the strongest inner urge to burn two Hare Krishna books which I knew were in her bedroom. After struggling with this for a while, I realized it was the Holy Spirit telling me to get rid of these things, so I took them outside and attempted to burn them. At first they wouldn't burn at all and it was only after I prayed, that they finally caught fire. It took one hour to burn two paper-backs!

'On arriving at the hospital the next morning, I found that all the pain had left C. in the night, and movement had returned to her arms and legs. Praise God. Although total recovery took some months, she is now perfectly healthy with no after-effects.'

The evidence is undeniable. The Scriptures, practical experience, the awareness of children, and the testimonies of parents all combine to present powerful evidence that the evil one is indeed very much involved in causing a vast number of problems among our children and teenagers.

But this does not conclude the evidence. Chapter twenty-one, will examine the biblical evidence of satanic designs to kill, cripple, dominate and bind children and young people.

SUMMARY

1. The Gospels show conclusively that children may become oppressed to a major degree.
2. The ministry of deliverance is very effective with children, and will bring freedom when other methods fail.
3. Children themselves can be very aware of demonic activities, and often know when they are oppressed.

4.   Mothers have been aware of their children becoming demonized.

5.   When traditional methods of controlling children's problems fail to be effective, a controlling spirit is usually the cause. What you call it is not as important as seeing the child freed in the name of Jesus Christ.

6.   The older a child becomes, the stronger the spiritual force or forces controlling the child become. What manifests itself in adulthood very often comes from heredity, or begins in childhood. A childhood deliverance will lead to blessing in adulthood.

Chapter 14

The School Where All Mothers are Students

(by Phyl Gibson)

At my stage in life, being a grandmother of nine lovely children, one is so much wiser. I wish I had accumulated all that wisdom when our own children were young, but there seems to be no escape from learning by experience. However God is gracious. He often allows us a 're-run' with our grandchildren. Let me assure you it is a real thrill to be a grandmother.

To become a grandmother though, you must first be a mother. With hindsight, although there are things I regret, the lessons I have learned from our own children have taught me much about the nature of God.

I sometimes shudder to think that as a young mother, I was so rigid in obeying the four-hourly feeding routine regardless of the baby's needs. I believed it had to be done by the book.

We wanted our first-born to be as nearly perfect as possible, all for the wrong reasons – most of them caused by our own awful pride. We over-disciplined our much loved daughter, causing her to become insecure and unsure of her ability to do things well. I wept at what we had done and cried out to the Lord – HELP! He faithfully and lovingly answered by revealing to me how to counteract the damage. After Adrienne had been sleeping soundly for 10–15 minutes I whispered into her ear 'you have nothing to fear' 'you *can* do all that is asked of you' (naming the thing that she was afraid of, and reassuring her she was loved very much). How my heart sang when she began to bounce up the stairs each morning after speaking to her subconscious mind those positive statements. She very soon became a very out-going, secure little girl. She never found out about my nightly prayer sessions in sowing faith seeds until she was married and had a child of her own.

Hundreds of mothers can testify to the protection of their children in dangerous circumstances. They surely do have a guardian angel. Jesus Christ said, *'See that you do not despise one of these little ones, for I say to you that their angels in heaven continually behold the face of My Father who is in heaven'* (Matthew 18:10).

One morning I felt compelled to go back to the kitchen where our little one was playing. She had pulled a chair up to the sink, climbed up, and turned the hot tap on. The sink was just about to run over with scalding water when I arrived. I knew the Lord had protected her from being scalded.

On another occasion when Adrienne was about twelve, she came home from school, weeping. Her outburst was 'I hate my Daddy being an open-air preacher.' I sensed immediately that persecution was doing its destructive work. One of her special girlfriends had ridiculed her because of her father's work. I gathered her into my arms and wept with her and told her I couldn't change things because that was what God had asked her Daddy to do. Like all mothers, I prayed with her that Jesus would heal the hurt. God not only heard that prayer, but answered in his own special way. About three weeks later she bounced in from school, full of smiles. The girlfriend who had been so critical of her had told her she had been on a beach one Sunday afternoon and had seen and heard a man telling a wonderful story. She had asked Adrienne, 'Was that your father?' Adrienne told me she was proud to say 'Yes, it certainly was my father'. From that moment the antipathy was dropped and personal warmth and respect were restored. Only God could have resolved the problem in such a beautiful way.

Our middle daughter, Aureole, was another much longed for baby. She was very loving and very determined. Everyone called her 'smiler'; her enthusiasm for life was unbounded.

When she was just three years old she told me one day she was going to run away. Something had not pleased her and she thought she could threaten me. But her threat was not just verbal, for she put it into action. She packed her little case with a book, teddy bear, and a jumper, and left by the front gate. I had told her how sad I was that she didn't want to live with us any more, and that she would have to sleep under the bushes at night. Adrienne was very upset so we prayed together. Being a practical mother, I followed Aureole, hiding behind the bushes until she reached a busy road at the bottom of a long hill. She stopped for some time, then slowly turned around towards home.

I quickly retraced my steps and waited. When at last she walked in the door, she went downstairs and put her things away, then came upstairs and ate her meal as normal, without a word being said about what had happened. Young as she was, she learned that manipulation did not work, and never again threatened me with running away.

The same little one was always wanting to help me. Mothers know it is much quicker to do it yourself, but involving them pays off well in the years ahead. Allowing them to help (even if you have to do it again when they are not looking), is worth while. Aureole, always doing everything in a hurry, brought in the milk bottles one morning. At least she almost did. The total loss was every milk bottle, my cool, and some very red blood from little cut fingers. All this seems so small and unimportant now, but I learned and am continually reminded of how patient God is with me. He never loses his cool!

Children are very discerning and forgiving. When I made a wrong judgement and confessed it, asking the girls' forgiveness, how quickly they forgave, and they never brought it up again. Children are mostly better at forgiving than adults. I never felt I had lost face by admitting a mistake. But I did gain their trust because they learned I would be fair. And it never hurt them to realise that their mother wasn't perfect!

After six years of motherhood we were blessed with the gift of a third beautiful daughter. How she was loved and tended by her two sisters! She became the one who asked all the questions. There had to be a reason behind everything she was asked to do. When a mother is tired, one doesn't want always to be giving reasons. But by exercising patience, and listening without interruption, it can become a revealing exercise. When a child feels free to talk without correction, you then often hear the true heart-beat.

At the age of four Yvonne our youngest played a game with me which she took very seriously. She was 'Mrs White' with two children, and her husband was always away. She went into great detail about how her children missed their daddy.

This went on for some time, until I began to be worried that she had too much fantasy, but slowly it decreased. The Lord showed me that she was working out her own emotions in missing her Daddy who was overseas for four months. The game certainly had a very healing effect upon her, and gave me some insight concerning her needs.

Oh dear, I made many mistakes. Some nights I went to bed and wept, confessing to the Lord that I had made a poor showing of representing him that day. A mother is the first impression of God upon a child's life.

Yvonne says even to this day, 'Mother, one of my vivid memories of you is that you were always on the phone.' I'm not proud of this, because I was foolish. We had a telephone counselling ministry and the demands were high, but if I had been wise I would have cut off the phone when the children came home from school and given them my full attention, instead of interrupted time. These things I cannot undo, but I am consoled by the fact that I loved them with all my heart. I also claim the Scriptures *'Love covers a multitude of mistakes,'* and *'Love never fails.'*

Let me encourage you; if you listen to the Holy Spirit he will guide you in the care of your children. He is not a God of confusion, nor does he cause us to be over-committed. We do that ourselves, and we often give up with frustration and disappointment. It is so easy to do damage to sensitive little hearts by not getting things in their right priority.

With Noel away from home so frequently it often fell to me to try to be mother and father. I felt inadequate for both roles, so constantly had to turn to the Holy Spirit who is the teacher.

When the children began to complain about their daddy being away so much, I called a family council so that each one could air their personal opinions. After some discussion I asked this question: 'Do you want your daddy to be able to tell people about Jesus, or do you want him to be home all the time?' I told them to think about it, then ask the Lord Jesus, and give me their answer when ready.

After a few days they all came to me separately and said 'Mummy we want our Daddy to tell people about Jesus, and we will spare him.' The amazing thing to me was that those little girls did not continue to complain about being without their Daddy. God stepped in and blessed them with a contented spirit. Noel was very impressed with the change. In fact, he could have felt a sense of rejection, because they asked him: 'When are you going away again Dad, so that we can pray?'

Our home was an open house for a large group of young people. I was concerned that the children may have felt neglected. Our own children can easily feel rejected while we are busy doing 'good works' for other people's children. We need the wisdom of the Lord because he knows the needs of the little ones. Since many young people were coming for counsel, we made it a rule that we would not be available until 8.30 each night. By that time the children had had quality time with me.

I have precious memories of the times the girls and I spent talking and listening to one another, reading books and praying. I did not read spiritual stories at night, but good clean healthy and exciting books. The girls loved to climb on one bed with me and have a close family time. They also had separate times for talking and sharing. Every child needs to have a special time with a parent.

When each of the daughters married, I asked them to tell me honestly if they had ever felt that they had been given second place with all the young people flowing in and out of the house. Each one said 'No, we knew we were first; we learnt to share our home, and we loved it.'

Let me encourage all parents, especially Christian workers, to keep things in right balance; if you do, God will bless your children, and they will have a richer experience of Christian living.

The Lord is faithful. He has given those precious girls a deep faith in himself, and when the tests have come they have proved they have a firm foundation. Now the joy of praying for and with those lovely nine grandchildren is beyond words. It is a very rich experience.

One Christmas time our youngest little granddaughter, then aged six years, said, 'Bamma, you are getting old and you will die soon, and I'll be sad, but where will you be?' I told her I would be in Heaven with Jesus, waiting for her. She was silent for a minute, then said quietly, 'Bamma, it will be a long time before I come!'

One of my grandsons was watching me doing the usual things that ladies do to their faces. He was very serious, 'Bamma, how come you have so many cracks on your face?' He informed me he did not have any. I told him I was getting old. He was a bit shocked, and burst out with indignation, 'You are not old – you are Bamma!' What a delight these children are; how they comfort and build one up when you think you are not useful as in the days gone by. One finds even greater fulfilment as one walks with the Lord in later years. He gives wisdom.

Of course I could tell many more stories, as every mother and grandmother can. We carry these treasures in our hearts, and it fills us with deep joy and thankfulness that we have been so blessed.

Phyl Gibson (still learning)

Chapter 15

How Parents Can Defend Their Children Against Satanic Attacks

Parenthood may be planned, accidental, or unwanted; family life may be welcomed, enforced, tolerated, evaded, or incomplete for the child who loses a parent by separation, divorce, or death.

Incomplete parenting is a bad launch-mechanism for a child.

In making recommendations for wise and effective parenting, Biblical principles must be given first priority.

Firstly, the positives:

● *Righteous parents bless their children and grandchildren.*

> *'But from everlasting to everlasting the Lord's love is with those who fear him, and his righteousness with their children's children – with those who keep his covenant and remember to obey his precepts.'* (Psalm 103:17, 18)

> *'Deliver me and rescue me from the hands of foreigners whose mouths are full of lies, whose right hands are deceitful. Then our sons in their youth will be like well-nurtured plants, and our daughters will be like pillars carved to adorn a palace.'* (Psalm 144:11, 12)

Secondly, the negatives:

● Depriving a child of the rights of life is sin. When Joseph's brothers plotted to kill him, Reuben the oldest brother suggested that the boy be thrown into an empty cistern because he planned to rescue him and take him back to his father. That plan was thwarted when the other brothers sold Joseph as a slave (Genesis 37:17–29). Years later as the brothers were confronted by an austere Egyptian official second only to Pharaoh, their consciences troubled them because of what they had done to Joseph. No one even imagined that the official could be Joseph, their brother, using an interpreter. Then Reuben said this:

> *'Didn't I tell you **not to sin against the boy? But you wouldn't listen!** Now we must give an accounting for his blood.'*

(Genesis 42:22 emphasis added)

With all his other faults, Reuben was at least tenderhearted, and recognised that it would be evil to kill the boy and break a father and son relationship which was important to them both.

● *Leading a child into sin is abhorrent to God* and will be appropriately punished (Matthew 18:1–9). The application of this teaching to the sexual defilement of children has already been covered. But the injunction can apply to any sin. Teaching children to rebel against any scriptural moral or ethical standard is what Jesus Christ obviously had in mind.

The greatest example of all

All parents need to read and note the attitude of Jesus Christ to little children found in Matthew 19:13–15; Mark 10:13–15; Luke 18:15–17.

(1) All writers agree that little children were being brought to Jesus to be blessed. Luke said they were babies (v. 15).

(2) All writers say that those who brought them, presumably their mothers, wanted Jesus to lay his hands on the children. Matthew adds that they were also brought to be prayed for (v. 16).

(3) All writers emphasise that the disciples rebuked the mothers for bringing their children to Jesus, actively trying to stop them. Obviously children didn't rank highly in their list of priorities. But they did to Jesus Christ.

(4) All writers show that Jesus considered the children were so important to him, that he immediately used them to teach important truths about how adults enter the Kingdom of God. Mark said Jesus was indignant at the way the disciples had acted (v. 14). Luke said that the disciples were told not to hinder the children coming to him (v. 16).

(5) All writers claim that hands were indeed laid on the children. Mark adds '*And he took the children in his arms, put his hands on them and blessed them*' (v. 16).

The attitude of Jesus Christ to children may be summarised as follows:

- Babies and children should have the highest priority when praying for people to be blessed.
- The simplicity, openness, honesty, and trust of a child are the basic attitudes required of adults for entry to the Kingdom of God.
- Special spiritual blessings may be communicated to children through the laying on of hands, and prayer.
- Adults who stop children from being blessed by Jesus Christ obviously offend him. He did not merely show displeasure to the disciples, he was indignant with them.

In the light of Scripture, the example of Jesus Christ, and from practical experience, here are a number of practical recommendations for parents:

Get right yourself

(1) *Look into your own spiritual mirror.* Maybe you don't like what you see. A list of works of the flesh is given by Paul in Galatians 5:19–21. But you may say 'I have tried my best to overcome these; I have wept, and asked for help. I have even fasted and prayed but still I am not free.' Have you ever considered that you may need deliverance from the irresistible forces which continually cause you to be defeated? You may reply: 'But I have always been told that you can't cast out the flesh.' That is right. The natural desires we have allow the sins of the flesh to be temporarily, or even permanently enjoyable. They can also become so much part of us, that only death can end them. There are three steps overcoming this problem:

(a) Recognise that because the flesh is capable of both bad and good responses, there must be spiritual forces which produce these results. If 'the flesh' can't be cast out, then the demonic powers which produce the wrong responses should be cast out of the flesh like pulling a hand out of a glove. These forces cause your lack of victory, your failures, discouragement and defeatism. But in the power of the name of Jesus Christ and the blood of the Lamb they can be forced to leave.

153

The sources, types and effects of Satan's works in believers are fully discussed, and the means of deliverance described in volume one of this series, *Evicting Demonic Intruders and Breaking Bondages*. If you are unable to find someone who can free you from these spirit caused problems, then ask God to lead you to someone who does have faith and authority.

(b) Once you have been freed, then you need to co-operate with the Spirit of God to kill off those fleshy responses of your personality. *'For if you live according to the sinful nature, you will die; but if* **by the Spirit you put to death the misdeeds of the body,** *you will live, because those who are led by the Spirit of God are sons of God'* (Romans 8:13, 14). That death commenced when we were born again in identification with the death, burial, and resurrection of Jesus Christ on our behalf. Few seem to realise it needs to be re-affirmed daily, so that sin no longer reigns in us. Romans Chapter 6 clearly teaches this. Paul said *'I die daily'* (1 Corinthians 15:31).

(c) To be successful in overcoming wrong responses to temptation, right choices of the will need to be made constantly to be victorious. Paul did it and recommended others to do so (2 Corinthians 4:11; Galatians 2:20; Colossians 2:20).

(d) Give the Holy Spirit unrestrained control in your total personality which determines soulish and physical responses, and allow him to produce in you what Paul calls *'the fruit of the Spirit'*, which is opposite to the fruit of the flesh (Galatians 5:22, 23).

In this way you become connected to God's supply of special ability to think, plan and act as he desires. The inner stimuli to sin which commenced in Genesis chapter three becomes reversed, and God's spirit provides the strength to live as a child of God is expected to live.

If you were not released from the desires and power of the kingdom of darkness at the time of new birth, then the three processes outlined (b, c, d) are a 'package deal' that God freely makes available to all believers.

(2) ***Examine the shadow you throw.*** Have you ever noticed how your children respond to you? Is it with pleasure, even excitement, or do you obviously turn them off? Are they wanting to spend more and more time with other people's children and in their parents' homes, rather than their own?

Wherever possible, avoid being a dark shadow which may cause your children to seek love, comfort, understanding, advice, guidance, or direction from others.

(3) *Adjust your priorities to include your children.* I have already confessed my obsession with God's work which at times pushed my family responsibilities into second place. We have also mentioned the problems of two-income families. But what about professional fathers and mothers who are not available when their children most need them? After school, and bedtimes are very important to children. This is when little worries are shared; assurances given; confessions made; confidences exchanged; and important advice given. Those are the times when fears are put to rest, children prayed over; relationships are deepened, and security given. Without them, insecurity, loneliness, withdrawal, anxiety, and habits of false comfort may commence.

When I was away for long periods I just longed to get home and share with Phyl. After eventually arriving home, I found that I couldn't get near her! There were three (not-so-favourite) daughters surrounding her! So I had to learn to wait until three little angels were tucked up in bed. Waiting was hard for me, but right for the girls. It was Phyl who helped me understand priorities from the children's point of view. Now that they are big girls, we all love the special times of sharing together.

Pay special attention to your home, and contents

(1) *The spirit influences of previous owners or tenants.* In many cases new owners or tenants may not be aware of the lifestyles of previous occupiers, and could become very troubled by demonic forces which remain on the property.

It is not generally realised that demons may continue to oppress buildings when the previous occupants have been involved in demonic activities. This is particularly so when seances, Satan worship, black-art rituals, or occultic and witchcraft practices have been carried out. Even articles of furniture from such premises may deeply disturb children whose parents have either borrowed, or purchased them. We have had to cleanse homes and a number of children's sleeping cots, to release the children from demonic influences. In one case, a girl went through a personality change; she became oppressed by fears after her family had moved home and she had to sleep in a room previously occupied by a lonely, rejected child. The boy of the former tenant used to return from the school daily to an empty house, and spent most of his time in his room alone. When the house was sold and the family moved out, the lonely spirit stayed on and oppressed the next child using the room.

Where strong demonic activity has been a regular practice, succeeding occupiers, particularly Christians, may experience a variety of disturbing events. These include unusual sounds in the dead of night, the sounds of doors being opened, or closed, the sound of footsteps, or drawers being opened and articles of clothing partly removed. Lights and water taps may also mysteriously 'turn themselves' on, and off. Children are particularly sensitive to spirit phenomena, and have often been too frightened to enter some houses, or return to others.

In all such cases, and also as a preventative measure, each room of a newly acquired home, and grounds, should be cleansed through the power of the name and blood of Jesus Christ. This is done by carrying an open Bible into each room while praying aloud to break all demonic influences and practices, and by claiming release and cleansing. By walking around the property at night-time with an open Bible, any embarrassment with neighbours will be avoided. But it will break any curse, or prevent the activity of evil spirits.

Where previous occupiers are known to have been violent, argumentative, promiscuous, alcoholic, or have separated or been divorced, the same procedure is most advisable for the whole family's sake.

(2) *Remove and destroy artifacts or items associated with indigenous forms of spirit worship.* These include anti-spirit face-masks, buddhas, totem-poles, Maori tikis, charms, Chinese dragons, temple lions, models or pictures of temples, and the like. Demonic art forms which feature dragons, snakes, witches, frogs, owls and unicorns need to go.

There is a Biblical basis for this. God clearly instructed Moses to warn his people about having contaminated things in their houses.

> '*The images of their gods you are to burn in the fire. Do not covet the silver or gold on them and do not take it for yourselves, or you will be ensnared by it, for it is detestable to the LORD your God. Do not bring a detestable thing into your house or you, like it, will be set apart for destruction. Utterly abhor and detest it, for it is set apart for destruction.*'* (Deuteronomy 7:25, 26 emphasis added)

From our own experience, and from the testimonies of others, we know that sicknesses and other troublesome activities stop when these links with indigenous spirit worship are thrown out or burnt.

(3) *Examine the contents of your books, magazines, and home videos.* Unless parents move home occasionally, the tendency is to accumulate possessions. The problem arises when children reach that inquisitive age and they investigate everything they can find in the family home. Even the private belongings of their parents are not exempt. If they discover explicit sex materials, or books on occultism and witchcraft which their parents had either forgotten about, or thought they had safely hidden, moral or spirit problems could well commence in the children who see them. Even Christians may have accumulated some of these spiritual 'time-bombs' before they came to Christ. We have seen the Lord liberate many adults whose sexual problems or involvement with evil spirits began in this way.

It is the duty of every Christian to destroy what belongs to Satan (see Acts 19:17–20).

(4) *Control your own and your children's TV viewing.* Some experts claim that television viewing can cause children to become materialistic, and cynical of the sincerity of adults. And because everything is spelled out so clearly on TV the child's reasoning power and imagination is given little chance of development. When the square box also becomes a de facto baby-sitter, sleeping times are unsupervised, and schoolteachers pay the price by teaching dreary pupils.

The increasing blatant exposure of children to violence, overt sexual acts, out-of-space fantasies, and witchcraft dominated horror movies certainly programmes today's youth to become tomorrow's sex-crazed and violent monsters. When times of transmission are limited to when children are supposed to be sleeping it is a blessing to every caring parent, but meaningless to those who don't care what their children see. Of course video viewing outside the family home may circumvent the best parental protection.

(5) *Carefully watch how your children are influenced by people who live with you, stay with you periodically, or visit frequently.* Generally speaking, we expect our 'friends' to be above suspicion, but some families have suffered sexual interference, tension, and manipulation by those who have been trusted. Parents need to be sensitive to any changes their children show, and be ready to deal with possible causes. No friendship or giving of hospitality should be allowed to prejudice the family.

Adjust your family activities

(1) *Adequate relaxation with the children.* Some families schedule one night a week when both parents spend quality time with their child, or each child. It is an exercise of listening, sharing and doing what the child wants, with the emphasis on having fun together.

One pastor of a busy church told me he had received a call one night from a parishioner urgently requesting a pastoral visit. The pastor declined, stating that he had a prior engagement. The caller, unwilling to take 'no' for an answer, asked what the pastor was doing that he could not interrupt it. The answer was simple. 'I'm having my weekly family time with my children, and I will not allow that to be interfered with.' The church member may have been offended, but it was a quality decision.

(2) *Holidays to remember.* Living by faith is a hand to mouth existence – God's hand to the family's mouths. God always supplied our needs but sometimes our wants had to wait. Unless kind friends made holiday cottages available to us as a family, we often went camping, usually beside the sea or a lake. Each family member loved living in tents, cooking over kerosene stoves or camp fires, fishing, and generally enjoying the outdoor life. Each of our daughters still recall these camping holidays as one of their greatest childhood memories. We were together, and joy of joys, particularly to the girls, no telephone! We went places, did things, and bought simple treats which made us all glad to be together.

(3) *Worship together.* Unfortunately, many parents regard 'Church' as a building rather than a fellowship of worshippers. The New Testament Church was a group of people owing allegiance to Jesus Christ, who met to worship, learn, interact and serve one another wherever they could. Children were never excluded. Modern 'crying-rooms' and nurseries make it possible for the whole family to be at church.

Many fathers feel that the pressures of business, sport and relaxation justify them sending their wives and children to worship while they are engaged elsewhere. But sooner or later teenagers will use their father's absence as a reason for not attending. Example is difficult to counter by mere argument. The cliché is still true – 'The family that worships together, stays together.'

As children grow older, parents need to ensure that their children's spiritual needs are being adequately met. It is better to change a place of worship than to lose the family unity.

(4) *Taking an active interest in your children's curricular and extra-curricular activities.* Many may watch and cheer when junior runs, plays in a recital or performs on stage etc., but if 'Mum' or 'Dad' are not amongst them, that special excitement is missing. As previously mentioned, during counselling some adults have shown bitterness, anger, and hatred towards a parent, particularly a father who has never shown the slightest interest in childhood activities. It is often impossible or inconvenient for parents to take time off to support their children, but for those who are able, the long-term dividends in family relationships will more than compensate. Grandparents are often acceptable substitutes.

Some personal recommendations

(1) Don't force your children's growth to maturity. The process of growing and developing should be gradual, interesting, and in line with their peers.

(2) Don't make a child take on more responsibility than they ought to bear for their age. For example, making children under ten years responsible for the needs of younger children.

(3) Don't force a child to do so much physical work in or around the house that they have no time for relaxation or playing.

(4) Avoid being heavy handed in applying Biblical principles. This may cause resentment to the things of God which could flare into open rebellion in teenage years.

(5) Don't inflate minor matters into major incidents, so that discipline becomes out of proportion to what originally happened.

(6) Don't over-spiritualise matters for children. Encourage natural faith so that it becomes meaningful, and a way of life.

(7) Remember your own awkward, turbulent, or troublesome teenage years, and be tolerant to your own children breaking out of the chrysalis of childhood into adolescence. Be a firm anchor for them, not a piece of driftwood. Listen, converse, and suggest alternatives, avoiding heavy-handed directions unless they become unavoidable.

(8) To apologise, ask for forgiveness, or back down when wrong, is not to lose face, but to gain the confidence of your children.

(9) Showing children how, is always preferable to telling them how.

(10) Don't be surprised if you feel that your son's girlfriend, or your daughter's boyfriend is just 'not good enough for your child'. They

seldom are! If God has made the choice, relax, and allow yourself to become agreeably surprised at how wrong you were. If you feel that God wasn't consulted in the partner-choosing process, pray about it. Don't 'play God' and lose a son, or a daughter.

(11) Prayer changes relationships, attitudes, habits and actions much more effectively than harsh words, or shouting, or manipulation.

SUMMARY

1.   Parents may cause or contribute to the satanic problems in their children. On the other hand they should be the first line in their children's defence.

2.   To get the best out of their children and teenagers, parents need to do some personal spring cleaning. If necessary, they should call for the help of others so that they can be freed from every bondage or dominating spirit which could affect their children.

3.   Parenting is an art-form which can be improved by studying Biblical principles and applying them by the power of the Holy Spirit.

4.   Time spent with children will pay eternal dividends, as children are the only earthly possessions we can take to heaven.

5.   Clean humour, fun, and laughter, are not sinful. They have saved many a parent's sanity, and may save the children from embarrassment.

Chapter 16

How Parents May Pray for the Freedom of Their Children from Demonic Activities

The forms of satanic oppression in children need to be re-emphasised:

Bondages

He prevents them from doing what they know to be right, for example, from saying they are sorry when they know that what they did was wrong, from forgiving others, or from being honest, obedient, respectful, and diligent.

Dominations

He makes them do what they know to be wrong, although they may not want to. Examples include displays of anger, temper, stubbornness, disobedience, deceit, and lustful actions.

Oppressions

Satan often troubles children by a variety of fears. He also makes them anxious for no apparent reason, causes them to oppose spiritual matters, or stirs up an insatiable interest in occultic and psychic matters.

Afflictions

Children may have an unexplained series of mishaps or accidents, and suffer from repeated sicknesses or allergies of all kinds. Children are often the first to fall victim to family curses causing blindness, deafness, and mental problems particularly when they occur as an established family pattern. Death may even result from these afflictions.

The 'buck' should stop at parents

Parents should always be a child's first line of defence. Most parents overlook the possibility that they themselves may be the basic cause of the problems in their children. Ask any schoolteacher, social worker, or police officer what reactions they normally receive when approaching parents about a troublesome child! What probably angers and frustrates parents most is recognising a repetition of their own childhood problems. Hurt pride only exacerbates the parents' inability to think and act objectively.

Of course all children's problems do not end in confrontation with authority. Unless parents are completely passive, or believe in giving children the unchallenged right of expression (a non-Biblical attitude), then the first confrontation will be between parent and the child concerned.

Parents need to be free from their own problems before they can set their children free

Children are very unimpressed by parental inconsistency ('Do as I say, don't do as I do'). We were asked to pray over a boy with a bad temper because his father's prayers were ineffective. No wonder! The father was an angry man.

One of the problems Phyl and I sometimes face in being asked to pray for children is that they return to the same environment. If the parents have caused the problems being prayed over, changes will be difficult to maintain. Parents themselves need to be right before God, before their prayers can be effective.

> *'If I had cherished sin in my heart, the LORD would not have listened.'* (Psalm 66:18)

The children's deliverance may well commence with the parents seeking freedom in Christ from demonic oppression. The causes are:

Heredity. An explanation of these generational causes may be found in series one, *Evicting Demonic Intruders and Breaking Bondages*. The list includes:

- Spirits of occultism and witchcraft.
- Addictions of all kinds.
- Anxiety, worry, depression and mental problems.
- Suicide.
- Sexual practices and problems.
- Religious spirits.
- Sicknesses and allergies.

Two further causes of hereditary problems are:

- Rejection.
- Freemasonry.

Demonic oppressions may be caused by pre-salvation activities

Apart from heredity, children may become oppressed through their parents' sins before being saved. If parents were not delivered when they were born again, demonic activities can afflict children conceived before this. Parents need to lead the way in seeking deliverance from spirit-controlled problems.

Family possessions which may be used by spirit forces to oppress children and teenagers need to be destroyed

Believing parents are strongly urged to remove and dispose of (preferably by burning) all articles which could lead to demonic oppression. They include:

(1) Ceremonial clothing worn by Freemasons, including sashes, aprons, belts, badges, degrees, and other written materials. Ignore their sentimental value. Satan will use them to bring oppression to all members of the family.

(2) Horoscopes, and written predictions with all symbols of astrology including star signs, birth stones and flowers.

(3) All written materials dealing with the black arts, spiritism, and paranormal activities. These include the writings of Edgar Cayce, Alister Crowley, Lob Sam Rampa, Shirley McLean, Anton le Vey, Jean Dixon, Ruth Montgomery, Arthur Ford, Eckhardt, Dennis Wheatley, Ram Dass, Jacob Lorber, and others.

(4) All rock and roll, punk rock, heavy metal, acid rock and New Age music tapes and records. In fact any music, including classical music, which has sensuous connotations.

(5) All forms of demonic, abstract, or surrealistic art, particularly those featuring snakes, dragons, scenes of witchcraft and unicorns.

(6) Pornographic materials of any kind including adult 'X' and 'R' rated videos dealing with explicit sex, or scenes of violence.

The mere existence of these materials can both cause, and maintain spirit oppression in children.

Personal holiness is a basic principle of discipleship which follows the new birth. Few realise that this principle also applies to all personal possessions. No contaminating influences should remain in the home.

Parents should find out what their children do when away from home

Children everywhere play at one another's homes after school and at weekends, and mothers who know the children concerned are usually quite relaxed about it. However, problems sometimes arise when no-one is home to supervise what they do. Some have been known to attempt seances, view X-rated videos, sample alcohol or drugs, and sexually investigate one another, leading to regular sex relationships. The damage these activities will do depends on the ages of the children, the degree of involvement, pressures used, and the frequency and type of behaviour involved. Children may become involved quite innocently but be unable to resist the pressures or desires which are stirred up.

Changes in behavioural patterns caused by sexual abuse have already been mentioned, but some may indicate other problems as well, including:

(1) Unusual quietness, withdrawal, secretiveness, and clamming up.

(2) Changes in eating habits and sleeping patterns, guilty looks, unexplained tears, lack of concentration, and falling school grades may also be distress signals.

(3) Other indications. Sudden demands for money, or the disappearance of money normally left around for household needs. Loss of appetite, the smell of alcohol, the appearance or hiding of questionable reading materials, or long periods of absence from home

for the flimsiest of excuses may also indicate control by addictive spirits.

Parents should not treat expressions of fear or anxiety flippantly. Root causes should be investigated, and if it appears that dominating spirits are oppressing a child, parents would be well advised to seek counsel and deliverance for him or her. Minor fears or anxieties can usually be resolved by talking things over, and by prayer.

Guidelines for parents who are willing to pray for the freedom of their own children

- **Never** use the word 'demons' in talking to children about their problems, talk about 'spiritual influences', or 'the bad things that came down in a family' which could spoil their lives. Avoid causing them to develop fears.
- Make sure they know you are not blaming them for hereditary problems.
- If you intend to pray for deliverance, take time to sit and talk with each child about what is going to happen. When they understand that mothers brought their children to Jesus Christ to be blessed and set free from things that troubled them, they will understand why you want to pray for them.
- If you are the type of person whose hands tremble when quickened by the Holy Spirit in prayer, tell the children what will happen when you put one hand on their forehead, and the other hand on the back of their head. Generally I stretch out my hands in front of a child and ask whether they think my hands are still, or shaky. Invariably they reply 'They are still.' I then tell them that when I pray, my hands will shake so that they will have a 'head-earthquake'. This means that Jesus loves them. So I pray a little, then stop. By that time they are usually grinning, and any tense feelings are gone. So after another little chat, I continue to pray over each problem root we have been told about, or have discerned. Parents who tell their children why they are praying, and what will happen, will have no problems with them.

1. Praying over children up to the teenage years:

(a) *Where to put the child?* With babies and small children, a parent's knee is ideal. Older children usually prefer to sit on a kitchen chair, by themselves.

(b) *Who should pray for the child?* Either parent may pray, provided they themselves are free from the problems being prayed for. With younger children, the parent to whom the child normally goes for comfort is the logical person to nurse the child. The other parent should then lay hands on the child and pray. Babies and very small children may also be prayed for as they lie in their prams, cots, or beds.

(c) *How to pray.* Place the hands on the front and back of the child's head. Some small children may object by trying to pull your hands away. If so the parent nursing the child should hold their hands firmly. Parents do not normally experience the physical resistance which often makes it very difficult for strangers to pray effectively. If this should happen, ask a pastor, or experienced counsellor for help.

(d) *What to pray over.* Write down a list of the obvious problems the child has.

Make sure you include what has been, or may still be a problem to you, or your husband, such as: anger, lust, rejection, fears, thoughts of suicide etc. Roots need to be removed.

Hereditary problem areas which have troubled parents and grandparents on both sides of your family (whether you have experienced them or not), need to be added. These sometimes miss a generation. Examples include addictions, particularly to drugs, alcohol, nicotine, gambling, and food. Mental problems should also be included in the list.

Any controlling spirits of known family involvement in all sources of demonic domination need to be added. These include Freemasonry, the black arts, and all witchcraft practices.

Finally, include the symptoms of rejection which your child obviously shows. These will commence with rejection, self-rejection, fear of rejection, and each appropriate item from the list which follows. Break the habit patterns which have accompanied the dominations.

A basic list of problems in associated groups is:

- Striving, achievement, performance.
- Self defensiveness, self pity, selfishness.
- Criticism, refusal to love or communicate.
- Emotional immaturity, crying.
- Withdrawal, independence, aloneness.
- Insecurity, inferiorities, low self-image.
- Anger, resentment, violence.

- Day dreaming, fantasy.
- Anxiety, worry, suicide, death.
- Fears of all kinds.
- Jealousy.

(e) *What to do in prayer.* You don't have to use old English terms or special prayer language. Simply talk naturally to the Lord, and thank him for his completed work at Calvary's cross in dying for our sins and destroying all the works of the devil. Thank him for the gift of your child (by name), then:

In the name of the Lord Jesus Christ (or Jesus Christ), bind, break, and loose the spirit of each problem you have listed. Remember that spiritual powers of the enemy are much easier to release in children than adults. The heel of a shoe or boot will snap the spine of a small snake after it emerges from its soft shell, but no one in their right mind would do the same to a fully grown reptile! (Tougher methods need to be used for them.)

Bondages can be broken, and even dominating spirits may be released from children without any manifestation normally seen in adults. But quite frequently a child being prayed for will sigh, or yawn, perhaps repeatedly. These are signs of release. Should the child spontaneously cough while being prayed for, don't reach for the cough mixture; this is also a sign of release. Pastors and counsellors quite often get this reaction, but it is not as frequently seen by parents.

The binding of the spirit of each problem in the name of Jesus Christ (Matthew 16:19) means that the power of his name prevents that spirit from operating any further. Breaking the spirit's power over the child prevents it from oppressing the child any more. Loosing the grip of each particular spirit over the child's life is in effect a command to either cease exercising a bondage, or in the case of a dominating spirit, to depart. The process of cleansing and renewal should not commence until all known causes of problems have been dealt with. If the parents are sensitive to his promptings, the Holy Spirit may even suggest some extra matters for prayer.

(f) *Finally, the cleansing and filling process.*

(i) *Cleansing.* Continuing the laying on of hands, ask the Lord Jesus to cleanse each part of the child's personality in which demonic habits have persisted. This will include the mind, heart, and will and could include parts of the body, particularly the sexual areas, or the respiratory system in cases of chest problems.

(ii) *The filling.* Ask the Lord to fill the child with his love, the assurance of his presence, and his peace. The faith of children is often beautiful to see, and sometimes shames adults.

(iii) *Healing.* Where appropriate, ask the Lord Jesus to bring physical healing to affected parts of the body. Ask in faith, don't demand.

(iv) *Special prayers.* Pray for special needs the children have expressed, or for any area in which you feel there is a need. Here are some examples:

- 'I pray that Alex will be able to understand what the teacher says; that you will give him a good memory, and help him to be able to express himself clearly when answering questions.'
- 'I pray that Susan will know that you are always with her Lord Jesus, and that she has nothing to fear, because you have promised never to leave her.'
- 'I pray that you will help Trevor to be strong and not let the other boys make him do wrong things, and that he will have the courage to say "NO" to what you would not like him to do.'
- 'I pray that Karen will not be bossy, but be gentle and kind to her brothers and sisters.'
- 'I pray that Cameron will have a clean mind, and will have no bad thoughts about girls. Please help him to be a good example to other boys, and to have nothing to do with the wrong things boys and girls do to each other.'

(v) *Plant good seed-thoughts in the subconscious mind.* Within the first half hour of children going to sleep (before deep sleep comes) positive seed thoughts may be slipped quietly into a child's mind. These may follow the pattern of the prayers suggested above, such as:

- Alex may be told: 'Jesus will help you to understand the teacher and remember what he says so that you will be able to answer the questions.'
- To Susan: 'There is nothing to fear, Jesus is with you all the time.'
- To Trevor: 'Jesus will make you strong to say "NO" when the other boys try to make you do wrong things.'
- To Karen: 'The Lord Jesus will help you to be gentle and kind to your brothers and sisters.'
- To Cameron: 'Jesus will keep your heart clean and make you strong enough to follow him and keep away from boys and girls who do bad things together.'

Phyl was once challenged by a man who claimed that speaking to the subconscious mind was a form of brain washing. She replied that God had taught her to do this, so he shouldn't be too concerned about it. As a splint to a green-stick fracture, or a calliper to a disabled leg, so the prayerful introduction of Biblical principles and positive encouragement to faltering minds and hearts will produce wholesome and changed attitudes and habits.

Some parents have prayed over their children as they have slept, and seen good results. The writer has watched some sleeping children toss and turn or become visibly restless when praying over bondages and dominations. This method may be helpful when a child or teenager strenuously resists a suggestion of prayer, or if the person praying for the children is unavailable during daylight hours. From personal choice, both writers feel that praying with a child and talking over problems is the best method. Follow-up prayer certainly may be made while a child is asleep. Should the child wake easily, bind demonic powers of oversensitivity or sleeplessness before going into the child's room to pray.

2. Dealing with teenagers:

Basically, the procedure is the same. However, there are two areas which may be taken to a deeper level:

(a) *Explaining causes*. Teenagers will understand the principle of hereditary sin particularly if they battle against the same habits they may have seen in their grandparents, and are sure to have seen in their parents.

Then there are the problems for which teenagers are themselves responsible. Experimenting with alcohol, nicotine, drugs, sex, occultism, and witchcraft may open doors to demonic dominations from which they need freedom. Ordinary counselling methods may give some measure of control, or force them to cover up their activities. Only deliverance removes root causes.

(b) *Manifestations of deliverance*. As children grow, so does the strength of their demonic dominations. While smaller children often sigh, or yawn as they are released, teenagers may show obvious movements in the area of the abdomen. Or they may feel a choking sensation.

In such cases the young person should be encouraged to cough. If demonic spirits have caused these symptoms, the child will spontaneously cough for a time until the spirit causing that particular problem has gone.

A twelve year old girl for whom the writer was praying recently suddenly showed signs of fear as she was being set free. We asked the Lord to fill her with his peace, and she was fine.

In praying for cleansing and wholeness with teenagers, they should be encouraged to breathe in by faith the love and peace of God. As God breathed life into Adam's spirit, soul, and body (Genesis 2:7), so the Spirit of God also renews those whom Satan has oppressed.

Follow-up care

1. Prayer for cleansing of the child's room:
With an open Bible ask the Lord Jesus to cleanse the child's room from the influence of every oppressive spirit from which he or she has been freed. The writers have seen the Lord cleanse rooms, homes, furniture and belongings, stopping further troublesome experiences.

2. Deal with continued problem habits:
Established habits may take time to disappear. When animals are killed, there is often twitching in the limbs for some time, and headless table birds will career around aimlessly, unless restrained.

In the same manner it may take time for any long-established bad habit to come to a final stop. Encouragement is an important positive influence in the recovery process. Discipline may also be needed to break habits. Remember also the value of speaking into the subconscious mind after the child has gone to sleep.

3. Keep the lines of communication open:
Teenagers need to talk. If parents are too busy, they will turn to their peers or outsiders whom they admire and trust. During this time of maturing, they form opinions, attitudes, and habits. They work out what political and religious beliefs they wish to hold. Wise parents will converse with them, and provide information from which choices can be made, based hopefully on their good example. Teenagers rightly resist pressure to become mere parental clones.

After the enemy has been defeated, young people will probably want to talk, and will need a sympathetic ear. Teenagers need parents who make themselves available and are willing to listen. It helps them to clarify their thinking, releases emotional pressures, and makes them open to receiving advice at the right time. Discerning parents will recognise the signs, and stand by ready to listen or discuss as needed. In this way further potential crises may be avoided.

4. Set aside a time for worship if it is not part of the family routine:
There is no better way to unite a family than by giving God first place in the home. The husband and father is responsible for the spiritual leadership of a family, and should initiate this activity. In his absence (or by rotation if mutually agreed upon), mother should participate. Single mothers should do the same.

The timing will need careful consideration. Breakfast is often a grab-and-run affair, so it may not be the ideal time. At lunch-time most family members have lunch at school or work. So the evening meal is often the only convenient time.

Even that may be difficult if Dad arrives home late, and insists on watching the evening TV news and current affairs programme. So the time needs to be made regular, interesting, and not too long. Family worship should include:

(a) *Worship and praise*. Children should be taught how to worship God for who he is, and praise him for what he has done in his world. They should also praise him for the family and their own lives. To learn to be thankful in childhood will be a great spiritual asset in later life. Regrettably, gratitude is very much of a missing ingredient in the lives of many adults, whether saved or unsaved.

(b) *Instruction in the Word of God*. *'These commandments that I give you today are to be upon your hearts. Impress them on your children. Talk about them when you sit at home and when you walk along the road, when you lie down and when you get up.'* (Deuteronomy 6:6, 7)

The home is the Christian parents' first line of defence against secular humanism. The children will face this philosophy in non-Christian primary and secondary schools, as well as university. Early Biblical instruction is the soundest protection against Satan's onslaught against Christian standards.

For some strange reason Christian fathers are often lax, even apathetic, about establishing systematic family worship and Bible instruction. Some Christian mothers have even encountered opposition in pressing for a God-honouring family time together. It is little wonder that teenagers who lack understanding of Biblical principles will often succumb to worldly standards.

Thank God for godly mothers who have often done what fathers have failed or refused to do. But it will be the fathers who will be accountable in the day of judgement. When Christian parents restrict a child's friends, games, music, films, and television viewing, explaining that their influences are against Christian standards, children may object, but will know in their hearts that this is fair.

(c) *Participation.* Family worship need not have the solemnity of a religious occasion; it can be enjoyed and anticipated with pleasure.

The reading of supporting materials geared to the children's level of understanding, the asking of questions suitable to their individual ages, and prayer together can make the devotional time both interesting and enjoyable. As the writers have stayed in many believers' homes it has been a delight to see how successful some fathers have been in communication, and how much the children have responded.

Engage in spiritual warfare over your children

The writer firmly believes that Job lived long before God gave Moses his laws for successful living, but he was an excellent example of ethical and parental uprightness. In Job 1:4, 5 we see an example of parental spiritual warfare circa 1520 BC, and Job's lifestyle and spiritual perception were pointed out to Satan by God in these words:

> *'There is no-one on earth like him; he is blameless and upright, a man who fears God and shuns evil.'* (Job 1:8)

Modern-day parents who maintain godly standards in a world which rejects them, and who shun the evil in which the world revels, will doubtless desire to be as sensitive to their children's spiritual welfare as Job showed himself to be.

A mother whose son's lustful associations had dishonoured himself and his Christian testimony, prayed constantly that chains would be placed around her son's feet. When later the Lord freed the young man he said to one of his sisters: 'You know, I always felt there were chains around my feet, and I couldn't go where I wanted to go.'

Another Christian teenager went to a discotheque with her friend. The friend was admitted, but she was refused admittance. Because she had an admission ticket, she demanded a reason. The young lady at the entrance simply said 'You are surrounded by angels, and we don't want your type in here.' Another answer to a mother's prayer!

Parents need to be sensitive to the needs of 'instant' spiritual warfare. On one occasion Phyl felt constrained to cry out urgently for our eldest daughter's safety. When she returned we learned that she and her husband had narrowly avoided a traffic accident.

Emergency treatment

Here is a prayer which Phyl has given to mothers needing to see their children released from the pressures of the evil one.

> 'I take authority over you Satan in the Name of Jesus Christ, and render you powerless in the life of ... (child's name).
> 'I bind your power, break your influence, and loose ... (child's name) from your grip. All harmful hereditary, and other spirits ... (name them) I break in the name of Jesus, and by faith I now take the blood of Jesus and cleanse the conscious mind, the subconscious mind, the emotions, the imaginations, the heart and will of ... (name child).
> 'I thank you for the power and authority of your name and blood, Lord Jesus, and ask you to keep the heart of ... open and tender to the leading of the Holy Spirit. Please fill ... with your everlasting love, your peace, and your joy, for your glory. I ask this in the name of Jesus. Amen'.

The greatest blessing of all

How true is the statement 'God has children but no grandchildren.' One presumption that parents cannot afford to make is that their children are automatically saved because they themselves are believers. This subject is so important that the next chapter has been devoted to helping parents lead their children to Jesus Christ.

Finally, write your own charter for bringing up your children, and stick to it

The following suggestions may be secular in origin (author unknown), but the points confirm many Biblical Principles. As the chrysalis is

173

essential to the full development of the butterfly, so a wise Christian family charter will be to a growing teenager.

(1) Meet defiance immediately with stringent punishment. Respect for parents (and other adult authorities) is a critical factor in child-rearing. This is the key to establishing parental leadership in the family.

(2) Start at a very early age to reprimand bad behaviour by suitable punishment when family rules have been broken. This discipline helps children learn the difference between right and wrong. The goal is to correct the behaviour before it becomes a habit or is assumed to be a right.

(3) Give children jobs of responsibility that increase with age or maturity. Require them to complete their tasks before recreation begins. The goal is to show children they are functional parts of family unity and that the family has the first claim on their time and energy.

(4) Be firm. 'No' means 'no'. When older, children should be allowed to present their 'case' to help parents understand their reasons for disobedience. But they need to know that understanding does not automatically imply that parents will say 'yes' to their wishes. The goal is to maintain parental control.

(5) Treat older children differently from younger ones, in line with their ages and behaviour. The goal is to teach maturity which earns privileges.

(6) Give children what they need but not everything they want. The goal is to help establish a sense of reality, the ability to separate need from desire.

(7) Monitor television, radio, films, and books according to family standards and the child's age and maturity. The goal is to teach selectivity and clarify values.

(8) Insist on knowing who your children's friends are, where your children are going, and the approximate time of their return. The goals here are multiple: To prevent you from unnecessarily worrying, to help control peer pressure, and to teach accountability and common courtesy.

(9) Show your anger when serious incidents occur. It is important for children to see that their misbehaviour disturbs you. The goal is to teach accountability.

(10) Insist that children face up to their mistakes at home, socially

and at school – even if this requires emotionally painful confrontation with other parents/adults. The goal is to teach honesty, self-possession, and courage.

(11) Make your own well-being and that of the family just as important as the child's own desires. The goal is to teach perspective.

SUMMARY

1.   Christian parents should be a child's first line of defence against any demonic activities in their lives. To be effective, parents need to be free themselves, and see that their family home and possessions do not cause children to become oppressed.

2.   Parents should keep a watchful eye on their children's friendships, and where they spend time outside of school hours. Any change of behavioural pattern should be investigated thoroughly.

3.   Parents can be very effective in seeing their children and teenagers released from bondages and dominations, and bringing them into new attitudes and habits.

4.   Parents have a God-given responsibility to institute and maintain a time of family worship, and to protect their children by engaging in spiritual warfare on their behalf.

5.   Discipline is essential to break habits associated with the problems from which the child has been set free.

Chapter 17

Become a Soul Winner in Your Own Home

Strangely, most parents will do everything within their power, even to considerable self-denial, to help their children reach the best goals in life, but few of them know how to lead them into the new-birth experience. That most important step of life is usually left to others, even complete strangers.

The writer was led to Jesus Christ by his own father who was spiritually sensitive to the signs of soul trouble. My partner Phyl was born again by her own bedside, convicted by her father's Gospel preaching.

To help parents experience the joy of leading their own children into the saving knowledge of Jesus Christ, and to guide them in the Christian pathway, the following has been reproduced from pages 149, 150 *The Fisherman's Basket*. (Written by Noel C. Gibson, and published by Freedom in Christ Ministries.)

Here is a simple plan of salvation

It is illustrated by a shepherd's care for his sheep, and will be helpful with young children.

(1) The Bible likens people to sheep (Psalms 79:13, 95:7, 100:3). Children will see themselves as lambs.

(2) The devil is the sheep thief who stole our hearts from God (John 10:10). Those who do wrong things are following his bad example. That is sin, and hurts God.

(3) When sheep get lost they can't find their way home. Sinners can never find God by themselves (Isaiah 53:6). Only Jesus can lead us to

177

him. Sheep are the only animals without a homing instinct. They need a shepherd.

(4) Jesus the Good Shepherd came to earth to find all lost sheep. He came to call them to himself, make them clean inside, and bring them back to God's true sheepfold – heaven (Matthew 18:11–14; John 10:11).

(5) The Devil who stole God's sheep tried to kill the Good Shepherd. He used Judas to betray him (John 13:2).

(6) God is stronger than the devil. He allowed Jesus to die for our sins before the devil could kill him. He came back to life again so that he could rescue us from the power of the devil, and give us his special quality of life (John 10:10).

(7) The Good Shepherd will make every boy and girl one of his special sheep if they ask him to be their Saviour (Revelation 3:20; John 1:12).

(8) The Good Shepherd will keep and protect his sheep from the sheep thief the devil, for ever (John 10:1–8; Psalm 23).

(9) The Good Shepherd expects every one of his sheep to recognise his voice, follow him, and obey what he tells them. His voice is heard by reading the Bible. (John 10:3, 4, 14, 27.)

Counselling children is similar to adults, but should be expressed in simple language. Remember that:

(a) Children are won by love and understanding; speak to them as Jesus would.

(b) Be sensitive to children who want to be saved but are shy, or don't know how to express themselves.

(c) Only use words that children understand: 'being naughty' or 'doing wrong things' will be more meaningful than 'sins'. 'Punishment' is better than 'judgement'. 'Taking our place' should replace 'substitution'.

The process of leading a child to Christ

When a child understands the Gospel, and is mature enough to pray alone, suggest prayer points, leaving them to choose their own words.

For example:

- 'Tell the Lord Jesus you are sorry for all your wrongdoing.' (Name some.)
- 'Thank him for loving you and taking your punishment.'

- 'Ask him to forgive you and make your heart clean.'
- 'Ask Jesus to come into your heart, and live in you.'
- 'Ask him to make you strong to live for him and to grow up as he wants you to do.'
- 'Thank him for hearing and answering your prayer.'

For children who do not know what to say, here is a simple prayer:

'Dear Lord Jesus,
I know I have done wrong things (name some) and I am sorry. Please forgive me, and make my heart clean. Thank you Lord Jesus for loving me, and dying on the cross to take the punishment I deserved. Please come and live in my heart and life as Lord and Saviour. Make me strong to live for you and to become the person you want me to be. Amen'

Check sincerity by asking this question: 'Where is Jesus now?' The answer should be 'In my heart'. If the answer is 'I don't know', then explain that when we open our heart's door, Jesus always comes in because he promised to (Revelation 3:20). When the reply is positive, ask a second question: 'How do you know?' If the answer is based on feelings, turn their attention to what Jesus said, and make sure they understand and believe because the Bible says so (1 John 5:10–12; Revelation 3:20). If necessary, go over the basics once more. If there is still uncertainty, pray with the child and check their understanding later. Don't try to pull unripe fruit from the tree.

For a child who knows that their prayer has been answered explain that Jesus does not leave us if we do wrong things after he becomes Saviour. Sin makes him sad, so we need to tell him how sorry we are and ask his forgiveness (1 John 1:9). Doing wrong spoils the friendship, but doesn't break the relationship. Bible reading and prayer should be encouraged. Make sure your child has a Bible of his or her own.

John's Gospel 10:27–30 is an ideal passage to assure a child that not only does Jesus Christ give them eternal life, but he and his father – God – both hold them close so that Satan can never snatch them away.

Follow up

If you need to buy your child a Bible, buy one which uses language they can understand. The Good News Bible with its line drawings, and the Living Bible with its simplicity are ideal. Encourage the habit of daily reading and some dialogue on the meaning of what has been read.

Encourage your child to talk to God as naturally and respectfully as they talk to you. Show them how to do so quietly under their breath at any time of need, particularly at school or in danger, and what to say as they kneel by their beds before going to sleep.

Be careful not to give the impression that they are expected to be perfect once Jesus has come into their hearts. You're not, so why should they be? Gentle dialogue, and the mutual evaluation of lessons learned will establish Christian principles of living.

Be constantly on the lookout for simple reading matter which will teach your child how to live and grow as a Christian. Daily Bible reading notes graduated to age group produced by the Scripture Union could also be very helpful. Many books are also available.

As a family united in Jesus Christ, learn to enjoy being Christians, and remember fun and laughter are not sinful. They are like spiritual medicine.

SUMMARY

1.   Parents should be able to lead their own children to know Jesus Christ as Saviour and Lord.
2.   Don't pick unripened fruit. Pray for discernment for the best times for harvesting the souls of your children.
3.   Lead, teach, and encourage spiritual growth and development.

Chapter 18

Demonic Oppressions from which Children and Teenagers Need Deliverance

The Japanese have given the world the bonsai art-form of miniaturisation of trees. Giants of the mountainsides and plains can now be grown indoors showing every outdoor feature, but even smaller than many indoor plants. When roots are confined, so is the growth of the tree.

Similarly children and teenagers can have their development to maturity impaired. It can happen through the way they are treated at home, or outside of the home, or by what happens to family members. While their physical growth continues normally, a traumatised psyche can easily be hidden under a flurry of physical activity and emotional effervescence calculated to signal 'all is well in my little world'.

Sometimes their troubles are abundantly obvious, but some parents are extraordinarily insensitive to their children's inner hurts, inferiorities, fears, confusion, and secret habits. Their blindness is not caused so much by failing to read the evident signs, but by refusing to accept any personal responsibility or by the assumption that their child 'would never ever do such a thing!' Family pride is never more repulsive than when it is used for self-justification: 'I have always been a good father (or mother)'; 'I have never done anything to cause my child to act like this'.

To some degree, every adult shows the fruit of seeds sown in his or her childhood. During counselling, we often ask a leading question: 'How do you feel about the way you were treated in childhood?' Sometimes we are almost swept away by a verbal tidal wave. Good and positive things are usually submerged by real or imaginary wrongs, injustices, grievances, or a torrent of resentment, bitterness and anger. Even the veneer of supposedly right relationships often gives under direct questioning, and the real truth comes out.

Surely it is not God's will that children should grow up harbouring feelings of rejection, insecurity, or lacking confidence? Nor is it his will that they should be chilled by fears, burn with lust, or be driven to addictions which have relentlessly afflicted their families for generations.

This chapter lists the types of oppression the evil one has exercised over children and teenagers who have been brought to us for spiritual release and wholeness. God has wonderfully blessed them, and we certainly commend deliverance and healing as the first step to release, not the last resort.

But before this, we need to share our own personal frustration and sadness at not having been able to see some types of young people freed and made whole. Our candour is deliberate; we want to repudiate any inference that the writers are some sort of 'deliverance gurus' with pat answers for every problem.

Firstly, those who are mute

We have not prayed with completely autistic children, who of course are unresponsive to their environment. But we have prayed with one or two whose only communication was by sounds or signs. These young ones warmed to us personally, and there was some improvement, but to our deep regret not one has been able to speak freely.

Just as there are disappointments in praying for the sick, there are frustrations in not seeing some receive the freedom which we are confident is ours in Jesus Christ.

Reference has already been made to the incident in Mark 9 centred around a father who was frustrated because the disciples were unable to cast a violent, destructive demon out of his dumb son (Mark 9:14–29).

In reply to the disciples' question as to why they were unable to drive out the demon, Matthew writes *'Because you have so little faith. I tell you the truth, if you have faith as small as a mustard seed, you can say to this mountain, "move from here to there" and it will move. Nothing will be impossible for you'* (Matthew 17:20–21 emphasis added).

Regrettably neither Phyl nor I have yet reached that level of discernment or faith, but we long to. I shared with the participants of a deliverance seminar in Auckland, New Zealand, my deep desire to see the teenage son of a friend begin to speak, and my frustration at my ineffectiveness. At the end of the day I was handed a piece of paper on which a man had written the name of a certain lodge to which the boy's ancestors had belonged. He said the Lord had revealed to him that this was the cause of the boy's inability to speak.

The mother responded to this by bringing the teenager to us again so that the curse could be broken. We prayed the prayer of faith, anointing him with oil. We still await the manifestation of God's power in full release.

Secondly, those with special health problems

From time to time we have been asked to pray for children with Down's syndrome, cerebral palsy, and enzyme deficiency. These little ones certainly bring forth extraordinary patience, love, dedication and physical endurance from their parents. While behavioural improvements were reported in some, as yet the Lord has not given us the keys to complete freedom. In each case we have bound, broken and released any possible spirit of infirmity, or affliction, then prayed for cleansing, love, peace, and healing. As with adults, we ask God to exercise his grace in answering prayer, but we never demand. A servant does not have that right.

Now to the promised list which recapitulates some of the earlier recommendations, and adds further subjects for release, cleansing, and healing.

Child abuse victims

Child abuse may be caused by an hereditary spirit which will pass on through the family. If there is no family record of this, the experience of abuse as a child can cause victims to later abuse, or want to abuse their own children. From then on, it becomes hereditary. Regardless of the source, all who do the abusing and those who have been abused, will need to be freed from:
- The trauma of their physical abuse.
- The spirit of child abuse.
- Fear of violence, anxiety and worry.

- A sense of rejection, self rejection, and fear of rejection.
- Anger, resentment, hatred, and revenge towards the person responsible.

Many countries impose legal obligations on counsellors to report child abuse incidents to police or child welfare agencies. If this were carried out, there would be far fewer deaths each year caused by violent parents, de facto partners or guardians. The guilty party obviously is in desperate need of deliverance.

It should not be presumed that child abuse is a crime committed only by non-Christians. Christians who are not being controlled by the Holy Spirit, are just as capable of this type of violence as anyone else.

Small children who are prayed for while they are young appear to grow up without showing long-term effects. But with some, continuing wise counsel and prayer may be advisable.

Ministry to the sexually abused has already been covered. Regrettably, we have not had many brought to us immediately after their trauma. But we have seen the Lord free and heal hundreds of adults whose lives and marriages had been emotionally and sexually crippled because of what happened in childhood.

Adopted children

Many, but not all adopted children have problems. Although most of them know that they were chosen to become family members, the sense of being abandoned or given away by their natural mothers often overrides this.

There are a number of potential problem areas:

(1) The bond with the natural mother needs to be broken, so that the new relationship will not be complicated by a double-parent identity. If this is not done, the invisible spiritual umbilical cord could cause an insatiable desire to find and make contact with the natural parent.

(2) In some cases there may be a sense of abandonment, even attitudes of resentment and anger towards the natural mother. These are not bondages, but are dominant spirits and need to be released.

(3) Feelings of low self-image and worthlessness are common.

(4) If the child's conception was pre-nuptial, or the result of a casual sexual partnership, a spirit of lust needs to be driven out.

(5) Surprisingly, many adopted children are very ungrateful, and

believe they have rights over what other brothers and sisters regard as privileges.

(6) The insecurity of adopted children sometimes causes them to become jealous and self-justifying.

(7) If little is known about the natural parents, it is wise to pray against possible family curses and spirits of occultism, witchcraft, anti-Christ and Freemasonry, in case they are hereditary. No harm will come to the child if these spirits have not been passed on.

(8) Rejection, self rejection, and fear of rejection.

Children of single mothers

Some single women do not marry the father(s) of their child(ren) and elect to bring up the child(ren) alone. There was a time when so-called 'illegitimate' children brought disgrace to the mother, but today's amoral society accepts single motherhood without question. A recent '60 Minutes' programme featured an eighteen year old unmarried mother of three children born to two different fathers. She said she wanted to have another child in four years' time. She explained she had been brought up in a foster home. The interviewer asked what she considered her future to be. She replied without hesitation 'Bringing up kids'. It would be easy to pass that off as environmental pre-conditioning, but what else did that lonely, longing-for-love teenager know about? Her children were her security, her reason for living, and the centre of her affections.

The problems from which these children will need release include:

(1) The feelings of rejection, self-rejection, and fear of rejection.

(2) Spirits of lust, and fantasy – lust particularly. With girls, spirits of seduction, fornication, adultery, and even prostitution should be prayed over in accordance with the mother's sexual history.

(3) Spirits of loneliness and withdrawal should also be released, also any bondage to the natural father. Where the natural father and child spend time together, spirits of confusion of identity, jealousy, and manipulation need releasing from the child.

Children of a deserted parent

Their special problems include:

(1) Senses of rejection, self-rejection, and fear of rejection.

(2) Spirits of loneliness, and withdrawal.

(3) A spirit of sorrow and sadness may need to be released, and any emotional bond which has tied the child to the deserting parent. Recently we were asked to pray for a girl aged twelve, and a boy aged nine. Their mother had walked out when her son was only nine months old, and had left the country. This had forced the father to give up his profession and spend his time in household duties bringing up his two children; he had done an excellent job. The daughter had only two complaints as we talked with her alone. 'My dad never buys me the clothes I like, and we disagree over this. And my brother embarrasses me by coming into my room at any time, without knocking.' A little chat with the father was all that was needed to solve both problems.

Children of divorced parents

Some couples stay together only for the children's sake – usually until they have completed their schooling. If the children discover this they will feel guilty and unhappy. They are usually the first to show the strain, both emotionally, and physically.

Divorce can shatter children's stability. They become confused when the ground of the family security suddenly gives way under them, and they find themselves struggling with choices of loyalty, often complicated by the loss of a home and standards of living. Sometimes they also imagine that they are personally responsible for the family break-up.

The sudden loss of a father may also cause daughters to look elsewhere for male comfort and support, often with tragic results.

These young ones need to be freed from:

(1) Their feelings of rejection, self-rejection, and fear of rejection.

(2) Their low self-image because they feel unloved, and insecure.

(3) Feelings of guilt imagining they are the cause of the divorce, feeling they were unable to prevent it.

(4) Unhappy and grieving spirits.

(5) Possible resentment and anger over what has happened.

Where a child shares time with both parents, it may be very difficult for them to resist a partisan spirit, especially if one parent is using money or gifts as incentives to get their allegiance. The child's tendency to manipulate either parent for personal advantage may also need to be dealt with.

Children who have to accept a step parent

In the joys of marriage or remarriage, single mothers, divorcees, or widows often overlook the possibility of jealousy, resentment, anger, even hostility being shown by their child or children to the new father. The same, of course, applies when fathers re-marry.

Resentment is really quite logical from the child's point of view. The new parent is seen as an intruder on everything the child and parent have done together. The child feels unwanted when there is someone else in the bed they used to go to for special times of togetherness.

Emotionally unresponsive or harsh step-mothers, and authoritarian step-fathers, will certainly add to a child's resentment. The step-parent, rightly or wrongly, is blamed for having intruded and spoilt the previous relationship.

Step-children mostly need freedom from:

(1) Spirits of rejection, self-rejection, and fear of rejection.

(2) Resentment, anger, and hostility towards the new parent.

(3) Withdrawal, self-pity, self-centredness, selfishness, and spirits of unhappiness.

(4) Manipulative spirits.

Those brought up in the care of other people such as foster homes, orphanages, child welfare institutions etc.

Whenever children do not have a warm and loving home-life they become independent and self-protective. If they run away, are thrown out by their parents, or removed by welfare authorities because of neglect, they may end up in foster homes or institutions where it can become a matter of survival by becoming the smartest, strongest, and most resourceful. The goal, of course, is to insulate themselves from society which they judge to be against them.

This should not be taken to suggest that those who care for them are heartless. In fact many who devote themselves to caring for these needy children do so out of love for Jesus Christ, or a pure motive of selflessness in serving those in desperate need. Some children have turned out to be a credit to their foster parents. Regrettably, we hear most about the rejects of foster care and institutional life. There is often not enough funding for staff to provide adequate person-to-person relationships in private, or government institutions.

Behind each child is a story of personal tragedy. Some are found-lings; others have suffered the death of a parent and the remaining parent is unable to cope with responsibilities of raising a child. Some have shown criminal tendencies, while others have had parents who have been mentally disturbed or hospitalised.

Such deprived children need to be released from:

(1) Strong spirits of rejection, self-rejection and fear of rejection. Most will also have hereditary rejection.

(2) Spirits of loneliness, independence, isolationism, and a distrust of adults.

(3) Spirits of self-protection and self-defensiveness.

(4) Spirits of ingratitude and emotional coldness.

In addition there may be:

(5) Spirits of dishonesty, lying and stealing.

(6) Spirits of anger, violence, bullying and belligerence.

(7) Sexual self-stimulation, and possibly heterosexual or homosexual aggressiveness.

(8) Possibly spirits of occultism and witchcraft, anxiety, worry, depression, fears and suicide.

(9) Fantasy and escapism with consequential learning difficulties.

(10) Addictions which manifest themselves at an early age, such as alcoholism, drugs, nicotine, gluttony, gambling and financial irresponsibility.

These children can be very vulnerable to people who show them kindness, because they deeply crave affection. A man who survived an unbelievably traumatic orphanage upbringing came for help at forty-seven years of age. His mind had blanked out all memories of those terrible early years, but he did remember the first home he stayed in as a teenager. The man was kind to him, but soon involved him in mutual sexual stimulation.

He grew up deeply rejected, sexually stimulating boys and then beating them up. Even in married life, he couldn't break the habit, and was violent to his wife. He was deeply repentant, crying out for help. The Lord heard him, set him free from his rejection, indecency and violence, then healed his marriage. He had such a wonderful renewed love relationship with his wife that it seemed as if they were on their honeymoon. To them both, God had done a miracle.

Children of working parents

Coming home to an empty house can cause a hollow feeling in the pit of the stomach, at any age. The warm welcome of a mother, or a partner is both comforting and heart-warming for child or spouse alike.

Children who come home from school to an empty house every day usually need release from:

(1) Spirits of rejection, self-rejection and fear of rejection.

(2) Loneliness, withdrawal, and sometimes isolationism.

(3) Low self-image, insecurity, and even worthlessness.

(4) Other problems such as anger or deception if the child has been covering up behaviour the parents would not approve of.

When both parents, or the sole parent work full-time, child-care is often taken on by grandmothers or others on a part-time or full-time basis. When there are strong family bonds the children usually have no ill effects. But should one be preferred to another, or punishment be unnecessarily harsh, the four problems mentioned above may manifest themselves.

Then there are those who employ help, even English style 'nannies', some of whom find immense fulfilment in looking after, and bringing up, their acquired family. The children respond well, and the fallout is minimal, except if they become confused as to their priorities in loyalty, love and obedience. When relationships with the natural parents are superseded, the bond between the nanny and the children should be broken.

When a child-minder has little or no emotional input, the little ones will in all probability show the four problems listed above. In addition, they may become manipulators of both parents and paid help, taking advantage of the situation for their own benefit. These spirits of manipulation must be released, otherwise they will continue to dominate the children.

Children who lose the security of their home and surroundings when the family moves house

Security is important to children. The three factors which contribute to security are the family home, the school, and personal friends. When families move, it may devastate a child.

Phyl and I joined a family of four in the dining room of an organisation that specialises in adult discipleship training. During the meal, I casually asked the twelve-year-old daughter if she was happy there or would she rather be back home. She quietly said 'Back home'.

I then asked if she had had a horse at home (having heard her parents say that they had come from a farm). She nodded, so I pressed a little further. 'What happened to the horse?' An obviously sad little girl hung her head and said quietly 'We had to sell it'.

While praying for children later in the week, the whole family came. Through hearing her daughter's answers to my questions, the mother had begun to realise just how deeply rejected her girl had felt. Both she and her husband asked their daughter to forgive them, which she did gladly. I then asked the Lord to free the girl from:

- Spirits of rejection, self-rejection, and fear of rejection.
- The low self-image syndrome.
- Spirits of loneliness, withdrawal, independence, and sadness.
- Spirits of resentment, anger, and grief.
- Hereditary spirits coming from both parents.

When I had finished, the girl left her mother, and coming up to me put her arms around my neck and her head on my chest. She then sobbed 'Please pray for me, I am so sad about leaving the farm.' Gently, I did so. The next day a happy mother and daughter were walking around with an arm around each other.

We have often found that ministering God's grace to children forges an emotional bond between them and ourselves, and as they grow up they continue to express openness and warmth should we happen to meet.

Another young man who came for ministry had shifted from house to house, and school to school, thirteen times as a child. He had rejected his parents, become withdrawn and independent. He was angry at continually losing his friends, so he rejected his parents, and modelled his life on his arrogant old grandfather who was somewhat of a showman.

He was freed from:

- A strong rejection syndrome including hereditary rejection, and parental rejection.
- Resentment, bitterness, anger and hatred to his parents. There were also spirits of withdrawal, perfectionism, criticism, and a spirit of emotional immaturity.

Parents certainly need to consider the potentially damaging effects which constant house moving may have on their children. Some parents seem to have a nomadic spirit which takes them from state to state or even country to country. Some family moves are of course essential, but special care needs to be taken to cushion the children from emotional trauma. One of our own grandsons whose parents had shifted several times had a special prayer request for us, 'Please pray that I will find a special friend'. We did, and he did.

Of course there are exceptions. Some parents have professional, missionary, or diplomatic positions in which they have to move around in their own country and overseas. Often there are no marked detrimental effects on their children. The excitement of new places helps to cushion them against the trauma of leaving familiar places and friends.

Some mission societies have researched this subject and are taking measures to prevent, or minimise potential problems.

Children who are traumatised by boarding school

Some children are glad to get away from home, or the isolation of country living, and go to boarding school. To the adventurous it is a challenge with the prospect of excitement.

However, to the shy clinging child, the rejected insecure child, and those who do not wish to go, boarding school can be a very bad experience. A number of adults have emphasised this when seeking deliverance.

One girl was so victimised by her house mistress for taking more than her permitted portion of breakfast cereal, that she had seriously considered knifing the woman. As a result, she grew up with a deep resentment to authority figures.

Many have harboured a sense of injustice for unfair discipline or treatment, harsh attitudes, or staff favouritism to a selected few. Some have spoken of having been bullied, made to endure sexual indignities, or forced to masturbate themselves, or others, publicly.

Anyone who has suffered in this way needs to be released from spirits of:
- Rejection, self-rejection, and fear of rejection.
- Worthlessness, inferiority, insecurity, and self condemnation.
- Withdrawal, loneliness and isolationism.
- Difficulty in giving and receiving love.
- Anger, resentment, hatred, and revenge.
- Anxiety, worry, tension, stress, and nervousness.

- General and specific fears.
- Injustice, hurts, and grief.
- If sexual indignities or abuse have occurred, then the particular type of spirit involved should be released, together with a sense of shame, guilt and degradation.

In the case of a very distressing childhood, it is not unusual for the person to have a complete memory blackout, and not be able to recall traumatic events. If possible, parents, and other family members may need to be questioned to complete a case history before deliverance can be fully effective.

Children who are adversely affected by the death of a parent, grandparent, or a family member

(1) *When death is by accident, or natural causes.* The death of a close family member always causes a child to feel rejected and unwanted. Anger is sometimes expressed towards the deceased person because the child feels he or she has been abandoned. Relatives should be careful not to say anything to a bereaved child which implies that God is in some way responsible for the death. For example: a little boy was told 'Jesus needed your father in Heaven, so he took him.' The boy then said, 'Well, I hate Jesus. He is selfish. We needed our Daddy here. I don't want to have anything to do with Jesus if he does mean things like that.'

Bereaved children should never be made to feel that they are expected to fill the shoes of a deceased parent. An uncle of a five-year-old boy said to his nephew 'Now that your father is gone you will have to be the man around the house.' When that boy grew up to be a man he told us just what that had meant to him. He said, 'My chest swelled up and I felt very important for about half an hour. Then the reality of what it meant, hit me, and I collapsed inside, realising how impossible it would be.' He said he felt defeated, and from that time onwards he had never been able to take responsibility.

Bereaved children often have a strong fear of losing their surviving parent, causing them to become very possessive, not wanting to let their mother or father out of their sight.

In ministering to these children, the following should be prayed over:

- Spirits of grief and sorrow.

- Spirits of abandonment, the fear of abandonment, and the fear of death.
- The three-fold rejection syndrome.
- Anger, resentment (depending on the age of the child).

(2) *When death is by suicide.* Hereditary spirits of suicide, destruction, self destruction, and death also need to be released.

(3) *When death is by murder.* Dependent upon the ages of the children, and in addition to the list in Section 1, pray against:

- Spirits of shame, guilt, humiliation and tragedy.
- Spirits of hatred, bitterness and revenge.

Children and teenagers who are attracted by the thoughts of suicide

Research has shown a close link between media coverage of the subject of suicide, and actual incidents.

There is often a false heroism associated with teenage suicides which draws others into following their example even at the same place. Recently a sequence of deaths by suicide occurred on a certain stretch of railway track in the Sydney metropolitan area.

Suicide is sometimes a desperate method of escape from a life of emotional unhappiness, even wretchedness. But it can also be an attempt to gain attention.

A rejected teenager whom we contacted through outdoor evangelism, and whom we were discipling phoned me about 2.30 a.m. one morning. His voice was thick and slurred. He told me he had taken a bottle of tablets (naming them) in an attempt to get his parents' attention. I obtained his address, told him what to do, then 'phoned the police and asked that an ambulance be sent to his address. He died on the way to hospital, was revived, but finally succumbed about daybreak. He died while still wanting to live.

All teenage talk of suicide should be investigated. They may have been dared to do it, or think that suicide is the only escape from threats of exposure or punishment. The thoughts may be only fantasy, but they need to be checked out.

Children and teenagers who talk about suicidal thoughts or desires, or have a family history of suicide need release from:

- Spirits of suicide, and if appropriate, spirits of hereditary suicide.
- Spirits of destruction and self-destruction.

- A spirit of death and the fantasy of death.
- A deceptive spirit of heroism.
- The whole rejection syndrome, and loneliness.
- Spirits of worthlessness, and uselessness.
- Bondages to siblings, members of their peer group, or any others who may be exercising undue pressure on them.

Regrettably, the numbers of young people who take their own lives are on the increase in most countries, particularly Japan, where there is such an emphasis on maintaining family honour.

One of the great contributory factors to the teenage suicide rate is the rock and roll industry where lyrics often feature death with violence.

The Dead Kennedys have these words in one of their songs!

> 'God told me to skin you alive . . .
> I kill children . . . live to watch them die . . .
> I kill children . . . make their mommies cry.
> Crush them under my car . . . I love to hear them
> scream . . . feed them poison candy . . . spoil their
> hallowe'en.'

The following are danger signals of which parents should be aware. They may indicate other problems already listed, but in case suicide is being contemplated, they need investigation.

- A normally outgoing child becomes withdrawn and sullen.
- A good student begins to fail.
- A child who has difficulty in sleeping.
- A change of eating habits, fasting, and anorexic or bulimic symptoms.
- A sudden tendency to drive dangerously.
- The taking of drugs, or alcohol.
- Promiscuity.
- Pre-occupation with death, or conversations which reveal morbid introspection.
- Any expression such as 'I wish I were dead.'

Children and teenagers who are overtly rejected by parents, siblings, school teachers or other authority figures

Some people believe that although sexual relationships are highly desirable and pleasurable, the prospect of having a baby is highly objectionable. Even marriage may do little to alter that attitude and if continued after a child is born, he or she will certainly feel rejected. If the birth of a baby interrupts a successful career, endangers the mother's health, overcrowds accommodation, overstrains meagre finances, hinders the 'good life', or is more than a mother can emotionally cope with, that child will feel unwanted.

A parent's thoughtless, hasty, or angry comments which are not withdrawn, or for which an apology is not given, will often push a child into the rejection syndrome. Examples of what we have been told include:

- 'I don't know why I ever had you'
- 'I could murder you!'
- 'You will never do any good, you will always be a failure.'
- 'I wish I could give you away, but no-one would have you.'
- 'Your brother was clever at school, but you are just a dummy.'
  Teachers may also have a similar effect on children. Examples:
- 'Everyone, just look at this disgraceful homework by Johnny; a five-year-old could do better.'
- 'What's the matter with you? Did your brother get all the brains in your family?'
- 'Stop talking Mary; you've got a mouth like a circus clown.'
  Peer comments and actions are equally devastating:
- 'I'm not going to be your friend any more. I'm going to be . . .'s friend,' (naming a rival).
- 'You're ugly and I hate you.'
- 'You can't come to my place any more; your father's only a garbage collector.'
  All this will only cause a child to:
- Feel worthless and totally rejected.
- Withdraw, become lonely, and be self protective.

   From this, tearfulness, aggressiveness, or other symptoms of the rejection syndrome may soon develop. Children in this category need the full spiritual release ministry previously mentioned for rejected children.

Those who have behavioural problems

(1) *Withdrawal into fantasy.* Causes may include:
- Real or imagined rejection.

195

- A hearing or eyesight problem which prevents a child from effectively doing his or her school-work.
- An hereditary spirit of occultism and witchcraft.
- Insecurity caused by lack of discipline.
- Overmuch exposure to television, or reading books on space adventures.

The treatment of hearing or eyesight problems, and supervision of a child's reading materials and TV viewing will resolve some problems. Otherwise, attention should be given to dominating spirit causes.

(2) *A swinging personality.* Causes may include:

- An hereditary spirit of schizophrenia.
- An hereditary spirit of Freemasonry causing ambivalence. We have prayed for a child in this category.
- A rejected child wrestling with confusion of loyalties.

In these cases it is desirable to obtain release from provoking spirits and then to follow with a prayer for wholeness and healing.

(3) *Children who continually tell lies, whether consciously or unconsciously.* Causes may be:

- Fear of punishment.
- Feelings of rejection; the child is looking for attention. Exaggeration is common amongst children; it is encouraged by films and books which make animals talk and act like super-humans. The fantasy of space films, books and toys also draw children into a state of make-believe. To overcome a feeling of rejection, children may imagine themselves to be someone else, and may not realise they are being untruthful.
- Hereditary spirits of deceit and lying which are operating in the child.
- Parents and other role models setting a bad example by being untruthful. Children cannot be blamed for considering it an acceptable way of life.

Lying may become a habit pattern to cover wrong doings or bad habits. It may also be the first reflex of self-defence. Lying may also result from threats of physical violence, or be a calculated method of getting others into trouble. The motive is personal spite, or revenge.

In affected young people spirits of deceit and lies need to be driven out, and habits broken.

Bondages, obligations, and fear of reprisals should be broken between any who have pressured the child to be untruthful, and the person being prayed for.

- Other associated spirits of stealing, immorality, rebellion, envy, jealousy, hatred, and revenge may also have to be driven out.

(4) *Those who steal.* Unless this problem is recognised and adequately dealt with in childhood, it may become more serious in later life. Children and teenagers steal because:

(a) Some families have a familiar spirit of kleptomania which has come down for generations, and the children are literally driven to steal everything they covet.

(b) Sudden impulse overcomes them. They have no need, but give way to temptation. Adults who are well known and highly respected in the community sometimes do this. The act is out of character and without rational explanation.

(c) Children brought up in poverty cannot resist the temptation to take something they particularly want but their parents cannot afford to buy for them.

(d) Sheer greed and covetousness motivates them.

(e) It is an act of bravado or the fulfillment of a dare under peer pressure.

(f) An adult may 'employ' a child to steal to escape suspicion.

(g) They want to gain attention because of feeling rejected.

(h) They want to give money or gifts to friends to gain acceptance. A twelve-year-old girl was recently brought to us who had taken several thousand dollars from the cash register in her parents' shop and given the money to her school friends.

(i) They are being bullied.

(j) They have not been taught to be honest, and to respect the property of others. They do not think it wrong to take something they need or want and will even justify their actions without any sense of wrongdoing. One Christian adult who came for deliverance from other problems admitted, without any sense of guilt, that she had received several thousand dollars from an insurance company by making a false claim. Up to that time she had made no restitution. We strongly recommended that she repay the stolen money.

Children and teenagers with a problem of stealing need deliverance from spirits of:

(a) Stealing (kleptomania), covetousness, greed, deceit, and fears of punishment or revenge.

(b) Hereditary family spirits, where appropriate.

(c) Bondages to peers and adults may need to be broken.

In the cases of rejection, the rejection syndrome should be dealt with so that there is no longer a driving need to gain attention, or acceptance of a peer group.

(5) *Thumbsuckers*. This problem has been mentioned previously but no prayer points were listed. Children, teenagers and even adults need release from:

(a) A spirit of insecurity.

(b) The cause of the insecurity, in most cases spirits of rejection, self-rejection, and fear of rejection.

(c) The habit.

(d) Spirits of withdrawal, guilt, and shame.

(6) *Bed wetting*. Unless indicating a urinary disorder needing medical attention, this highly embarrassing problem which may continue to adulthood has already been mentioned. Two additional causes need to be added:

(a) Bed wetting may indicate subconscious insecurity and fear. If a child is loved and accepted at home, enquiries should include possible causes at school, the attitudes of the friends the child plays with after school or in any home where he or she may play.

(b) It has been found that bed-wetting can be a child's method of showing displeasure for a real or imagined hurt or wrong. One mother told us that after she had apologised to her child for a wrong attitude, the bed-wetting stopped immediately.

Suggested ministry:

(a) In the event of some trauma having been the cause of the problem, pray for release from the dominating spirit involved, together with spirits of insecurity, fear and withdrawal. Break the habit, and pray for cleansing and wholeness.

(b) If rejection has caused the problem, release the spirits of rejection, self-rejection, and fear of rejection. Break the habit and pray for cleansing and healing.

(7) *Nail-biting*. As already stated, this habit may come from rejection, insecurity, anxiety or nervousness. These driving spirits need to be freed, and the habit broken.

(8) *Sexual self-stimulation*. When this commences between the ages of two and five years, an hereditary spirit of lust is often the cause. Pleasurable sexual awareness is certainly not normal at such an early age. Boys, even girls, sometimes learn this accidentally by lying on their stomachs and pulling themselves up and down.

Self-stimulation and masturbation may also commence through children handling themselves as they reach puberty, or from the normal games they play which lead them to investigate one another's sexuality. The possibility that the habit may have commenced through incest should not be ignored.

Children need deliverance as soon as the problem manifests itself because of its habit forming power. As they grow, their mental fantasy could be stimulated by pornography, and they will doubtless come across older children and teenagers who will try to involve them in full sexual activities. The following spirits need to be driven out:

(a) spirits of lust and fantasy lust.

(b) spirits of self-stimulation and masturbation.

(c) any hereditary spirits known to have been active in the family. These include spirits of lust, incest, molestation, exposure, seduction, promiscuity, homosexuality, lesbianism, bestiality, and obsession with pornography.

(d) spirits of uncleanness, impurity, guilt and degradation, particularly in cases of incest.

In addition, bondages of false comfort and habit need to be broken.

(9) *Children showing excessive fears of the dark.* This is a wider perspective than 'Controlling Fears' outlined in chapter 8. The possible causes of this problem include:

(a) a severe fright at night caused by a violent storm, an intruder, or even an over-active imagination.

(b) an hereditary spirit of occultism and witchcraft.

(c) bad dreams or nightmares.

(d) bad television programmes.

(e) the activities of a spirit of poltergeist popularly called a 'ghost'.

(f) the reading of 'ghost' stories at bed time.

(g) siblings trying to frighten one another by sharing weird stories, or appearing at night in draped bed sheets making appropriate moaning sounds.

This problem should be dealt with:

(a) by making sure that activities which have caused the problems are discontinued.

(b) by prohibiting disturbing reading materials or TV viewing.

(c) by deliverance from spirits of anxiety, nervousness, fear of the dark, fear of being alone, and oversensitivity.

199

(d) by praying for cleansing, and that the child will be filled with love and peace.

A small night light may be helpful for a while.

Children of alcoholics

(1) Symptoms of this widely prevalent problem amongst children (some of which may have been mentioned before) include:

(a) showing a liking for alcohol, such as draining the glasses left on a table.

(b) a tendency towards other addictions, particularly gluttony.

(c) impulsiveness.

(d) always seeking approval.

(e) having difficulty in sticking to a project.

(f) a tendency to tell lies.

(g) shame because of a father's public behaviour, or what he has done to his child under the influence of alcohol.

(h) fear of brutality. (Sometimes physical scars can be seen.)

(2) To bring these young ones into freedom in Christ, they need to be delivered from spirits of:

(a) alcoholism, and hereditary alcoholism.

(b) all spirits of addiction.

(c) the rejection syndrome, together with insecurity, worthless-ness, and difficulty of giving and receiving love.

(d) hereditary physical, emotional or sexual violence to which they have been subjected.

(e) specific problems which may be obvious such as brutality, shame, unforgiveness, anger, revenge, etc.

Pray for cleansing, and the filling of God's love and peace to conclude.

Children or grandchildren of Freemasons

As outlined in *Evicting Demonic Intruders and Breaking Bondages* the following spirits need to be released:

(a) the curse of Freemasonry and the Luciferan heresy.

(b) idolatry, occultism and witchcraft, false religion, deception, and mockery.

(c) apathy, passivity, confusion of mind.

(d) hardness of emotional life.

(e) scepticism, doubt, and unbelief.

(f) sicknesses, infirmities, and allergies.

Where parents or grandparents have been involved in the higher degrees of Freemasonry counsellees also need to be released from:

(g) the third eye, and false wisdom.

(h) spirits of disaster.

(i) spirits of poltergeist.

Children who are overworked in childhood, or loaded with heavy responsibilities

This may happen through the continuous sickness of a parent, a large number of children having to be cared for, or because their leisure time is taken up working to help the family income. A lazy parent, or one intent on enjoying the good life may also load a child with heavier responsibilities than is normal. Generally speaking, there can be three effects:

(1) the child is robbed of the normal privileges and joys of carefree childhood.

(2) the maturing process is accelerated by the untimely workload, and by the anxiety of having to perform like an older person. They grow up with a serious or heavy spirit.

(3) it is possible for the child to grow up with a resentment towards parents, and an aversion to marriage, and having children.

A child with little or no joyous memory of childhood will make 'heavy weather' in life generally. They need to be released from:

(a) the rejection syndrome, and a sense of worthlessness.

(b) spirits of heaviness, seriousness and 'being old before their time'.

(c) a resentment or bitterness towards parents.

They need cleansing, renewal, and to be made aware of the love they may receive from God the perfect Father, his Son Jesus Christ and the Holy Spirit.

Homeless children

The recent alarming upsurge in numbers of child and teenage 'street people' should tug at everyone's heart-strings. The trauma of parents rejecting their children, and in turn being rejected by their children, will never disappear just by the provision of institutional care. What is needed is the power of God to save and set these young ones free.

They need to be delivered from the spirits of rejection and all its complications; spirits of both heterosexual and homosexual activities, addictions, drug dependency, occultism and witchcraft; and anti-social attitudes such as rebellion, violence, deceit and stealing. These young people need deliverance, cleansing, and wholeness before they will be able to enjoy normal relationships.

Children who had delivery problems at birth

Readers are referred to the contents of chapter six which outlines potential problem areas.

A reminder of some teenage problems which need special understanding, tlc, and prayer

(1) Injustice, real or imaginary, which surfaces as rebellion, resentment, and anger.

(2) Adolescent confusion as teenagers grow. They often feel alienated, withdraw, and blame their families.

(3) The fear of getting fat caused by the media and fashion industry emphasis on the concept that 'thin is beautiful'. Anorexia nervosa may be the next step.

(4) Ambivalence amongst Christian young people confronted by having to decide whether to stick by their family's biblical ethics, or join their unsaved friends. Enjoying alcohol, drugs, and sleeping around is made to sound like the good life.

SUMMARY

1. While medical and psychological treatment have been the standard means of helping children and teenagers to overcome their problems, spiritual release has mostly been misunderstood, neglected, or refused.

2. Experience has shown that spiritual release from compulsive forces followed by cleansing and renewal, are most effective.

3.   The God who designed man and gave him personality is the One who is most able to bring release and freedom at any age from Satan-inspired bondages and dominating spirits. He is also able to bring mental, emotional, and physical healing after such releases.

4.   From experience, spiritual release has an important role to fulfil in association with medical sciences, in bringing children to wholeness of personality.

Chapter 19

How Parents Can be Blessed by Their Children

In an earlier chapter keys to good parenting were suggested as both short and long-term investments in the growing child. The results of investing these spiritual values should be seen progressively and continuously.

By rejecting biblical standards, humanists have had to produce their own 'how-to-do-it' kits on bringing up children. The rationalisation of past moral standards with the 'enlightenment' of present day permissiveness, together with the encouragement of child independence places our Christian families in jeopardy.

The only defence a Christian parent had to this drug-crazed, sex-orientated, rebellious and independent generation, is a Christ-honouring home where the example and behaviour of the parents demonstrates to the children the effectiveness of biblical standards.

The recent upsurge in the establishment of church-orientated and non-denominational schools throughout the world illustrates the alarm Christian parents feel about secularism. Christians are spoken of in negative, and often derogatory terms. They are called 'spoil-sports', 'narrow-minded bigots', 'Victorian in attitude', and 'religious

4 5 6
3 THE BLESSINGS 7
PARENTS SHOULD
RECEIVE FROM
2 CHILDREN AND 8
TEENAGERS WHO
1 GROW UP IN 9
GOD HONOURING
HOMES 10

Parental Input (Ch. 3)
Fair Discipline Faith Godly
Fairness Patience Example
LOVE TRUST
Encouragement
Adequate Time
Biblical Teaching

freaks'. Their non-swearing, non-smoking, non-drinking, non-drug taking, and non-immoral behaviour, is a light in the world's darkness, and it is being resisted more and more. The children of Christians often suffer in the fall-out and some of them succumb to the ever present and increasing pressure to conform.

Despite the problems, it is true today that many from Christian families are glorifying God and honouring their parents. The most visible signs in the family home are:

Spontaneous love and affection

As soon as a child is old enough to respond to love a deep and warm mutual bond is forged. Discipline, and even fair punishment will not disturb the security forged by warm and tender love. In early childhood, little arms around a parent's neck, and a quiet voice saying 'I'm sorry', usually triggers an affectionate response. This should continue into teenage years, even if a trifle muted!

The absence of spontaneous demonstrations of love may not mean that a child (later a marriage partner) does not love. They may show their love by extreme loyalty, or a spontaneous willingness to help around the home.

The biblical principle of sowing and reaping applies also to human hearts. Because Phyl and I have always spontaneously shown our love and affection to one another, our daughters and their families do just the same. It gives us much pleasure to receive love and see it shared so freely in our greater family.

Obedience

Children ought never to be allowed to set their own 'obedience-time-clock'. Nearly every male of the human species has an inbuilt capacity to 'switch off' when called! But right training should produce spontaneous responses, and these may be crucial in times of danger.

Of course children are always on their best behaviour in front of visitors. When the guests comment favourably on the obedience and good behaviour of the children, it is a mother's reward. Discipline calls for patience, fairness, persistence, and the appropriate measures of reward for obedience or punishment for disobedience.

Despite popular belief, there is really no such person as 'a self-made man.' One medical specialist reading the manuscript had this excellent comment – 'A self-made man is a product of unskilled labour!' Sure, there are people who have become outstanding in their professions or public life, but seldom does the spotlight focus on the dedication of parents in forming the character of those children. Parents do not desire this, as their fulfilment comes in seeing the fruit of the seeds they planted.

The spirit of the age is rebellion, self-opinion, and stubbornness. Many parents have contributed to this, more than they may care to admit. If accused, they will deny it.

Submission to God's principles commences by children obeying their parents. (Ephesians 6:1–3.) Parents bless their children by insisting on obedience. Children bless their parents by being obedient. God is blessed when both parents and children obey him.

Parental respect

Age, experience, and family ties don't count for much today. The terms the 'old man' and the 'old woman' may be true in actual age differences, but often their use is intended as a put-down.

There is indeed something special about children who in adulthood continue to seek the opinions or guidance of their parents over important decisions. I have always felt honoured when a daughter or her husband has phoned to say: 'Dad, I want your advice please.'

Men so often put their wives down in front of their children and publicly. The women usually respond by criticising the children's father openly at home and when they get together, and so a 'stand-off' situation develops. This should change when people are born again, but the habit often remains. Spirit-filled parents should constantly show respect for one another, setting standards which their children will follow. As a result, many will later call them blessed.

Honesty

In our youngest daughter's home, a lie is treated as the scarlet sin which 'Mum' will never tolerate. As a result there are four boys who can be counted on to be truthful. My natural instinct as a growing boy was to lie to prevent punishment. (I was usually guilty.) I could do so without a blush, looking my mother straight in the eyes. But I didn't fool her, so I was generally booked for one of those dreadful front-room episodes when my father came home. I learned to be honest by example, biblical teaching, and the rod of correction applied to the 'seat of learning'.

Telling tales about other family members may be technically honest, but it is often motivated by spite and vindictiveness. When the truth is blurted out at the wrong time to the embarrassment of a family member, it is in spite, not honesty. If parental instruction causes children to grow up truthful and sensitive about when to speak, they and their parents are blessed.

Openness, and a willingness to confide

Parents who listen to their children, and give advice wisely, will have avoided causing them to turn to outsiders for help. Many readers who had difficulties in talking to their parents, can recall with gratitude the advice and understanding given by non-family members during those 'awkward teenage years'.

When children trust their parents and don't feel threatened, they will chat openly about any subject, and a delightful bond of mutual openness will be forged which will last for a lifetime.

Spontaneous willingness to help

'I'll help you Mummy (or Daddy)' is usually just what a parent does not want to hear when short of time. But that investment can produce big harvests. Children who are given responsibilities which assist in the smooth running of the family home (and not just to earn money) will grow up with helpful spirits.

Jesus Christ summed up man's earthly responsibility as loving God and one's fellow (Luke 10:37). This class of love motivates action, as Jesus Christ illustrated by telling the story of the good Samaritan. The place to commence is the family home.

Thoughtfulness and consideration

During school holidays, two of our grandchildren often come for the day while their mother works. When it comes time for 'us oldies' to take a rest, they play quietly, and never disturb us. We did not teach them this, nor do we need to enforce it; they were brought up to be thoughtful and considerate. Gentle character forming discipline in early life leads to children learning to keep noise levels in check. And that blesses parents, grandparents and neighbours!

As we have travelled, we have sometimes been pressured by some who have driven us relentlessly to counsel people, and blessed by those who have been thoughtful and protected us from self-centred people obsessed with their own problems. Considerate attitudes are learned in childhood, and those who have blessed us also honour those who taught them.

Purity

While nothing a parent can do will guarantee a child will not give way to life's moral temptations, parental example, the teaching of biblical standards, and intercessory prayer will prove to be the greatest protection possible.

Today's children and teenagers are subject to greater pressures than in any previous generation. Teenage daughters are put on the pill (usually to prevent their mothers from the indignity of a daughter's unwanted pregnancy). The teaching of moral purity is also generally regarded as being out of date. Peer pressure, the flood of pornography, and the fear of being branded a 'goodie-goodie', are challenges difficult to resist. And then there are paedophile human ghouls who sexually prey on the young, as well as those driven by lust caused by drugs and alcohol. Our growing young people are certainly facing a battery of moral pressures, but Christians can be victorious.

Children and teenagers who have been given right standards, warned of dangers, and had their television viewing, reading, music and friends supervised will generally respond positively, and maintain purity. What blesses parents is a spontaneous determination to remain pure, motivated by right reasons, not just fear of rejection. Children given a feeling of protection and security will respond by rejecting what is wrong.

Diligence in their studies

It seems that most children have to be 'encouraged' (if that is the most appropriate word), to do their homework and take their schooling seriously. Laziness in studying seems to be the norm during school years. It was in my generation, and nothing seems to have changed.

The diligence of parents has encouraged children to aim at selecting and fulfilling the best objectives. Knowing that their parents have succeeded in their particular field of endeavour is the greatest encouragement to children to aim for the highest standards.

A willingness to submit to Jesus Christ as Saviour and Lord

This is surely one of the greatest ways children may bless their parents.

Parents cannot force the Gospel seed to germinate in their children. The new birth experience is solely the ministry of the Holy Spirit. The time span between sowing and fruit bearing may be short or long (even after a parent has died), but the greatest blessing parents may receive is when their children choose to walk the way of salvation. Phyl, myself, our girls, and our grandchildren have all experienced new birth in Jesus Christ through the example, prayers, and encouragement of parents or grandparents.

The perfect parent, and the perfect child are only to be found in story books. In real life, some families may come close to the ideal, but most parents give God the glory when they see their parenting has been effective in the generations which follow.

SUMMARY

1. The principle of sowing and reaping is not just for outdoor life; it is a life-moulding force in bringing up children.

2. Children's lives are like a good investment. The return may far exceed what was invested, but it will take time.

3. Parents should not invest advice, encouragement, and prayer in their children for selfish gratification, but to fulfil divine requirements, and glorify God.

4. As a beautiful flower blesses more than just the person who planted the seed, so the spiritual returns from godly parenting will bless many others to the glory of God.

Chapter 20

WARNING!
A Spiritual Predator is at Large, Attacking
Babies, Children and Young People

All forms of life face survival problems from the time they are born.

A baby's first protective line of defence is of course its mother, closely followed by the father, and other family members. Even the household pet dog 'gets into the act' at times.

But the greatest danger to children and adults comes from an unseen source. Satan and his demonic hordes have an obsession to stop God's love, grace, and power from bringing spiritual life to every living person. That Satanic oppression may commence at conception, during the forty-week period, or from birth onwards. One thing is certain. The domination will only increase. Satan has no respect for age or sex, and aims to dominate us humans from the cradle to the grave. There are no exceptions.

From Eden onwards, children have been at risk. From ripping open pregnant mothers in early historical records to the holocaust of Jewish families in World War II, we blush to think of the countless numbers of children slaughtered by genocide, infanticide or religious sacrifice.

The family of our first parents

The first two children born in the human race emphasise the tragic reality of his destructive power. When Adam and Eve were banished from the Garden of Eden, they still had two great spiritual blessings. Firstly, their sins were covered by atoning blood, and their bodies covered by skins of the animals. Secondly, God promised Eve that she would have children, and that a future female descendant would give birth to a child who would crush the head of the serpent who had deceived her (Genesis 3:15).

The Bible does not say how long it was before Cain and Abel were born, and we know nothing of their early lives. What we do know is that Satan manipulated Cain to murder his brother, just as he had successfully used Eve to incite Adam to rebel against God.

> '*Do not be like Cain **who belonged to the evil one**, and murdered his brother. And why did he murder him? Because his own actions were evil, and his brother's were righteous.*'
>
> (1 John 3:12, emphasis added)

Other translations include:
Weymouth '... *who was a child of the evil one* ...'
J.B. Phillips '... *who was a son of the devil* ...'

The first child born after Eden showed that Adam was no longer able to control his family. Although Luke's genealogy records Adam as '... *the son of God*' (Luke 3:38), the children born to him certainly were not. Abel was assassinated, and Cain's family line was obliterated by the flood (Genesis chapters 6–9).

The only human survivors were the descendants of Seth, the next recorded son born to Adam and Eve. Thousands of years later, Jesus Christ said to Seth's heirs and successors '*you belong to **your father the devil**, and you want to carry out your father's desire. He was a murderer from the beginning, not holding to the truth, for there is no truth in him. When he lies he speaks his native language, for he is a liar and the father of lies*' (John 8:44, emphasis added).

The repercussions of Eden's spiritual fall is clearly seen in the first generation born after sin began its reign of death. Original sin (Genesis chapter 3) became hereditary sin in the children (Genesis chapter 4). The evidence of this is outlined in the 'Cain Syndrome' in, *Evicting Demonic Intruders and Breaking Bondages.*

In order to understand the devil's designs on the lives of our children, we need to examine the biblical record.

(1) The Genesis fall was but the first battle in Satan's unending spiritual war against God on this earth which will not end until he and his demon powers are destroyed in the lake of fire (1 Corinthians 15:24, Revelation 20:10).

In the end times, the Satanic trinity of evil (Revelation 16:13) will reign on and over the earth with fearsome demonic manifestations, and will delude mankind into worshipping him and defying God (2 Thessalonians 2:3–10; Revelation chapters 9–18). To do this, Satan must control the nations. He began with the first family and still aims to bring every family in the world under his control.

(2) It is evident that Satan was the architect of Abel's murder plan. The divine revelation that a child would be born who would defeat him in conflict may indeed have triggered the events which followed.

Satan must have been infuriated when Abel's sacrifice of firstborn fat lambs was accepted by God (Genesis 4:4). He may have reasoned that by killing Abel he would prevent any promised child from being born. He knew that Cain was totally under his control, and would never produce 'holy' seed. So Abel was but the first of countless numbers murdered in a vain attempt to stop God from carrying out his word.

And so, because of Satan, Adam and Eve were bereaved of their first two children at unknown ages. One by death, the other by exile. From then on, Satan's evil ambitions knew no bounds, culminating in the extermination of mankind for continuously practising evil, wickedness, violence, and corruption (Genesis 6:5–13). While God saved eight adults, every other man, woman, baby, child, and teenager perished. Satan rejoiced.

The family of Jacob

Joseph was not only his father's favourite son (Genesis 37:3), but was also set apart by God. The dreams he shared with his family were actually God's revelations of his future. They made his brothers angry and disquieted his father (Genesis 37:5–10).

The incredible saga of Joseph's early life could not have been merely a chain of unfortunate events which happened to come right in the end. The writer suggests that Satan prepared and implemented a master plan to crush this young man and stop him from becoming a future saviour of his own family, and a type of Jesus Christ himself.

The babies of the Hebrews in captivity

A little more than 430 years after Joseph and his family had been re-united, they had increased so greatly in numbers and prosperity that

Pharaoh became concerned. Fearing the Israelites might betray Egypt in a time of war, he ruthlessly forced them into slave labour. Still concerned, he announced a diabolical plan. (Diabolos is a Greek word for the devil, meaning 'accuser, slanderer'.)

Simply stated, it was to force Israelite zero-population growth by the murder of every newly born baby boy. Two Hebrew midwives named Shiprah and Puah were instructed to kill each boy they delivered (Exodus 1:16). The midwives however feared God, and were smarter than the king gave them credit for. Ancient Jewish tradition claims they called upon the name of the LORD, and that he helped the Hebrew women to have their children before the midwives arrived.

Pharaoh appeared to be unimpressed by the midwives simple explanation. Doubtless they just happened to omit any reference to praying! They certainly earned God's blessings (Exodus 1:20, 21), but the obvious distrust of Pharaoh. He then introduced phase two of his male-baby extinction campaign.

All Egyptians were ordered to throw every Israelite baby boy they could find into the river Nile, but to spare the baby girls (Exodus 1:22). So child murder became obligatory and justifiable in Egypt.

The reason is obvious. Witchcraft was openly practiced in Egypt, and Pharaoh's top advisers were experts in the use of demonic powers, as Moses and Aaron later discovered in giving Pharaoh God's ultimatum to free his people (Exodus 6:11). Pharaoh's plan was not his own, but merely the fulfilment of Satan's determination to wipe out the Hebrew nation to prevent the promised 'favoured child' from becoming a reality.

God interpreted Pharaoh's death edict against the Hebrew baby boys as an attack against Himself. He instructed Moses to tell Pharaoh *'This is what the LORD says: "Israel is my firstborn son, and I told you, 'Let my son go, so he may worship me. But you refused to let him go: so I will kill your firstborn son"'* (Exodus 4:23, emphasis added).

Moses was in an unenviable situation. Firstly, he had to stand before the very court which would have been his had he not chosen to reject his dual citizenship and revert to being an Israelite. Secondly he had to issue an ultimatum to Pharaoh that if he didn't release God's son (the Israelites), he would lose his own son, and by implication, the eldest son in every home in Egypt. But first of all God had to give Moses a personal lesson so that he would not just be a message-bearer to the Egyptian king, but a living part of the message.

During an overnight stop on the family's journey back to Egypt, God himself came to kill Moses. His wife Zipporah then 'suddenly' remembered that her own eldest son had never been circumcised in obedience to God's covenant with Abraham (Genesis 17:9, 10, 23). Quickly taking a flint knife she circumcised her own son on the spot, and splattered her husband's feet with blood. And so the covenant was fulfilled, God was satisfied, and Moses was spared. He was then able to speak to Pharaoh with the authority of a man whose life had been spared through the blood of his own son.

So Pharaoh's campaign against Israel's future existence began by murdering potential fathers. God stepped in, and delivered his *'son Israel'*, by the blood of the passover lamb.

The children of the idol worshippers at Bethel

After Elisha had received Elijah's mantle of prophetical authority, he returned home via Bethel. As he approached the city, a jeering mob of juveniles followed him (2 Kings 2:23, 24). They were obviously intent on belittling the new prophet and jeered at him in contempt.

These were the children of idolatrous parents who worshipped demon idols (1 Corinthians 10:19–20), and Elisha called down a curse on them in the name of the Lord (verse 24a). When two bears came out of the woods and mauled forty two of the youths (verse 24b), it was a deliberate judgement on the children of idolatrous parents. Satan shows no mercy to the children of those who worship him.

Influences of the heathen practice of child sacrifices

While God required animal sacrifices to atone for sins throughout the Old Testament, Satan, the great deceiver, demanded human sacrifices, preferably children.

Some names by which Satan is worshipped through child sacrifice include the Moabite 'Chemosh', the Ammonite 'Molech' (1 Kings 11:7), also known as 'Milcom', 'Malcham', or 'Malchan'. Other idols to whom children were sacrificed by burning were 'Adrammelech', and 'Anammelech' (2 Kings 17:31). For a much more detailed and informative background sketch of the Babylonian trio of Baal, Semiramis and Tammuz and their domination of heathen worship practices, readers are referred to the first four chapters of *Devil Take the Youngest* (Winkie Pratney – Huntington House Inc).

The pagan religious ceremonies of ancient civilisations were certainly thinly disguised times of demon worship. The worship of both masculine and feminine deities had sexual overtones. Fertility rites, sexual experiences as an expression of worship, male and female temple prostitution, and sexual deviance of all kinds, soon became a normal part of religious expression. The climax of such religious blasphemy was the offering of children as sacrifices to heathen deities. By the time Israel conquered Canaan, Satan already had established child sacrifices as a normal part of idolatrous worship. He knew it would only be a matter of time before the Israelites could be enticed to kill off their own children in the fire.

The Israelites had one piece of history which Satan may well have used to encourage the practice. At God's request, Abraham, their greatly revered patriarch, had offered Isaac, his son of promise, as a burnt sacrifice on Mount Moriah through a sacrificial ram God had tethered nearby (Genesis chapter 22).

Because Abraham was willing to glorify God by sacrificing his son, Satan may have deceived the God-fearing Hebrews into following his example literally.

God's attitude to the heathen custom of infanticide was never in doubt:

- *'Do not give any of your children to be sacrificed to Molech for you must not profane the name of your God. I am the LORD'* (Leviticus 18:21). See also Leviticus 20:2–5.

   But history shows that the demonic practice of neighbouring nations was more appealing to the Israelites than their fear of God's judgement.

- *'Israel sacrificed their sons and daughters in the fire'* (2 Kings 17:21). See also 2 Kings 23:10, Jeremiah 19:5 and Ezekiel 23:37–39.

And so, by following demonic religious zeal, Israel became the tool of Satan in destroying their own heirs and successors.

Other incidents involving the killing of children and young people

- Abimelech was the son of Gideon (Jerub-Baal) by a slave mistress. He connived with the citizens of Shechem to make himself king, and to rid himself of family rivals, he butchered seventy of his half-brothers on one stone in Ophrah. Only Jotham, the youngest son, escaped death by hiding. Because Abimelech's treachery, and the murder of seventy innocent and obviously young men was so offensive to God, he sent an evil spirit against him and the treacherous people of Shechem and wiped them out. In doing this God fulfilled Jotham's curse (Judges chapter 9:56, 57), and affirmed the sanctity of all life.

- Athaliah was a daughter of the infamous queen Jezebel. When her son King Ahaziah died, she murdered all the royal princes so that she could be queen. But a family member removed Joash, a one-year-old child from amongst the intended victims and sheltered him in the temple for six years. He was crowned king at the age of seven years (2 Kings 11:16). The number of royal princes who were murdered is not recorded, but the female butcher suffered a similar end for her villainy (2 Kings 11:16).

In an attempt to kill the child Jesus, King Herod slaughtered many children

Herod is notorious for the murders he planned and committed. When the Magi failed to return with directions as to how to find the newly-born king, Herod's frustrations and fury caused the murder of the innocents to be planned. Consequently, all children under two years of age in Bethlehem and environs died, except the intended victim, the baby Jesus whom God had sent to Egypt for safety (Matthew 2:13–18). Jeremiah had prophesied that particular child slaughter would take place some six hundred years before it happened (Jeremiah 31:15).

Teenagers and young people are still at risk today

The Apostle Paul well knew that young people were a special target of the evil one. When writing to his spiritual son Timothy in Ephesus, he made three vital recommendations. They make excellent advice to teenagers coming to grips with the reality of having to use the principles of spiritual warfare to be spiritually victorious: **Flee – Follow – Fight** (1 Timothy 6: 11, 12). They are:

- **Flee** the temptation to love money and be drawn into all types of evil (vv. 10, 11).

- **Follow** *'righteousness, godliness, faith, love, endurance and gentleness'* (v. 11).
- **Fight** *'the good fight of faith. Take hold of eternal life to which you were called when you made your good confession in the presence of many witnesses'* (v. 12).

Scriptural warnings of the predator's deceptive strategy

Something of the subtlety and variety of Satan's spiritual oppression may be clearly seen in the New Testament. Parents are responsible to guard their children from birth to the age of maturity. Young people are then accountable for their own actions, and need to know:

(1) Satan uses cunning schemes to outwit Christians of all ages (2 Corinthians 2:11).

(2) Satan troubles some believers by a spirit of fear (Romans 8:15, 2 Timothy 1:7).

(3) Satan pretends to be an angel of light (2 Corinthians 11:14).

(4) Satan causes some believers to reject their faith. He uses deceiving spirits and demonic doctrines (1 Timothy 4:1).

(5) Satan is given a foothold in our lives when we give way to anger (Ephesians 4:26).

(6) Satan fires arrows of temptation at us all (Ephesians 6:16).

(7) Satan (the believer's enemy), prowls around believers like a roaring lion looking for prey (1 Peter 5:8).

(8) Satan controls the world in which we live (1 John 5:18).

Satan's basic kit of tools is certainly extensive. He is able to oppress a baby, child or teenager directly through their parents, guardians, teachers, friends, or aquaintances. From womb to tomb, there is no let up.

But victory over him and his hordes of demons has been given to us through Jesus Christ.

> *'I write to you, young men, because* **you have overcome the evil one** *...'*
>
> *'I write to you, young men, because you are strong, and the word of God is in you, and you* **have overcome the evil one.***'*
>
> (1 John 1:13, 14 emphasis added)

SUMMARY

1.   Babies, children, and young people have always been the target of the destroyer. Apart from secular historical records, the Bible shows a clear pattern of Satan's murderous intent.

2.   New Testament warnings of Satan's activities are even more urgent today than when they were written.

3.   Spiritual warfare in the authority of the name of Jesus Christ, and the power of the Holy Spirit, is as effective today as it was in the first century.

Chapter 21

'To Our Children, We Give, Devise, and Bequeath . . .'

So reads the legal wording of the last will and testament which becomes effective on the death of the testator. In this way parents direct the disposal of their lifetime savings, belongings, and property as they wish.

Material possessions are not all that children inherit. There are non-material spiritual blessings and problems which are passed down from parents. Only God has the power to release children from transmitted bondages and dominations which so often hinder, control, and limit their lives.

Having looked at the practical principles of parenting, let us turn our attention to four things which parents pass on to their children, as revealed in the Scriptures.

Problems which come from heredity

A brief summary of this subject from *Evicting Demonic Intruders and Breaking Bondages* is as follows:

(1) Because Satan deceived Eve into sinning against God and Adam deliberately disobeyed him in yielding to his wife's persuasiveness, every person born since then has suffered or yet will suffer death as the hereditary curse of that original human sin (Romans 5:12).

(2) The first-fruits of original sin, are clearly seen in Cain's behaviour in Genesis chapter four. God confirmed the punishment of the sins of parents to the third and fourth generation when he addressed Israel from Mount Sinai (Exodus 20:4, 5).

(3) When Noah's son Ham dishonoured his father he caused a curse to fall on his whole family, but his youngest son Canaan was the one most affected (Genesis 9:22–27; 10:15–19).

(4) Isaac inherited a spirit of lying and deception from his father who lied about his wife (and half-sister) (Genesis 12:11–13; 20:11–13). Up to sixty-five years later, he, in turn, lied about his wife (and cousin) to Abimelech the Philistine King in Gerar. He too feared for his life, as Rebekah, like her mother-in-law was also a beautiful woman (Genesis 26:7).

(5) Other illustrations quoted included Jacob's deception of his father (Genesis 27:1–29); and of his uncle Laban (Genesis 30:31–43). Later Jacob was himself deceived by his sons over the assumed death of Joseph (Genesis 37:33).

The descendants of Korah, Dathan, and Abiram died because of their father's rebellion (Numbers 16:27–32), and the family of Aachan were stoned to death for their father's sin (Joshua 7:1–26). Other examples listed were, Jereboam, son of Nabat, Eli the priest, King David, and his son Solomon.

But it was not all negative. The descendants of others were blessed because of the faithfulness of their fathers. Examples included Phinehas (Numbers 25:10–13); and Jehonodab (Jeremiah 35:6–8, 18, 19).

(6) Further examples.

(a) *Ahab's sin caused his descendants to die prematurely and often violently.* Of Ahab it is written:

> *'There was never a man like Ahab, who sold himself to do evil in the eyes of the LORD, urged on by Jezebel his wife. He behaved in the vilest manner by going after idols, like the Amorites the LORD drove out before Israel.'* (1 Kings 21:25, 26)

When Elijah confronted King Ahab about murdering Naboth in order to seize his property, he pronounced what was probably God's most chilling judgement on any family:

> *'... because you have sold yourself to do evil in the eyes of the LORD, I am going to bring disaster on you. **I will consume your descendants** and cut off from Ahab every last male in Israel – slave or free ... Dogs will eat those belonging to Ahab who die in the*

city, and the birds of the air will feed on those who die in the country.' (1 Kings 21:20–21, 24 emphasis added)

2 Kings 9:24 and 2 Kings 10:10 & 11, show that Elijah's prophecy was totally fulfilled.

(b) *Gehazi caused his descendants to become lepers.* Gehazi was Elisha's servant when the leprous General Naaman was healed. He hurried after the general to collect the reward his master had refused (2 Kings 5:20). In 2 Kings 5:25–27, we see that because of covetousness, greed, deception, lies and cover up, Gehazi's descendants were all cursed by leprosy. If any have survived, wherever they live, they will still be lepers. God said so.

(c) *King Hezekiah told the people of Judah that they were suffering because of their father's sins.* Hezekiah was a reformer. He restored temple worship and said to the priests:

*'Our fathers were unfaithful; they did evil in the eyes of the LORD our God and forsook him. They turned their faces away from the LORD's dwelling place and turned their backs on him . . . This is why our fathers have fallen by the sword and why **our sons and daughters** and our wives are in captivity.'*

(2 Chronicles 29:6, 9 emphasis added)

As children can become the innocent victims of their father's evil behaviour, so nations may also be cursed by the sins of their leaders.

(d) *Job knew God's principle that children would suffer for their father's wrongs.*

'If a man denounces his friends for reward, the eyes of his children will fail.' (Job 17:5 and Job 27:13–15)

(e) *Jeremiah and Hosea confirm the principle.*

*' . . . Remember that I stood before you and spoke on their behalf to turn your wrath away from them. **So give their children over to famine; hand them over to the power of the sword.** Let their wives be made childless and widows . . . '*

(Jeremiah 18:20, 21 emphasis added. See also Jeremiah 29:32 and Hosea 4:6.)

'... because you have not set your heart to honour me ... I will rebuke (or cut off) your descendants.' (Malachi 2:2, 3)

God also promises blessings.

'The righteous man leads a blameless life: blessed are his children after him.' (Proverbs 20:7)

'I will give them singleness of heart and action, so that they will always fear me for their own good and the good of their children after them.' (Jeremiah 32:39)

It is not until God's final order on this earth has been established that the hereditary curse principle will be reversed.

*'They will not toil in vain **or bear children doomed to misfortune** for they will be people blessed by the LORD, they **and their descendants with them**.'*

(Isaiah 65:23 emphasis added. See also Jeremiah 31:29, 30.)

(f) *Present day examples of hereditary curses.* A young man had a grandfather who was a Freemason. Both his grandparents and parents had been involved in occultism and witchcraft. His grandmother, mother, and aunt taught him how to do astral travel and remain in that condition for eight hours at a time. He was also able to move objects just by looking at them, and by mind control. He grew up to become a warlock, and was totally under demon control. He was born again at twenty-five but not freed until he came for ministry one year later.

A teenager with a family background of Freemasonry and witchcraft practices, grew up addicted to drugs, alcoholism, nicotine, gambling, food, excessive physical exercise, inability to save money, and lustful habits. He had been extensively involved in the black arts, consulted mediums, attended spiritist meetings and had psychic experiences. He said his father had appeared in front of him after his death, saying he was going to live inside his son. The young man was suicidal, adulterous in marriage and made an idol of sport. After he became a Christian he had some deliverance, but backslid and made a pact with Satan. When he came to us for further freedom, he manifested a false air of happiness, and spoke strongly in what we discerned was a demonic tongue. After Jesus Christ had fully freed him, he was a totally new person, and spoke joyfully in a new tongue, this time obviously a gift from the Holy Spirit.

The power of parental example

The positive side of this subject was dealt with in chapter three. In this chapter the focus is more on the adverse effects that parents may have on their children, through negative or bad influences.

Learned habits feature significantly in animals of higher intelligence and human beings. As cubs follow the mother lioness on hunting expeditions and learn skills by observation, so children observe and follow parental example.

Parents who are good examples will have their children bless them and glorify God. King David was a good example to his heirs and successors. (See 1 Kings 9:4–7 and 2 Chronicles 17:3.)

(1) *The tragedy of unbelief at Kadesh.* By the time the Israelites had reached the borders of Canaan God had fulfilled everything he had told Moses he would do (Exodus 3:7, 8). What stalled them was simply a matter of credibility, God's credibility. Ten tribal leaders looked at the visible obstacles and rationalised. Only two believed God and expected him to fulfil his promise. All the adults over twenty years of age (with the exception of Caleb and Joshua) were consequently cursed, because they followed bad advice instead of believing God (Numbers 13:31–33). Then God said:

> *'As for your children you said would be taken as plunder, I will bring them in to enjoy the land you have rejected. But you – your bodies will fall in this desert. Your children will be shepherds here for forty years, suffering for your unfaithfulness until the last of your bodies lies in the desert.'*
>
> (Numbers 14:30–33 emphasis added)

One of the greatest blessings children may receive from parents is an unshakeable belief that God will fulfil every promise he makes.

(2) *Lack of parental discipline.* Solomon says *'He who spares the rod, hates his son'* (Proverbs 13:24). One might add – 'and other people will soon hate him too!'

Even King David fell down in his fatherly duty to Adonijah. This showed up as soon as David died, when Adonijah put himself forward and said, *'I will be king.' (His father had never interfered with him by asking, 'Why do you behave as you do?')* (1 Kings 1:5, 6 emphasis added.)

If we individually were not disciplined as children, we will probably not discipline our own children. Whatever we do as parents depends largely on the role models we have known. One woman receiving freedom in Christ confessed that she had not physically loved her children after they reached five years of age. When questioned about her motive, she replied: 'Well my mother stopped loving me when I became five years old, so I thought that was the thing to do.'

Problems which arise through parental duplicity in the family home

When parental example conflicts with parental direction there will be trouble. Authoritarianism and self-justification are just two of the many nasty little cover-ups we parents sometimes use to bridge the credibility gap.

What we are seen to be, may also be just a 'shop window' display to gain the acceptance, or approval of others. It may be genuine, but it is more often deceptive. Parental example is really character expression which can bless, or blight children. The first cigarette or can of beer given by a parent is seen as justifying the indulgence from then on. Some people have told us that their lust commenced when their father allowed them to watch an explicitly erotic TV film with him, or when he did not stop them from watching a harmful movie.

Child molesters usually present a squeaky-clean public image to deceive others. Some mothers have even refused to believe their daughters' complaints of a father's incestuous behaviour because they genuinely believed in their husband's truthfulness and purity. Personal behaviour behind the scenes shows what we really are.

No matter what conclusions may be drawn from how parents treat their children in public, what happens between a parent and each child makes the greatest and most lasting impression. Prayer, Bible reading, and practical devotion to Jesus Christ as Saviour and Lord are the best character building traits children can learn from their parents.

Problems often commence when parents fail to teach and live out a God-honouring way of life

There is indeed much truth in the old saying 'Virtues are learned at mother's knees, vices at other joints!'

The Hebrews were expected to teach their children God's words, and his ways.

> *'Fix these words of mine in your hearts and minds; tie them as symbols on your hands and bind them on your foreheads.* **Teach them to your children, talking about them when you sit at home and when you walk along the road, when you lie down and when you get up.** *Write them on the door frames of your houses and on your gates so that your days and the days of your children will be many in the land that the LORD swore to give your forefathers, as many as the days that the heavens are above the earth.'*
> (Deuteronomy 11:19–21, emphasis added. See also Psalm 78:4–8.)

Probably one of the clearest examples of parental evil influence is found in 2 Chronicles 22:2–5 (emphasis added):

> *'Ahaziah was twenty-two years old when he became king, and he reigned in Jerusalem one year. His Mother's name was Athaliah, a granddaughter of Omri. He too walked in the ways of Ahab, **for his mother encouraged him in doing wrong.'***

Her strong matriarchal domination had obviously caused the boy to be weak-willed, and vulnerable to bad advice and influence. Athaliah murdered all Ahaziah's sons after his death, except Joash.

Children must never be ignored just because they are smaller in size than adults. When Nehemiah governed Israel, Ezra the priest gathered all the people together in a large square by the Jerusalem Water Gate to hear a special reading of the law of Moses. No-one left their children at home (Nehemiah 8:2, 3). The priests also explained the readings so that everyone would know what God was saying (v. 8). Without question, the earlier the teaching begins, the more effective is becomes. That was Timothy's heritage (2 Timothy 3:14, 15).

Regrettably, many parents adopt a hands-off approach to their children's Bible knowledge, simply telling them to read the Bible, or giving them commentary notes prepared to encourage regular reading. Our middle daughter's husband Tony, adopts a much more direct approach. He, or his wife reads a portion of God's word aloud at either the breakfast or dinner table, when the whole family is together. Then each child is asked some very searching questions, and comments made on their answers. Questions usually go something like this:

- 'What did the Lord say personally to you from this reading?',
- 'What did you learn from this passage?',
- 'How does this lesson apply to your life?'.

I have often been delighted at the depth of thought the children have shown in their answers and their subsequent spiritual growth. Bible instruction, discussion and prayer with children may take time a parent may feel they can ill afford, but it is a lifetime investment which pays great rewards.

King David did the right thing by his son Solomon, who later wrote:

> *'When I was a boy in my father's house, still tender, and an only child of my mother, he taught me and said, "Lay hold of my words with all your heart; keep my commands and you will live. Get wisdom, get understanding; do not forget my words or swerve from them, do not forsake wisdom, and she will protect you; love her and she will watch over you ..."'* (Proverbs 4:3–6)

Grandfather David certainly didn't score well. He passed on his lust to his boys; and gave a shocking example when he covered up his adultery by having Bathsheba's husband murdered. However, throughout the life of his son and grandson, his family example, behaviour, and teaching were exemplary.

Solomon's spiritual and philosophical decline in later life are clearly seen in the book of Ecclesiastes. So his son Rehoboam was left with just a fraction of the inheritance he should have had, because of his father's conduct, compounded by his own stupidity.

We twentieth-century parents not only have the teachings and examples of the Scriptures to warn and instruct us, we have something much greater. The Holy Spirit is willing to remove hereditary curses and problems, and help us to be faithful in example, in behaviour and in teaching God's principles to our children. No other power can preserve our children in the climate of humanism, scepticism and moral depravity in which they live. The greatest heritage parents can leave behind is practical godliness in every level of living. Let us give, devise, and bequeath a good and godly heritage.

SUMMARY

1.   Hereditary problems are unavoidable, but spiritual release is readily available.

2.   Positive parental example and behaviour are two of the greatest character and personality building factors in the lives of children. Negative or destructive attitudes and habits may ethically, morally, and spiritually hinder or prevent quality character development.

3.   The Bible is not just a book children should be left to read and interpret for themselves. It needs explanation, illustration by example, and practical application.

4.   Parents may leave their worldly possessions to their children, but the greatest inheritance which parents may leave behind is the clear imprint of God honouring footprints which their heirs and successors will choose to follow.

Chapter 22

When Pastors, Counsellors, and Youth Workers Minister Deliverance to Children and Teenagers

Today's children are growing up in a society which is ethically, and morally confused. This first affects believer's children from the time they begin to play with children of unsaved families. Our eldest granddaughter said to her mother one day 'I don't suppose it will be long before we get a new daddy!' In astonishment, her mother asked why she had said that. The answer was simple. 'Some of the girls in our class have new dads, so I thought we would too!'

Sometimes the junction of two rivers produces turbulence and discolouration. Similarly, when children from Christian homes begin to mix with others from unbelieving backgrounds, the language and conduct they are exposed to, may challenge or confuse them. Bad example and peer pressure often bring out hereditary weaknesses and habits to form explosive emotional pressures. This may even cause them to defy parents or teachers who insist on biblical standards, and result in sinful habits which grieve those who love or care for them. Children from ethically and morally upright non-Christian families face the same challenges.

Of course most Christian parents encourage and help their children to follow biblical principles. Others may have faithfully taught their children, and even prayed for them as set out in Chapter 16, but know that further help is needed. Regrettably, there are also distraught Christian and non-Christian parents, foster parents, and teachers who have come to their 'wits' end' and who desperately desire help from anyone who has special understanding of children's problems. These needy children and teenagers present a challenge to Spirit-filled pastors, counsellors, and youth workers able to minister in the power and authority of Jesus Christ.

In depth ministry to the more needy children and young people

Phyl and I recommend the following procedure. It has been found effective when traditional counselling (even including prayer) has proved inadequate.

Where possible, obtain permission from the adult responsible for the child or teenager

In most cases, this will be the child's parents.

For those who have been disowned and put out of the family home, or who have run away and refuse to return, this may be impossible without breaking trust. For those in foster homes or child welfare institutions, there is usually someone with sufficient authority to grant permission for a prayer and deliverance session.

Carefully and wisely explain to the parent or adult responsible what you wish to do with the child. Because of ignorance or prejudice, the word 'deliverance' might need to be replaced by an explanation of what you intend to do, such as 'a prayer for release from dominating or hereditary habits'. The word 'demon' should not be used in speaking of children as it may be highly offensive to some adults; others may feel threatened, or 'put-off'. Acceptable alternatives are 'spiritual forces' or 'the power of hereditary influences'. This is not spiritual dishonesty, but an inoffensive expression of truth. It is usually most effective.

To be effective, compile a list of all undesirable attitudes and behavioural patterns

This can be obtained as follows:

(1) *Talk to the parent or guardian first.* Learn as much as possible about the family background, known causes of problems, and details of the problem behaviour. During this session the child should not be present.

If possible ask the parent or guardian to bring a list of the child's

232

problems when the child is brought for prayer. Be prepared for a 'rambling' document from which you may need to extract your own list of deliverance needs. A comprehensive list of problems frequently mentioned may be found in Chapter 19.

Those who are praying for deliverance should constantly remind themselves that the objective is to 'pull roots' not 'pick fruit'. Fruit systems can be traced to their root sources from the information available, or by discernment given by the Spirit.

Obtaining background information for adopted children may be difficult when the adopting parents know little or nothing about the natural parents. In this case, it is better to pray over potential curses, family spirits, and addictions, and regard obvious bad habits as having come from heredity. For example, to pray only against a spirit of lust could be merely to 'pick fruit'. The basic cause is usually hereditary lust, so the root also needs to be dealt with to ensure lasting freedom.

(2) *Talk to the child.* From the age of four years, a child is able to clearly answer key questions which will help you in knowing how to proceed. For example you can ask:

- 'Is there anything you are frightened of?'
- 'Do you have bad dreams?'
- 'How do you get on at school?'
- 'Does anything worry you?'

The answers may indicate other problems which the parents or guardians are not aware of, and which need investigation or prevention. An example of this (mentioned previously) would be the need to deal with a sibling whose ghost stories and antics are obviously causing fear of the dark.

From seven years of age a child is usually able to tell you his or her concerns and fears, and possible causes for wrong behaviour. Sometimes a child may need gentle prompting by asking direct questions. The counsellor needs to be sensitive to the possibility of real or imaginary injustice, either at home, at school, or in the community. Every effort should be made to make each one feel at ease, and not under pressure to be disloyal. Avoid a stand-over authoritarian attitude. This may make a child withdraw. Any obvious specific bondages and dominations should be added to the list compiled by the parent, or guardian.

When a child reaches ten years of age, or a little younger in the case of early development, it is important to ask whether he or she would like to talk to you alone. Many do not want an accompanying parent to leave, because they feel more secure in the presence of someone they trust. But frequently a child is glad to be alone. Sometimes he, or she feels important, or wants to talk about things the parents or guardians know nothing about. A child may even wish to confess to having been emotionally, physically, or sexually hurt by the adults themselves, or others. It is important that he or she knows that confidences will be kept. Key information sometimes emerges from these sharing times which indicates prayer needs.

If it becomes necessary to speak to the parent or guardian about a problem the child has revealed, obtain his or her permission first. This would apply to allegations of cruelty or sexual harassment by family members, school pupils, acquaintances, or friends. If the child does not want to give permission, or expresses fear of the consequences, ask the Holy Spirit for wisdom in making suggestions to the parent or guardian which could change attitudes or actions causing the alleged problems. The possibility of fantasy should never be excluded. But remember that a promise to a child 'not to tell' needs to be observed. Oblique suggestions, or carefully worded questions are often all that is needed to change the situation.

If a child shows an unhealthy obsession about people's bodies, death, or suicide, or if it is indicated that such an obsession may be developing, excuse yourself briefly. Then question the parent or guardian (where the child cannot hear you), about any known hereditary causes.

(3) *Watch, and listen to any accompanying adult.* While you talk to any person(s) accompanying the child or teenager, you may observe:

(a) that he or she is over-protective, authoritarian, threatening to punish at the slightest provocation, or obviously using strong discipline. This usually causes rejection and fears. Not only does the child need releasing from the appropriate problems, but a parent or guardian may need to be 're-educated' about their attitudes and conduct (not, of course, in the child's presence).

(b) that the child clings to an adult and is obviously fearful of other people. This may indicate that the child is terrified of being abandoned, or has been abused by a stranger.

(c) other attitudes of rebellion, defiance, and stubbornness in the child's behaviour which may not have been listed as problems. (Add to your own list.)

(4) *Be sensitive to the Holy Spirit's voice.* Some pastors and counsellors see a mental picture revealing something about the child to be prayed for. Others hear the voice of the Holy Spirit in their inner personality, revealing specific problems from which the child needs to be freed. Add these to the list you are compiling. When it comes to prayer time, pray in the Spirit (1 Corinthians 14:14, 15; Ephesians 6:18), over demonic causes of problems you prefer not to speak aloud. No-one will be alarmed, or offended because they will be unaware of the subject matter of your prayer. Positive, or helpful insight may of course be shared for the encouragement of everyone.

(5) *Ask the older ones for permission to pray for them.* With mature children and all teenagers, it is essential to get their permission to help them, otherwise it may be a waste of time, and put them off any future prayer sessions.

It should be noted that where a child has a family history of Freemasonry, occultism, or witchcraft, he or she may well be dominated by a spirit of anti-Christ which will cause resistance to any suggestion of prayer. A child in this category will usually refuse to pray personally and object strongly to anyone praying in their presence, either privately or publicly.

Of course fear can also cause a child to want to avoid prayer. Generally speaking with smaller children, either the parent's assurance, or our gentleness wins co-operation. With the older ones, the gentle art of persuasion will usually cause them to co-operate.

One ten year old boy refused to come when his parents asked him. I went downstairs and found him standing a little self-consciously outside the front door. I chatted with him, and offered to let him go if he didn't like being prayed for. Reluctantly, he returned with me, sat still while we prayed over him, then jumped up and ran out to play. But I had a secret weapon. I discovered we both had a common interest in postage stamps, so with that as a bait, we became friends. With one arm around his shoulders, I was later able to pray casually with him, asking the Lord to release him in every area he may have resisted when we first prayed.

With younger children, resistance can be overcome physically in the parent or guardian's presence, and with their permission and co-operation. Intransigent teenagers should not be forced to submit to prayer. You should explain why they need freedom, and the possible consequences of refusal; they should then be asked to reconsider the matter with a view to making a further appointment.

The Ministry itself

(1) *The presence of a parent or guardian.* A good number of teenagers prefer to be prayed for alone. Provided the parent or guardian agrees, this may be helpful in their recovery from a low self image. This may make them feel 'special', or 'important'. Most teenagers, however, are more than happy for a family member to be present.

With younger children a parent, or the accompanying guardian, should be present throughout.

Counsellors must show the highest ethical code of conduct in touching children, particularly teenagers who have been subjected to emotional, physical or sexual abuse. Because Phyl and I generally work together, problems don't arise, but where we operate separately, we like to have someone else with us, if a family member is not available.

With children from the same family, our normal procedure is to have the father accompany the boys, and the mother bring the girls. In cases of favouritism, or by a child's own choice, it may be the parent of the opposite sex.

Most requests for help come from concerned parents, and they are generally willing to co-operate in any way possible to see their children freed.

(2) *Seating.* The procedure is the same as outlined for parents in Chapter 16. Small children will normally sit on a parent's knee, where they feel more secure in front of a stranger. The more independent ones like to sit by themselves. In that case, make sure that the parent or guardian is able to see the child clearly as you pray. A straight-backed chair is ideal.

(3) *Praying for release.* The procedure is similar to praying over an adult, but generally less intense because demonic powers are only beginning to establish their control over a young life. Unlike an adult, a child will not usually have made the type of deliberate wrong choice which opens the door to the more powerful kind of demonic domination.

(a) *Procedure*

• Assure any child old enough to understand that because you are going to pray over causes of problems a mother, father or grandparent may have had, that it does not mean that he, or she is personally to blame for having them.

- Gentleness is also needed in some cases. A brother and sister were brought for ministry. The older boy was prayed for first. The girl then looked at me with big eyes, and said 'Will it hurt?' I assured her it would not. Being a grandpa, and in the mother's presence, I lifted the little one onto my knee, and put my arms around her. She put her head on my shoulder and one arm around me. Placing one hand on her forehead, I began to pray. By the time I had finished, her eyelids had drooped, she was nearly asleep, and her hand had slipped down my back. It made me wonder what the children must have felt after Jesus Christ had prayed for them.
- By the laying on of hands and in the name of Jesus Christ, bind and break the power of each demon causing problems and order them to leave the child. It may be helpful if someone holds your list where you can easily read it.

Ministry to children is normally short. From the drawing up of the list of problems to the prayer for cleansing, up to thirty minutes is the average time taken. There are exceptions of course. While adults need progressive release, counsellors praying over a child may normally bind, break and release the power of the enemy in each problem from the beginning of the list to end without a break. Exceptions will be dealt with under 'problems sometimes encountered'.

(b) *Manifestations*

(i) The majority of children prayed for, show no outward sign of anything having happened. But not infrequently one of them will say something like this afterward:

- 'I feel good inside'
- 'I feel all nice and warm'
- 'I feel all light inside'

Because all deliverance is ministered by faith based on the substitutionary work of Jesus Christ, and in the authority of his Name, evidence of freedom should not be expected as a proof of effectiveness. It is much more encouraging to hear later that a change has taken place in the child's behaviour. Regrettably, most people who bring a child for prayer suffer from the 'nine-leper-syndrome' (Luke 17:17). They don't return to tell of the changes, and so give glory to God.

(ii) *Yawns*. Yawning is probably a child's most frequent manifestation of release. Some children yawn continually during prayer. Yawns are not like some other reflex actions, they cannot be turned on and off at will. So when a child who is not yawning before ministry commences to yawn during prayer, and sometimes cannot stop it until the prayer is finished, something out of the ordinary must be happening.

(iii) *Sighs*. A child may give the biggest sigh imaginable during the prayer for release (also when a child is being prayed for while asleep).

(iv) *Coughs*. On occasions the oppression is so strong that a child will cough during release. A parent or guardian will usually confirm that the child had no cold or cough prior to the ministry.

One ten-year-old boy spontaneously commenced coughing as we began to pray over him, and continued to do so throughout the time of prayer: His father had openly rejected his son and constantly disciplined him, even brutally at times. It was no wonder the lad looked so dispirited. It took an hour to pray through his list of needs, and for cleansing and healing. Every time we came against a new demonic power, he was doubled over in pain.

(v) *Body movements*. Restlessness may be an indication of demonic resistance. As with adults, children who have strong hereditary spirits sometimes feel unusual movements in their stomach area. During ministry Phyl will usually place her hand on the stomach of the girls, and I will do the same with boys and teenagers. When we feel unusual movements, we ask the child to cough, and release spirits of domination.

We normally make this a competition to see whether the child is able to cough louder than one of us (usually me). Any adult accompanying the child is invited to judge who coughs the loudest. On the count of three the child and I cough together. I make sure mine is muted, so the child always wins. Sometimes we repeat the action. When the child continues to cough spontaneously it is obvious that controlling spirits are being released. *Note:* Many children regard the whole experience as some sort of game. When you first lay hands on them, some giggle, while others sit bolt upright, perfectly still, only their eyes moving. A quick smile, or a question as to how they are feeling will usually break any tension.

(c) *Cleansing and renewal*. When their list of problems has been

238

prayed through, continue the laying on of hands and pray for cleansing and renewal. Pray for each area of the body and soul which has been affected as set out in advice to parents in chapter 16.

Each child needs to be filled with God's love (particularly when they have been rejected). This will help in being able to receive love, and share it with others. There is also need to be filled with peace (especially if the child has been fearful or hyper-active). Finally, pray that joy will also become evident.

(d) *Emotional bonding*. Some instances of this were given in chapter 9, but the need for it, and the 'how' of ministry is particularly important to pastors, counsellors and youth workers who desire to renew family relationships after the deliverance of a child overtly rejected by one or both parents. This is particularly so when an emotional block has developed between them, and neither one is able to express love to the other. When a parent really wants to be different, both parent and child need to be bonded together. If a child is old enough to understand, the father or mother (mothers particularly), will often tearfully tell a child how sorry they are for having rejected him, or her, and ask for forgiveness. If an apology has not been spontaneously offered, suggest that this be done. Tender scenes often follow with a parent and child locked in a warm embrace. At an appropriate time the counsellor should place one hand on the parent, and the other on the child, and pray for their emotional bonding, and the release of God's love between them.

If no spontaneous love is evident between them, the child (even teenager) should be asked to sit on his or her mother's or father's knee, and parent and child asked to put their arms around one another. Lay a hand on each person as before, and ask the Lord to remove emotional barriers, cleanse and warm cold hearts, and bond them emotionally so that each can express love to the other. If there is still no spontaneous reaction, ask each one to say to the other 'I love you'. A second prayer for bonding will usually bring release. Because love is an emotional commitment, not just a fleeting expression of feelings, don't be discouraged if the renewed relationship gets off to a slow start. Counsel them on the need for expressing love to one another to break the old habit.

A parent or guardian who asks for help from persons experienced in the deliverance ministry may not be aware of the need to pray for the spiritual cleansing of a room in which the child sleeps. If the adult responsible for the child's welfare is not sufficiently spiritually aware to be able, then the counsellor should (if in the home):

(i) Renounce and resist all demonic powers which may have oppressed the child in the room. There is no need to name them individually. (James 4:7)

(ii) Pray that the room may be cleansed from all demonic oppression by the power of the shed blood of Jesus Christ (Revelation 12:11), and the authority of his name (Mark 16:17).

When a child is set free, the quality and direction of that life changes, sometimes dramatically; the family is blessed, and doubtless schoolteachers will breathe sighs of relief! Our hearts certainly rejoice when we hear of immediate behavioural changes, and long lasting results, even if we have to wait years to hear of them!

Chapter 23

Some Real and Potential Problems in Young People's Deliverance

If ever proof were needed that Satan is without mercy and gentleness, this chapter will provide it. With most children deliverance is quick and effective. With some, Satan fights and resists the power and authority of the name of Jesus Christ, one step at a time.

Babies may cry and resist prayer

The reality of hereditary demonic oppression is never more clearly seen than when asking the Lord to set babies free. Even the most placid and happy ones can instantly change when hands are lightly laid on them, and prayer begins. They may commence to cry loudly, even bitterly, and twist their heads from side to side to avoid the hands being laid on them. It is advisable to tell mothers what could happen so that they will be prepared for such a reaction.

While Phyl was praying over a particularly placid baby being held by her mother, she discerned that the baby had a spirit of death. While releasing her, the baby cried loudly and the mother became agitated because 'her baby never cried' and wanted to know what Phyl was doing to cause the tears. She was asked to 'hang in there' until the prayer was finished. When the baby was once more full of smiles, the mother admitted that both she and her father had had a spirit of death. Two days afterwards the baby underwent a general anaesthetic for an operation and came through without any problems. Had that spirit of death not been dealt with the results may have been different.

Demons could hinder deliverance in children simply by playing on the emotions of parents.

Babies with hereditary spirits of Freemasonry have either visibly jumped, or become very restless when being set free.

Small children may fight strangers praying for them

Not infrequently children (mainly boys), up to five or six years of age will strongly resist prayer for deliverance. Hereditary spirits will often cause them to try and run away, yell, or even bite, scratch, and kick. With the parent's permission, I have sometimes found it necessary to sit a boy on my knee, pinning his legs between my knees, and holding each hand while praying. On one particularly bad occasion, the child did everything he could to break free, then suddenly stopped and smiled. All resistance was gone. The evil one must never be allowed to win with children. They, like adults, may need to be restrained.

A two and a half year old boy who was prayed for recently was the rejected child of a de facto relationship. The father left after he was born. The boy was extremely hyper-active, very destructive, dumb, and resisted any demonstration of love. During the time of prayer the mother nursed the boy and held his hands while I held his feet on my chest to lessen his struggling. He cried loudly while we came against the power of Satan. Before the mother and son had left, the boy spontaneously kissed Phyl on the lips. We have heard that he has quietened considerably. Had the prayer for deliverance not been successful the mother felt she would have had to have placed the boy in an institution.

While I was praying over one of our grand-daughters several years ago, she constantly resisted and tried to pull my hands off her head. During my prayer, I happened to use both her given names. She immediately stopped resisting, and smiled at me through her tears.

Both of us have found that when children have had to be restrained, they seem to remember nothing of it afterwards. In fact they are usually particularly friendly to us and often spontaneously give us a hug or kisses as they leave.

Older children, and teenagers sometimes react like adults

Children of all ages may react to deliverance just like adults. By body movements and spontaneously coughing as you pray, they continue to do so until they are freed. In such cases, ensure that all oppressive spirits are released, by praying systematically through all the known causes of problems and challenging any other forces of evil to name themselves. The child or teenager will tell you what comes to mind, if the Spirit of God has not already shown you.

Full freedom may not follow immediately after deliverance

Parents sometimes expect a child to change before their eyes during a deliverance session. Sometimes they do. Sometimes they don't. Doubtless some write deliverance off as a failure because they don't see what they want to see. But if there is any failure it is often in the attitude of the person or persons who bring the child for prayer. If a parent or guardian does not really believe that Jesus Christ is able and willing to release that child, and does not expect the child to be freed, then that lack of faith suits the devil just fine. In some ways deliverance is somewhat like physical healing. Miracles are immediately evident, healings usually take time to be recognised as such. It certainly may take time for well established behavioural patterns to change so that evident problems disappear. I have often heard Phyl counsel a parent 'Give God time to work'.

A six-year-old girl was brought to us by her parents. The mother was a born again and Spirit filled believer. The father was an unbeliever, obviously antagonistic to the Gospel, and totally frustrated by his daughter's behaviour. He thumped the table and demanded to know what would happen if 'this thing' didn't work. I suggested a psychiatrist, and he didn't appear impressed. The girl herself had had a very traumatic birth, and obviously felt very rejected. She was jealous of her younger sister, ordering her around, and deliberately did the exact opposite to what her parents told her to do.

The mother stayed with us as we prayed for the girl, and was asked to call us and give a progress report on her daughter a week later. When she phoned, she said that there were some good changes, but she felt the girl needed still more prayer. Because we were about to leave the city for a while, Phyl told her to trust the Lord, and promised to ring her again after returning home. When Phyl did call, the mother couldn't understand why she had done so. When reminded of the request for further prayer for her child she said 'Oh she's wonderful, just a delight to everyone in the family. There is no longer any problem'.

One deliverance session may be insufficient for full release

A young married couple who had attended one of our seminars on deliverance telephoned for advice concerning a nine year old. He had been sodomised twice by the age of five years, was fearful, angry, and violent. He was very rejected, heard voices, had twice been in a mental hospital and had incestuous dreams about his sister. He also had obsessive behavioural problems. He needed to be prayed for several times because the oppression was so severe. When for the first time the father began to discipline the boy, the habits declined and freedom increased. The father held the key to the boy's total freedom.

Sometimes one or both parents need deliverance before a child can be totally set free

The emotional link between a parent and child may be so strong that the child's full release may be delayed or even prevented until that parent, or both parents submit themselves to deliverance. One child for whom we prayed showed improvement, but was not totally set free until the mother who brought him for prayer confessed adultery to another counsellor who ministered deliverance to her. The biblical principle is found in Psalm 66:18: *'If I had cherished sin in my heart, the LORD would not have listened'*. One cannot but wonder how many children today are afflicted by the evil one because of a parent's wilful sin. If a child is not released after faithful prayer in the name of Jesus Christ, this possibility should not be overlooked.

Some recent case histories

During the writing of this chapter three children belonging to two separate families were brought for ministry. Both mothers brought comprehensive lists of problem areas.

Case History 1:
The girl was eleven years of age. Her mother thought she may have been influenced by family spirits causing mental problems and lust. The mother also confessed to having been involved in yoga in the past, and she also suspected that a curse had been put on her family. So we commenced our list by writing down hereditary spirits of psychiatric problems, occultism and witchcraft, the family curse, and lust.

The child's personal problems included:

(1) An induced birth which commenced the rejection syndrome. She was showing strong signs of self-rejection, and rejection of others. She also rejected God. This attitude was caused by a spirit of anti-Christ coming from the family's involvement in occultism and witch-craft.

(2) Other rejection symptoms included self-indulgence, scepticism, unbelief, jealousy of her younger sister, low self-image, inferiorities, inadequacy, insecurity, a sense of injustice, and an insatiable desire to accumulate things. She had convinced herself she was a failure, had no motivation, was apathetic, and lazy. She was also rebellious, aggressive, and would fight quickly in self-defence. Needless to say, she was very argumentative. The girl had become a loner, was self-centred and showed little affection. Food was her only comfort.

(3) Fear was a major factor, particularly at night. She suffered from bad dreams, and often had to sleep with a parent.

When all these problem areas were written down, it was quite a list for an eleven year old! During the session she showed considerable abdominal activity, and coughed willingly when asked to do so. She responded well to ministry and to us personally.

Case History 2:

The six year old sister was the next. She was obviously hyper-active, and was busy rushing around the church property while waiting to be prayed for. Twice she opened the door where we were praying for the older sister, and wanted to come in. Although her father was looking after her, we gained the strong impression that she was unresponsive to discipline.

Her personal list commenced with the hereditary problems already outlined. Unlike her sister she was open and very loving, but having also had an induced birth, she had:

(1) the rejection syndrome, including low self-image, insecurity, self-hatred, meanness and a manipulating spirit.

(2) rebellious symptoms included disobedience, anger tantrums, defiance, fighting, cruelty, aggressiveness and destructiveness. She ground her teeth, showed respect for no-one, and had outbursts of swearing.

(3) bad sleeping pattern; she told us she had bad dreams.

(4) a habit of touching her genital area; she continually changed her panties during the daytime.

(5) a sense of the presence of evil powers in the games she played at school.

Electing to sit in a chair by herself during ministry, the girl rested the back of her head in my left hand, and yawned constantly. Her parents told us they saw her twist her mouth into all sorts of queer shapes during the time of prayer. Her behaviour was excellent during the session.

Phyl had promised the mother that she would phone her during the afternoon to pass on a name and telephone number. The mother quite spontaneously said that there had been a considerable change in her daughter since the morning prayer time. She was neither screaming, or rushing around as usual, but was sweet and pleasant, quietly playing by herself.

Case History 3:

The child was a nine year old daughter of a divorcee. We were given a three page list of the problems the mother was experiencing with her daughter, plus the family history. From that background we selected the following matters requiring urgent prayer.

(1) Spirits of Freemasonry (the Masonic Lodge).

(2) Strong spirits of occultism and witchcraft. There had been extensive family involvement in the black arts, resulting in psychic visions, ghosts, and poltergeist happenings around the grandparents' home. Some family members had also practiced parakinesis (the movements of objects by the will, or mind), and there had been extensive readings of writers like Edgar Cayce, and the practice of ESP and mind control.

(3) Hereditary spirits of Karate and the martial arts.

(4) There was a family record of schizophrenia, anorexia nervosa, and bulimia.

(5) Family addictions included alcoholism, cigarette smoking, gluttony, gambling, valium tablets, and uncontrollable spending.

(6) There was a long and sad list of family involvement in sexual activities.

(7) Family sicknesses included heart problems, stress related sicknesses, asthma, allergies, and cancer.

(8) The ethnic background included five nations.

A number of significant factors affecting the girl were present.

(a) There was a spirit of death caused by an abortion before this particular child was conceived.

246

(b) The pregnancy was traumatic, with frequent arguments between the parents.

(c) The birth had been traumatic. The baby's blood was changed three times. This was followed by a period in the humidicrib under ultraviolet light.

(d) The child had a history of bad colic.

(e) There was a history of traumas. The parents had separated when the child was three years of age. The grandmother had died of cancer. An accident had left the girl with a scarred face.

(f) She suffered from fear of the dark, rejection, antagonism towards her mother, a lack of concentration at school, and memory loss.

(g) The girl loved rock-and-roll music, liked to watch karate movies, and disliked prayer and going to church, although she had invited Jesus Christ to be her Saviour.

For a child of nine years, she struggled against a formidable list of oppressions. We carefully went through the list. We broke bondages and bound, broke and loosed hereditary and dominating spirits.

When we had finished, we found she was still resisting prayer. So together, we came against the strong hereditary spirits of anti-Christ, originating from Freemasonry and witchcraft practices which were against prayer, Bible reading, church attendance, and the joyfulness of being a Christian. During this second spiritual assault, the girl spontaneously coughed and was obviously released. After prayer for cleansing and renewal the mother and daughter left, the girl still coughing from time to time. Phyl enquired as to whether she had had a cough before ministry, and the mother emphatically assured her that this was not so.

The Spirit of the Lord had forced those strong dominating spirits to leave the child, just as he does to adults.

Ritualistic sexual abuse, a specialised area of ministry

Where pastors and counsellors have the responsibility of ministering to children who have experienced sexual traumas, and those who have been ritualistically sexually abused (through witchcraft practices), a deeper understanding of the areas requiring ministry is needed.

The writer recommends a book entitled *Satan's Underground*, written by Lauren Stratford and published by Harvest House. The foreword is written by Johanna Michaelson, the author of *The Beautiful Side of Evil* (Harvest House). It was Johanna and her husband who were used by God to minister freedom to Lauren Stratford. Lauren's mother had traded her as a sex object to evil men to gratify their sexual lust in return for money, and work around the house. Unbelievably denigrated from the age of four years, the girl was taken over totally by a ring of pornographers, and sexually abused during the degradations of Satan worship. The only light in this private hell of sexual abuse and the witnessing of child sacrifices (even of those born to her during her sexual slavery to others), came from the Sunday School stories she remembered. She knew that Jesus loved people. She desperately clung to this hope, despite feeling too defiled ever to be able to receive such beautiful love. Her perseverence finally brought her into the fullness of redemption, deliverance, cleansing and healing.

Even the concept of writing about her experiences was traumatic, but encouraged by friends, and with God's grace, she has done this. For those who care for sexually traumatised young people, the book provides specialised information, and deals with subjects such as:

(1) How occultic principles and witchcraft practices systematically destroy a child's belief system.

(2) The tragic result of sexual 'spirit abuse'.

(3) What parents should watch for in their children.

(4) How to resolve fears and ritualistic abuse.

(5) Foundational counselling and ministry techniques to adults who have been drawn into sexual satanic rituals.

This chapter has been included not to convince the sceptic, but to encourage and help those who long for deeper understanding of releasing children from the grip of the evil one. Without doubt many of tomorrow's adult population will rise up and bless every one who storms the very gates of hell, and releases them from a fate which is beyond anything we may imagine.

SUMMARY

1. Some children need the expertise, spiritual understanding and authority of mature and responsible believers to see them effectively set free from the grip of the evil one.

2. Just as some parents brought their children to Jesus Christ because they were frustrated by the general lack of understanding

about the causes of spirit-caused problems, so today's parents can receive help from Spirit-filled counsellors.

3. Ministry to children should be with the parent or guardian's consent, and co-operation. The practice of listening, looking and sensing in the Spirit co-ordinate children's deliverance into a Holy Spirit initiated and controlled recovery programme.

4. In ministering to children, gentleness, sensitivity, and wisdom are needed to discern between what is an evil oppression and what is just bad parenting. Sometimes parents need freedom also.

Chapter 24

Wanted – A Future Generation

The present national tide of child and teenage dropouts and rebels must be stemmed. If not, the present trickle will become a tidal wave which will engulf, and destroy our traditional family heritage, our way of life, peace and security, social order, and all respect for human decency.

A recent survey dealing with today's children and teenagers was published by the Sydney Morning Herald. Both the SMH and journalist Frank Walker have kindly given permission for the reprinting of these articles. The alarming fact is that underneath the thin crust of society's 'All's right in my world' attitude, there is a potentially lethal condition. The first article was as follows:

'POVERTY, SUICIDE – OUR LITANY OF SHAME

Do you want to know the truth about Australian children? Not the cuties who appear in TV ads grinning over cereals or tinned pineapple.

Real kids – kids who grow up in the house next door, who play in the park, who sleep in the streets, kids who die young.

The cold hard facts about Aussie kids are shocking.

Some are hard to believe – but we can no longer turn a blind eye. This is Australia's litany of shame:

- Up to 40,000 children in Australia are homeless, sleeping in refuges if they can get in, otherwise on the street, in parks or on the beach.
- There are 27,000 State wards throughout Australia.
- The number of children living below the poverty line has doubled during the past 10 years to one in five. The Australian Council of Social Services says there are 750,000 children living in poverty. The institute of Family Studies says the figure is higher – 825,000.

- At least 100,000 children in NSW live below the poverty line.
- Half of Australia's three million children are looked after by outsiders during working hours, according to the Bureau of Statistics. Most go to the pre-school or child care centres, the rest to relatives.
- 250,000 youths are unemployed – about 19 per cent of people that age. (These figures have since greatly increased.)
- Since 1983 the suicide rate for teenage boys has increased from 248 to 290 a year. The number of teenage girls killing themselves almost doubled to 71 a year. An estimated 20,000 kids attempt suicide each year.
- Teenage prostitution is rife, with some as young as 11 and 12.
- Alcohol abuse is rampant among teenagers. Surveys have found 87 per cent of 12-year-olds drink – and by the time they are 15 and 16, 30 per cent go on regular binges of more than five drinks in a row.
- The number of kids killed by drugs has doubled this decade. Hard drugs killed 283 young people in 1985'.

This horrifying sea of young flotsam and jetsam is but one of the many 'people oceans' in which modern churches float, often unaware of the cries of those who sink around them, some tragically, never to re-surface. But the orchestras continue to play, the choirs sing, buildings are re-furbished and more powerful sound systems installed, and the same prayer is continually and fervently offered … 'Lord bring them in.'

Parental delinquency

Another recent statistical release concerned the number of recorded cases of child-abuse during 1987, compiled by the NSW Department of Family and Community services. (New South Wales has a population in excess of five million people.) The frightening figures were:

5390 cases of neglect.
4110 cases of sexual assault.
3675 cases of physical abuse.
2236 cases of emotional abuse.

(Sydney Morning Herald December 8, 1988)

What applies to Australia, and New South Wales, is without doubt reflected all around the world.

If there is to be a future generation, a piercing alarm needs to be sounded to shatter complacency. Parents must learn to become fathers and mothers who genuinely love, listen to, and converse with their children. But more importantly whole families need to learn the principles of God's Word and put them into practice. It has to be back to the basics. Let's make Jesus Christ the spiritual magnetic core of all family relationships.

When John the Baptist was born, his father prophesied that he was destined to

> '... *turn the hearts of the fathers to the children.*'
>
> (Luke 1:17)

As the return of Jesus Christ approaches, that message is even more urgently needed.

Social research is highlighting this need. If the world passes by the Church today without realising the wealth of divine revelation it is rejecting, perhaps it will listen to the sound advice of its own researchers who unknowingly, or otherwise, often reflect Biblical principles.

Moses in his day, instructed the people to read the written laws of God to their families every seven years. The reason?

> '... *Their children who do not know this law must hear it and learn to fear the Lord your God as long as you live in the land you are crossing the Jordan to possess.*'
>
> (Deuteronomy 31:13 emphasis added)

The responsibility was then upon the child to obey God and parents. Solomon speaks of the dire consequences of rebellion:

> '*The eye that mocks a father, that scorns obedience to a mother will be pecked out by the ravens of the valley, will be eaten by the vultures.*' (Proverbs 20:17)

There can be no fruit without a root system. Self defensiveness, excuses, and wrong priorities will never excuse an inadequate parental responsibility.

253

The answer to having a future generation does not lie in commissioning a fleet of ambulances to do twenty-four hour surveillance at the foot of the precipice, but by re-erecting a substantial protective system along the cliff face. Its ingredients include:

(1) a nationwide commitment to repentance from sin, self-centredness, greed, and the gratification of hedonistic pleasures.

(2) a nationwide return to biblical ethics and morals, and personal faith in Jesus Christ for salvation and discipleship, to the glory of God.

(3) a nationwide willingness to counter evil in every level of society through God's guidance and power, so that our children will grow up in an atmosphere of love, peace, and security.

This may be regarded as wishful thinking in today's low-ebb of spirituality. But to spiritual eyesight it is both practical, and possible. It has worked in times of revival and only the evil one blocks it today. Through guile and deceit he controls this world (1 John 5:18), and his demonic power actively campaigns against God's authority in a world created for his glory, and expressed through his kingdom on earth.

But that should not hinder the members of the kingdom of God making a personal commitment to follow these steps in personal and family living.

Conclusions of This Book

1.   Christians need to seek God's guidance in selecting a marriage partner who will bring his blessings to the union of sexes known as married life.

2.   Married partners should aim to fulfil the highest objectives when conceiving children.

3.   Mothers-to-be should turn their pregnancies into a precious time for conveying positive and beautiful things to each unborn child.

4.   Mothers, fathers, and new-born babies need a strong emotional and physical bonding together, as soon as possible after birth.

5.   Children should be given the privilege of growing up in a family in which God honouring principles of behaviour are standard practice.

6.   One of a parent's greatest joys is to lead their own children to a saving knowledge of Jesus Christ.

7.   The regular reading and teaching of God's word to children is the greatest means of counteracting the devil's temptations and lies. Intercession for the children should be a daily habit.

8.   Parents should protect their children from the evil one's snares by keeping their homes free of his influences.

9.   As Jesus Christ freed children from Satanic oppression in the first century, and instructed the church to follow His example in the power of His Name (Mark 16:17); parents, pastors, and counsellors alike should apply the principles of spiritual warfare against the bondages and oppressions shown by babies, children and teenagers in this century.

10.   A whole family living for the glory of God will be the greatest encouragement to children to follow their parent's godly example when they themselves marry.

11.   The greatest responsibility for the future generation is not with government, or social agencies, but with born-again, Spirit-filled, Spirit-controlled parents and those who minister to our children and teenagers.